A PSYCHOANALYTIC STUDY OF THE PSYCHOSES

A Psychoanalytic Study of the Psychoses

THOMAS FREEMAN

M.D., F.R.C.P.E., F.R.C. Psych.,

Consultant Psychiatrist, Holywell Hospital,
Antrim, Northern Ireland and
Hampstead Child Therapy Clinic, London

FOREWORD BY ANNA FREUD

INTERNATIONAL UNIVERSITIES PRESS, INC.

New York New York

Library of Congress Catalog Card Number: 72-80551

ISBN: 0-8236-4977-6

MANUFACTURED IN THE UNITED STATES OF AMERICA

CONTENTS

Foreword

When dealing with the neurotically disturbed, psychoanalysts are known to follow their patients' lead rather than to guide them, and to base their interventions on intuitive understanding rather than on cold reasoning and logical deduction.

Such behavior, though often criticized as unscientific, remains indispensable for a technique of treatment where the free association of the analysand needs to be matched by the free-floating attention of his therapist. Nevertheless, it does not, by any means, sum up the psychoanalyst's entire attitude. Once the patient's material has come to the surface, and once outside the analytic sessions in which it has been gathered, its data are accommodated within the theory which is specific for psychoanalysis. The pathological manifestations are grouped under a number of viewpoints: according to the conflicting forces which have given rise to them; according to the origin and relative strength of these conflicts and forces; according to their psychic qualities which range from the fully conscious to the deep unconscious; according to the part of the personality structure where the pathological process is located. It is these dynamic, genetic, economic, and structural aspects of the material which, when combined with each other, construct the framework for the analyst's systematic thinking.

When turning from the neuroses of the adult to the numerous disturbances of childhood, these considerations have to be extended further to include scrutiny of the drives, the intellectual, aesthetic and moral functions, from the aspect of success or failure of growth or of their pathological regressions from age-adequate to primitive, reduced levels. This leads to the blending of two approaches, the metapsychological and developmental, and it creates a useful tool for assessing patients which can be employed either at the time of initial diagnosis when the spread of pathology in the personality has to be weighed against its healthy remnants, or at the termination of treatment when the nature and extent of the therapeutic results need to be judged.

A Profile Schema of this kind has been drawn up in the Hampstead Child-Therapy Clinic in 1960, has been used consistently since then for diagnosing problem children, and has been modified subsequently to serve the assessment of infants, adolescents and neurotic adults as well. What Dr. Freeman undertakes to do in the present publication is to test how far the same schema, if suitably amended and extended, proves applicable to the psychoses. He illustrates with numerous examples the manner in which it does, in fact, help to reveal the far-reaching differences in the intactness or dissolution of personality in cases of hospitalized psychotic patients. Such differences are shown to exist in various areas of the patients' structure: with regard to the maintenance, qualitative change or loss of libidinal cathexis of the patient's own body or self and of the human objects in his external or internal world; with regard to the upkeep or failure of important defenses such as repressions, reaction-formations, sublimations and impulse-control in general; with regard to the efficiency or failure of important ego functions such as the use of speech for communication, the differentiation between fact and fantasy (reality testing), conscious control of motility, etc. Dr. Freeman hopes that such additional insights will improve differential diagnosis by preventing disparate mental states from being grouped under the same diagnostic label and subsequently being regarded (and approached therapeutically) as if they were identical.

In his chapter on "Some Comparisons between Childhood and Adult Psychoses," Dr. Freeman brings further fresh information to a topic which has been the subject of much controversy in the psychoanalytic and psychiatric literature of recent years. He is able to show under the Profile headings that, in spite of overt differences, there are unexpected areas of identity between the disturbed functioning and symptomatic manifestations of borderline children and chronic schizophrenics. It is this, in many ways surprising finding which leads the author to the interesting hypothesis that the prehistory of every schizophrenic patient may include not only the developmental weaknesses and failures which promote breakdowns and regressions in later life, but actual transitory episodes of psychotic functioning which during infantile life have gone unnoticed.

It is to be hoped that the author's argumentation, his carefully chosen clinical illustrations and his sample profiles will leave the reader with the impression that the approach which he has chosen is a profitable one.

ANNA FREUD
London, March, 1972

Acknowledgments

I would like to thank Miss Anna Freud and Mrs. Dorothy Burlingham for enabling me to participate in the research activities of the Hampstead Clinic. This book is the outcome of work carried out during the period 1966-1971 as part of a research project of the Hampstead Clinic financed under Grant No. 5 RO1MH05683 by the National Institutes of Mental Health, Washington, D. C.

The clinical studies were conducted initially at the Royal Dundee Hospital, Dundee, Scotland (1966-1967) and later at Holywell Hospital, Antrim, Northern Ireland (1968-1971). The clinical phenomena along with theoretical formulations were presented and discussed at monthly meetings held at the Hampstead Clinic, London. The opinions expressed at these meetings provided a stimulus for the clinical studies and for the formulation of views on the nature of psychotic illness from the psychoanalytic standpoint. Many staff members participated in these discussions over the five-year period. I would particularly like to acknowledge the contributions made by Miss Freud, Mrs. Burlingham, Dr. H. Nagera, Dr. Clifford Yorke, Mr. E. Freud, Dr. S. Wiseberg, Dr. A. Hayman, Dr. J. Humphrey, Dr. J. Novick, Miss I. Elkan, Mrs. I. Hellman, Mrs. H. Kawenoka, Mrs. Sara Rosenfeld, Mrs. M. Sprince, Mrs. H. Kennedy, Mrs. R. Edgecombe, Mrs. M. Mason and Miss Ruth Thomas.

Finally I wish to thank Mrs. Mary Cowan of the Hampstead Clinic for typing the manuscript.

Introduction

The centerpiece of this study is a profile schema, the purpose of which is to provide a systematic evaluation of a psychotic state. This schema is based on schemata which Anna Freud constructed for use with child and adult patients suffering from neuroses, behavior disorders and "borderline" states. The author, on the basis of extensive clinical experience (Freeman, Cameron and McGhie, 1958, 1965; Freeman, 1969a) has adapted the original schemata to accommodate the great variety of symptoms and signs which appear in the psychoses. The completion of profiles may be undertaken at the onset of a psychosis, in the acute phase, when the illness is well established, at relapse after remission and in chronicity. The more prolonged the contact between patient, psychiatrist, nurse or social worker the more plentiful the data on which the profile will be based.

In the course of completing profiles on established cases of schizophrenia, mania, paranoid psychosis and other psychotic states which cannot be so easily categorized except under such headings as mixed manic-depressive psychosis, schizophreniform or reactive psychosis, it became apparent that the schema offered the means for a wider examination of drive activity and ego-superego functioning in the different psychotic states. The studies which are described in Chapters three to nine indicate that when cases of psychosis are scrutinized in terms of the concepts which constitute the schema, clinical description is extended and refined. In transcending the purely descriptive approach to the psychoses the schema highlights the intrapsychic changes which provide the predisposition to the illness and which lead to the clinical manifestations.

While this book is primarily for psychoanalysts, particularly for those who work with patients suffering from psychotic illnesses, it is to be hoped that it will be of interest to general psychiatrists who spend much of their time engaged in the diagnosis and treatment of these severe mental disorders. In common with other psychoanalytic writers the author has submitted the clinical data to an assessment and evaluation in terms of psychoanalytic theory. The aim has been to arrive at formulations where there is the closest relationship between the clinical phenomena on the one hand and the descriptive and explanatory concepts on the other.

Classification schemes based on psychoanalysis are always in danger of culminating in theoretical expositions which overshadow the clinical observations from which they were initially derived. These schemes have proved disappointing and have found few advocates. The clinical psychiatrist has continued to base his nosological approach on symptoms, signs and the course of the illness in spite of his recognition of the fact that only a small number of cases consistently present an identical symptomatology (schizophrenia, manic depression). The vast majority of patients present combinations of symptoms belonging to one or another of the major psychotic states. This unfortunate situation for classification is the direct result of the inadequate state of knowledge as to etiology and pathology of the psychoses on which a generally acceptable nosological system could be derived.

It is against this background that the psychoanalytic approach to diagnosis and classification should be evaluated. All psychological theories of mental illness—and psychoanalysis is no exception—are limited by the special nature of the material with which they are concerned, namely, mental events. Psychoanalytic concepts are inexact and refractory to precise definition. They lend themselves to misinterpretation and to disagreement over meaning. Such unhelpful consequences are most in evidence when the concepts have their status elevated to that of irrefutable truths and dogmas. Then they are no longer regarded as instruments which have been devised for the sole purpose of inquiry, to be abandoned when no longer of value.

At the level of clinical observation there is little disagreement between analytic and nonanalytic psychiatrists. There is even a considerable acceptance by psychiatrists of psychoanalytic formulations regarding the mechanism of symptom formation where emphasis is placed on the role of regression and the failure of the ego organization. Serious controversy and rejection of psychoanalytic views only make their appearance when the explanation of symptom formation is extended to include a "reconstruction" of those aspects pertaining to the mental life of infancy and childhood which may have created much of the predisposition to the illness. Concepts such as fixation and repetition have a prominent place in these formulations. Hypotheses of this kind will be found throughout the current book.

Objective verification of such reconstructions can never take place to the satisfaction of all even when there is supporting evidence available from many sources quite apart from transference manifestations and the recall of memories and fantasies. The value of these hypotheses is twofold—first, in directing attention to the study of the acquired aspects of predisposition and second, in pointing to the necessity for undertaking research into those mental disturbances of childhood which show similarities to the reconstructions made in the case of the adult patient. In Chapter 10 a comparison is made between the psychoses of adult life and those which occur in early childhood.

Given the present state of knowledge diagnosis and classification must rest on observations made during states of illness and during complete or partial remissions (defect states). Psychoanalysis has a part to play in extending the range of clinical observation through many of its theoretical concepts. Clinical studies based on psychoanalysis need not step beyond the bounds set by the scientific method; to do so renders them at best unproductive, at worst incomprehensible.

CHAPTER 1

The Metapsychological View of the Psychoses

The Profile schema for the psychotic patient which will be described in Chapter 2 is based on the Adult Profile which A. Freud and her co-workers (Freud et al., 1965) devised for the adult psychoneurotic patient. The present schema is designed to provide a means of explanation and classification for every aspect of the symptomatology of psychoses as well as the healthy mental life existing in the patient. This becomes possible by adopting a metapsychological approach to the clinical phenomena, which must then be examined from the dynamic, economic, developmental and structural standpoints.

The purpose of this outline of the metapsychological view of the psychoses is to describe those psychoanalytic concepts which are relevant to the construction of a profile of a patient suffering from one of the many different forms of psychotic illness. Psychotic symptoms appear when stable defenses (e.g., repression, reaction formations) fail and are replaced by defenses belonging to early phases of the individual patient's mental life. The majority of delusions, hallucinations, the disorders of affect, the disturbances of thinking, perception and memory as well as those of motility can therefore be understood as the result of a defense against certain types of drive representation. The dynamic factor thus comprises a description of the conflicts existing within the patient and the nature of the defense organizations, the means whereby the proscribed drive representations are deflected from their aim and object.

In many cases of psychosis it is possible to uncover traumatic experiences, discern the resultant fantasies, trace out pathological identifications with their origin in object relationship conflicts and gain some insight into fixations which occurred in the course of drive development. In all this there is little to distinguish the psychotic from the neurotic patient. However, despite this identity of content, little or no similarity exists in their respective symptomatologies. It is generally agreed therefore that the dynamic factor alone is incapable of providing an explanation of the characteristic features of psychotic symptoms.

The symptoms to which reference has been made do not remain in the steady state throughout the course of an illness. They wax and wane in intensity, disappearing only to reappear in exactly the same form as before. Some symptoms are transient; others show a remarkable fixity. The affects are no less predictable in their expression. They may be absent for long periods and then make an explosive reappearance. This variation in the intensity of symptoms, object attachment, wishes, affects and fantasies requires the introduction of the economic point of view. The economic concept is designed to forge a connection between these changes and the fluctuations which occur in the intensity of the drive derivatives (the ideation and affect by which the drive finds representation). Clinical observation underwrites such a relationship. It is well known, for example, that the appearance of delusions and hallucinations is often associated temporally with genital arousal.

The observation of patients suffering from psychoses indicates that the differences which exist in the individual case between the abnormal phenomena and the remaining healthy mental functions must be due to qualitative and quantitative differences in the underlying mental processes. Wishes, feelings, needs and attitudes toward the objects which comprise the content of delusions and hallucinations have a special quality and intensity when compared with relationships to real objects, except insofar as the psychotic reality permeates external reality. The thinking through which the content finds representation is again of a different order from that found necessary for communication and environmental adjustment. Affects are less amenable to regulation and control. Perceptions and memories no longer give an accurate representation of present or past experience or of external reality.

Such differences require concepts through which a form of explanation may be made. The concept of drive representation or drive derivative is used to represent the mental processes (thought processes and affects) which impel the individual toward external reality and its mental counterpart. The intensities (cathexes) of sexual and aggressive drives vary in quantity. The quality of the libidinal or aggressive drive derivatives, i.e., the affect and ideation, will primarily depend on whether or not they have been affected by regression or a process of dissolution. The intensity of the drive representations will in its turn depend upon innate factors, the degree of activation of the drive and the extent of its expression or frustration.

The employment of the concept of drive representation within the context of a theory of psychosis suggests that the differences in the nature of the phenomena referred to above result from the activity of different forms of the drive derivatives. The psychotic process is perpetuated by the action of drive derivatives which are less advanced in development than those which underlie the healthy mental functions. It may be further hypothesized that the former variety of drive representations has closer affinities to bodily needs, affectivity and primitive modes of thinking. Hence, it belongs to that mode of mental activity described by Freud as the primary process. The latter forms of drive derivatives are associated with a greater distance from and control over bodily needs and affects and advanced forms of conceptual thinking—Freud's secondary process.

The concept of cathexis, drawn from the libido theory, provides a method for describing the changes which affect symptoms and the intensity of the attitudes which the patient adopts to the self and others in terms of drive cathexes. The investigation of the symptomatology therefore requires an assessment of the current status of the libidinal and aggressive drives and of such changes as may have occurred with regard to their intensity (hypercathexis, decathexis) and with regard to their aims and objects.

As psychoanalytic theory (metapsychology) regards the mental functions of the adult as the end product of a developmental process, the profile schema is constructed to accommodate a description of the extent to which these functions have deviated from the normal adult range. The deviation may appear first, as a loss of a level previously achieved, as in the case of the sexual organization, and second, by the substitution of an earlier mode of function as with magic thinking replacing reality-oriented thinking.

The developmental approach requires for its completion an account of the functional level of the drive cathexes, the affects and the cognitive functions as they appear in the individual case. Its employment necessitates the use of the concepts of regression, fixation, arrest and persistence. The concept of arrest refers to the observation that certain individuals fail to reach the final stage of drive and ego development. That is, their progress has been halted at a preliminary phase. The concept of persistence, however, was introduced by Freud (1917) to account for the continued effect of early forms of drive cathexis on later modes of drive expression as, for example, in a case where genital activity serves as a vehicle for the satisfaction of oral drive derivatives. This concept is applicable to those psychoses where the patient appears at first sight to have reached the phallic-oedipal stage while object relations, prior to the illness and during it, do not have the characteristics of that phase. The material necessary for a statement of the developmental aspects of the patient's personality and symptomatology is usually difficult to obtain in cases of psychosis. Sometimes information is obtained from the patient but this is almost always limited and can be unreliable. Parents and relatives usually bring some relevant data concerning the patient's childhood and adolescence. Although the reconstruction of a patient's development, even under the best of circumstances, is a hazardous task, a speculative hypothesis can sometimes be derived concerning the interaction between the premorbid personality and the illness itself.

Modeled on the profile for the neurotic patient the schema for the psychotic follows the same general layout. Once such topics as reason for referral, description of the patient, family background and personal history are taken care of, attention is directed successively to the state of the instinctual drives, the status of the ego and superego and the part played by fixations and regressions in the genesis of the symptomatology. There are inevitable differences in the placement of emphasis in the two profiles. In the case of the profile for the psychotic patient greater attention is paid to the disorganization of drives, ego and superego. Insofar as the part played by fixations and regressions is less easy to ascertain, other possibilities must be considered to account for the origin of certain psychotic manifestations.

Libidinal Cathexis of the Self

The schema is designed to examine the connections which exist between the disorders of the perception of the self, disorganization of cognition and defense (the ego organization), on the one hand, and the changes in the cathexis of the ego and the self-representations, both bodily and mental, on the other. Here Federn's (1927) distinction between the cathexis of mental "ego" and bodily "ego" gives the observer the opportunity to recognize that alterations may affect the one and not the other. Thus in psychoses the bodily self may be subject to a decathexis while the mental self may be hypercathected and vice-versa. Apart from the fact that the self may no longer be perceived as a separate, integrated entity it may also be experienced in a variety of abnormal ways. This is dependent first, on the intensity of the self-cathexis, second on the nature of the self-representation (mental, bodily, ego-ideal, superego) which is the focus of the cathexis and third, on the quality of the cathexis involved.

The regulation of bodily and mental sensibility as well as self-esteem is dependent on the state of the self-representation. In psychoses the representations of the self are subject to change and their cathexis fluctuates between hypercathexis and decathexis both in the same patient and from patient to patient. In schizophrenia and paranoid psychosis different self-representation systems will be affected. In the former the representations of the bodily self may be subject to derangement while in the latter it may be the representations of the mental self alone which are most affected. In mania there is a great increase in the libidinal cathexis of the self-representations with an exaggerated sense of well-being, self-esteem and power. In depression the self-representations are depleted of libidinal cathexis insofar as they have become the object of aggression arising from the superego.

For purposes of description, self-representations and the representations of real and fantasy objects must be differentiated from each other. It is a fact of clinical observation that withdrawal of interest from external reality and the resultant preoccupation with the self occurs not only in schizophrenia, mania and paranoid illnesses but in severe depressive states (manic-depressions) as well. In the schizophrenias and allied states the cathexis of the self-representations results in a pathological narcissism. In severe depressive states there is a withdrawal of drive cathexis from external objects (real persons). Psychoanalytic work with these patients reveals that it is the object representations, past and present, which have become the recipients of this hypercathexis. In that the drive derivatives do not change in quality, there is no evidence of the development of a delusional reality, except in those cases where the self-reproaches become unrealistic due to a hypercathexis of the superego with aggression. This has the effect of falsifying judgment and causing an impairment of reality testing. From a descriptive point of view, a preoccupation with the self is associated with a complete or partial disruption of ties with external objects irrespective of whether or not self or object representations are the focus of the cathexis and regardless of the quality of the drive cathexis.

The hypercathexis of one or more aspects of the self-representations implies a heightened narcissism with an impairment of object-libidinal cathexis. This impairment of object cathexis varies from case to case. A continuum exists between those psychotic states where the cathexis of real objects is abandoned and those where the object cathexis is maintained. An instance of the former is the withdrawn, self-preoccupied, inattentive schizophrenic patient while the latter is illustrated by the patient who is worried lest the spouse, for example, be injured by unknown persecutors. In both cases there is an increased cathexis of self-representations. In the former this pathological narcissism is reflected in grandiose delusions while in the latter it is expressed in an exaggerated egocentrism with the patient believing that he is the focus of unwelcome attentions. The clinical phenomena suggest that an inverse relationship exists between cathexis of self and cathexis of objects.

In all psychoses there is a pathological narcissism, based on instinctual libido, which is reflected in an egocentrism which varies in its expression from ideas of reference and misinterpretations to delusions with either an omnipotent or persecutory content. The grandiose ideas which typify certain patients whether schizophrenic, paranoid or manic can be traced to ego ideals, themselves an expression of the narcissistic state. The aims of the ego ideal, which has its origins in the narcissism of childhood (Freud, 1914), are based on wishful fantasies and the omnipotence of thought. In psychoses, wished-for ideas about the self are believed to be true. The nature of the ego ideals which come to the fore is dependent on the extent and kind of pathological process. The relation of regression to this process will be discussed later. Where the narcissism is not influenced by the superego, depressive affects or reality the ego ideals overshadow the true evaluation of the self.

The alteration in the distribution of the libidinal cathexes between self and object representations, which comprises the essence of the psychotic process, has the most drastic effect on the integrity of the secondary identifications. In psychosis, the self-representations which are based on these identifications are subject to a disorganization, the extent of which varies from case to case. In some the identifications are so deranged that little trace is to be found of their presence. In others there is adequate evidence of these representations some of which may have provided a source of neurotic symptoms in the prepsychotic period. The extent to which there exists a mental life uninfluenced by the psychosis—the nonpsychotic part—can be partially judged by the presence or absence of these secondary identifications.

LIBIDINAL CATHEXIS OF OBJECTS

It is also necessary to examine the state of the object representations. These representations may be defective, first in their psychological structure (size, shape and distance constancies) and second, in their capacity as recipients of object cathexis. The distinction which must be made between perceptual constancies and object constancy (the maintenance of object cathexis) is most clearly seen in the diffuse cerebral degenerations. Perceptual constancies can be severely deranged in these conditions and yet object constancy remains. Object cathexis continues to exist even in the absence of a stable preconscious image of the object. Clinical observations support the view that ". . . the two processes are different from each other" (A. Freud, 1968).

In the schizophrenias the transient alterations in perceptual constancies which appear are due to fluctuations in the cathexis of the mental representations while in organic mental states these disorders are due to an actual disintegration of the verbal and pictorial representations of objects. In cases of schizophrenia there can be a lack of correspondence between the external object and its psychic representation. This indicates that in functional psychosis the object representation periodically loses its cathexis. This state can be contrasted with that existing in diffuse cerebral degenerations where the object representation, however defective, retains its cathexis (Freeman, 1969b).

The quality of the drive derivatives investing the object representations in psychosis fluctuates in a given case and varies from case to case. In one patient there may be a "remnant" of these drive derivatives which follow the secondary process investing the object representations, the remainder of the drive derivatives following the primary process. The former allows the patient to maintain some contact with real objects while the latter activates the representations comprising the delusional reality. These are representations of real or fantasy objects. The primary process can lead to the condensation of external objects and object representations and to the condensation of two different representations as occurs in the dream. Reality testing breaks down with the appearance of misidentifications and false perceptions and must therefore be regarded as depending, to some extent at least, on the quality of the drive derivatives which invest the object representations.

The degree to which object representations are invested with drive derivatives of secondary process type will reflect the presence and strength of the remaining healthy mental functions (the nonpsychotic part of the personality). When patients, in whom this nonpsychotic part is reasonably developed are offered the opportunity of psychotherapy, transferences will appear which have the characteristics of a transference neurosis. Identifications which have escaped involvement by the psychotic process are resolved and the object representation revived in the transference. The cathexis is directed to a real object, the object representation having been externalized, as a consequence of the repetition, onto the person of the therapist. Whether the treatment will continue and reach a favorable outcome will depend on whether or not the nonpsychotic part retains its integrity. This is lost whenever the libidinal drive derivatives are affected by regression, thereby regaining their instinctual quality. When this happens cognition falls under the influence of the primary process and the cathexes invest object and fantasy representations with the development of a delusional reality. This penetrates the therapeutic relationship and frequently destroys it.

Reality testing can be assessed from either the standpoint of the ego or from the standpoint of object cathexis. The former provides a descriptive statement of the defective function, while the latter offers an explanatory formulation. Reality testing is dependent upon drive representations which have secondary-process qualities. Once these are lost and replaced by drives having the characteristics of the primary process, reality testing will be held in abeyance. The intrusion of the primary process into ego functioning is in part a consequence of the return of drive cathexes to the self, following upon the operation of projection and total identification. Cognition—speech, thinking, perception, memory—is influenced by condensation, displacement and the tendency toward the hallucinatory revival of memories.

SEXUAL ORGANIZATION

The derangement in psychoses of the libidinal drive cathexes, both with regard to their aims and objects, is reflected in the disturbance of the sexual organization. All manner of changes may occur. In some cases there is clear evidence that the libidinal cathexes belong to the genital-phallic phase. In other cases this phase, having apparently been reached in the prepsychotic period, is abandoned and replaced by the oral and/or anal organization of the libido.

In recent cases where the onset is acute the phallic organization is cathected with libido. This results either in the drives cathecting fantasy objects, with ensuing masturbation, or their object-directed sexual aims. In long-standing cases of psychosis the phallic level of the sexual organization may remain cathected once again with continuing autoerotic activity, or this particular organization may be decathected —the patient showing no sign, at any time, of genital arousal. It is in this last group of cases that the pregenital expressions of the libido are observed either in the direct or indirect form. The patient's libidinal position must therefore be specified, particular attention being given to indications of a direct expression of the sexual drives, including the component instincts.

In the psychoses regression may lead to the revival of fantasies and drive attitudes appropriate to different levels of the sexual organization. In this respect there is no difference from what happens in the neuroses. Hence the similarities between hysteria and schizophrenia which have frequently been commented upon. The major difference between the two states is the manner in which the libidinal cathexes are distributed between self and object. In the psychoses the objects and their representations are either depleted (decathexis) or overinvested (hypercathexis) with cathexes, while similar alterations affect the self and its various representations (sense of identity, body scheme, etc.).

AGGRESSION

The expression of aggression in psychoses, either overtly or in an indirect form, is usually associated with alterations which have affected the libidinal drives. Aggression is therefore typically related to the frustration of libidinal wishes, disappointments and object loss. Nevertheless there are occasions when aggression becomes manifest quite apart from the libido as the "pure" expression of the aggressive drive itself. Care must always be taken to ensure that the direct expressions of the drive are not reactive to stimuli which have been overlooked. This may easily occur in schizophrenic states where a latent interval occurs between the external stimulus and the aggressive act itself. The aggression may be directed outwards or against the self. In the preneuroleptic drug period this aggression was to be observed in the destruction of inanimate objects or less often in self-injury. A case in point is that of a patient who systematically removed all his teeth over a period of years.

Additions had to be made to the original profile schema in order to accommodate all the different ways in which aggression may manifest itself in psychotic illness. This is, as has been mentioned above, necessary because in the psychoses the mode of expression of the aggressive drives and the means of dealing with them differ in several respects from those found in the neuroses. Not only does aggression have a direct outlet but it also finds expression less obviously in the content of misinterpretations, delusions and hallucinations.

Over and above the defenses of projection, introjection and externalization, a method of reacting to aggressive drives peculiar to psychosis must be referred to. This is the appearance in motility of catatonic manifestations—namely, the hypertonia of the limb musculature, alterations in posture and ambitendency. Clinical observation has shown that a reciprocal relation exists between the expression of aggression and catatonic signs. The questions which appear in the profile are designed to allow for the recording of such data when they appear.

THE EGO ORGANIZATION AND DEFENSES

The ego organization is examined from a descriptive as well as a dynamic aspect. This supplements the economic evaluation of the ego functions to which reference was made earlier. The extent of the ego defect varies from case to case. At the same time the abnormalities which affect the ego functions are subject to alterations either in the direction of normalcy or towards exacerbation. The changes may be transient or permanent and frequently the movement toward "healthy" function is accompanied by strong needs or affects. Similarly a deterioration is associated with affectivity.

In cases of acute onset and in chronic states speech loses its communicative function, memory is disordered, perception becomes defective, thinking no longer maintains an advanced level of abstraction and connections between thinking, speech and motility are deranged. The ego functions become deficient because of the changes which affect the ego libido. The change in its quality is a result of the loss of the ego-id differentiation. Once the libidinal cathexes become organized in terms of the primary process, advanced forms of cognition are no longer possible. Thinking, perception and memory fall under the influence of the primary process.

In this review of ego functions the status of the defense organization is given special emphasis. Here it is again insufficient to limit consideration to the dynamic aspects of the defensive process. This only provides information about the manner in which the direction of the drive representations has been altered with respect to their aim and object. The dynamic interpretation does not throw any light on the fate of the intensities (the cathexes) of the drive representations after they have been influenced by the defense mechanism in question. Neither does it offer an explanation of why certain defenses appear concomitantly with the arousal of drive cathexes in psychosis. As will become clear in the following discussion, the economic consequences of the defenses which operate in a psychosis are such as to indicate that these defenses are of a completely different nature to those which relieve a danger situation in the healthy or neurotic individual.

The defense concept has a descriptive and explanatory value for the psychoses no less than for the neuroses. Defense mechanisms are ultimately set in motion by the consequences of danger situations which in turn lead to anxiety. These danger situations are no different from those that initiate the process of symptom formation in the neuroses. The most common danger situations arise from libidinal frustration, object loss and pressure from the superego. The essence of the danger situations comprises increasing quantities of libidinal cathexes which are denied the possibility of "discharge" onto external objects. These cathexes threaten an impending trauma. Object loss and pressure from the superego also lead to this potential trauma. The internal frustration, which arises from an inability to procure an outlet for these cathexes to the exterior, leads to a regression and consequently to a change in the quality of the drive derivatives. In the case of the neuroses this alteration affects drives which continue to be barred from conscious expression because of the integrity of repression. Their effects are experienced only indirectly in the symptomatology. In the psychoses the drive derivatives whose quality has been changed by the regression manifest themselves in the disturbances of object relations, in the disorders of cognition and in the content of delusions and hallucinations.

Repression is generally understood as "repression proper" (Freud, 1915) and distinguished from primal repression. The former is concerned with the derivatives of drive representations and does not act directly on the "mental representation of instinct" as does the latter. In the case of primary repression a permanent anticathexis bars the drives from consciousness. With repression proper the derivatives of the drives have approached consciousness or reached preconscious representation but their preconscious cathexis has been withdrawn following on the signal of anxiety. This cathexis is employed as an anticathexis. Repression proper, therefore, is a form of "after expulsion" (Freud, 1915), in contrast to primal repression. Withdrawal of preconscious cathexis is a decisive step in the development of repression. In Freud's (1915) words: ". . . the different mechanisms of repression have at least this one thing in common, a withdrawal of energic cathexis (or of libido if it is a question of sexual instincts)." Repression is specific in its function, acting against specified derivatives of the instinctual drives. It also has a mobility which ensures that those drive derivatives which provoke a danger situation can be opposed at any time. Repression is not a "once and for all" process. A constant expenditure of energy (anticathexis) is required to maintain the repression of the repudiated instinct derivatives. Repression guarantees inability to achieve motility. Withdrawal of preconscious cathexis does not guarantee the stability of the repression; that is dependent on the establishment of the anticathexis. A serious disorder of repression leads to the intrusion into consciousness of the drive representations and their expression in action.

In order to be completely successful, repression must act first against the ideas through which the drive derivative finds expression and second against the affect (sexual affects in the case of libidinal drives). The withdrawal of preconscious cathexis is effective against the former but not against the latter which are in the nature of "discharge" phenomena. Repression consisting solely of withdrawal of preconscious cathexis enables the individual to dissociate himself from an interest in or wish to carry out the drive derivative in question. It is only with the establishment of the anticathexis that the affect as well as the ideational content is completely removed from consciousness. Repression, being in the nature of an after expulsion, cannot come into play as a defense mechanism until the mental apparatus has achieved a considerable degree of differentiation—i.e., until there is an ego organization distinct from the id. Until this point, other processes influence the course of those mental representations of instinct which create situations of danger for the developing individual.

In psychoses repression is the first defensive maneuver initiated to annul the danger created by the drive derivatives. This danger may arise directly from the heightening of drive cathexis (active/passive sexual aims) or from the loss of an object the representation of which provided the focus for libidinal cathexes. In the acute phase of a psychosis repression first leads to the withdrawal of cathexes from the drive and object representations. This decathexis is not sufficient however to neutralize the danger as it is not supplemented by the anticathexis necessary for permanent repression. Clinical observation of long-standing cases of schizophrenia both in the chronic state and in remission indicate that a form of repression is operative, thereby allowing for some degree of freedom from symptoms, facilitating the expression of the delusional reality and permitting a measure of environmental adjustment. This repression must be in the nature of a decathexis in view of the ease with which it is abolished. In any assessment of the defense organization in a case of psychosis it is necessary to record not only the fact of repression in the descriptive sense but also whether this repression is limited to decathexis of drive and object representations or is completed by the addition of the anticathexis.

These mental processes which alter the aim and object of the proscribed drive representations are, like repression, dependent for their appearance on the presence of an ego which has reached a sufficiently advanced stage of development to make the distinction between inner and outer. The activity of these mechanisms presupposes a boundary, however imperfect, distinguishing self from object. Identification, which is one of the mechanisms falling within this category, has been described as an instinctual vicissitude by Fenichel (1935). As a result of its influence changes arise in the aim and object of the drive derivative.

Identification may occur whenever an object cathected by an instinctual impulse leads to a danger situation. Subsequent anxiety results in an abandonment of both the real and the endopsychic representation of the object. Simultaneously the active aim is given up as well. The ego now assimilates the endopsychic representation and partially or wholly models itself upon it. The ego then offers itself as a substitute object to the drive cathexis. This mechanism of identification is based on an earlier version of primary identification which functioned prior to the distinction between self and object and between ego and id.

As with identification, projection has the effect of influencing the aim and object of an "unpleasure-evoking" drive derivative. Its operation is also dependent on some degree of ego differentiation. Projection is more than the externalization of an unwanted drive representation or affect. Through its effect on the drive there is a distortion, the result of which is the abolition of an internal stimulus and its replacement by an external perception (Freud, 1911). The fact that the drive representation is barred from consciousness led Glover (1949) to emphasize that projection has some similarities with repression and displacement. In projection the aim of the drive representation is interfered with and there is an ensuing passivity.

Novick and Kelly (1970) distinguish between projection as a defense against unconscious drive derivatives and externalization which describes "the subjective allocation of inner phenomena to the outer world." Of relevance here are two forms of externalization, first, generalization and second, attribution of cause or responsibility. Generalization describes a mode of mental functioning characteristic of the young child. Conscious thoughts and feelings are attributed to objects. Later it may be employed defensively, as for example, in the warding off of painful emotions concerned with separation. The defense finds representation in the fusion of self and object representations. Generalization, common in psychoses, particularly in mania, is the result of a loss of discrimination between self and object representations.

Attribution of cause or responsibility is also a frequent occurrence in psychotic states—the patient being aware of a thought, emotion or action but declining responsibility. This is attributed to some person or machine. These are the so-called passivity experiences. The patient complains that he is forced to entertain certain ideas or emotions and to initiate actions against his will under the influence of some external agency. Here there is externalization of stimulus, intent and responsibility. Attribution of cause is also to be found in the normal child. It is part of that developmental phase where the child believes that the responsibility for all his thoughts and feelings lie with his parents. Both generalization and attribution of cause arise originally as modes of mental functioning and not as defenses. They belong to a very early phase of ego development. When employed defensively they are not primarily set against the drives but against the recognition of painful emotion. In this respect they differ from projection which is solely concerned with defense against unconscious drive derivatives. Finally reference should be made to a third form of externalization, namely externalization of aspects of the self-representations. This mental process has both an adaptive and defensive function in childhood. It is frequently encountered in psychotic states.

In contrasting identification and projection Nunberg (1955) has stated that these mechanisms have one common characteristic—i.e., the displacement of cathexis. Viewed from the economic standpoint however in both identification and projection the cathexes of the drive representations return to the self as a result of the reversal of instinctual aim. The cathexis of both ego and self-representations is heightened. Under ordinary circumstances projection and identification act solely in a defensive capacity, influencing drive derivatives which are unconscious. Relations with objects are maintained in accordance with the demands of reality. In psychoses projection and identification not only have a defensive role but they are the means by which the libidinal drive cathexes find their way to objects. Projection and identification thus have a restitutional as well as a defensive function in psychotic states.

Certain aspects of aggressive behavior in psychotic as well as neurotic patients can be understood as a consequence of externalization. The preconditions for the operation of these mechanisms are first, an identification with parental figures who have adopted critical attitudes to the expression of instinctual drives and second, a ready capacity to externalize those aspects of the self which harbor the prohibited drives. The result is an aggressive response whenever the forbidden instinctual contents are made manifest by an object. Identification with parental representations is an important stage in the development of the superego. Although the capacity to experience guilt feelings is present there is a lack of the self-critical attitude. The guilt feelings which are activated lead to a criticism of the object who brought forward, in speech or action, the condemned drive derivatives.

In cases of schizophrenia and paranoid psychosis the awareness by the patient of affects connected with sexuality leads to an aggressive reaction towards the individual, who as a result of externalization, is believed to be their cause. In these patients there has either been only partial development of the superego or a falling back from the mature to the immature stage. The very presence of this mechanism means that the superego is still partially internalized and operative. Identification with the aggressor also involves a change in the aim of the drive insofar as the criticism or aggression which was experienced passively in the original object relationship is repeated actively against the new object. In this instance introjection into the ego of the psychical representations of the parental figures leads to a reversal from passivity to activity in contrast to other forms of identification which involve an abandonment of active aims.

In the course of describing the defense mechanisms of identification and projection attention was drawn to the alterations which affect the aim and object of the prohibited drive. These changes which affect the drive derivatives and their objects may occur independently of any other mechanism. From a dynamic point of view, the drive is turned in on the self with a reversal of instinctual aim. The reversal affects both aim and content. These mechanisms influence the direction of the drive and are not concerned with changing the object.

This account of the processes of defense may be completed by reference to the mechanism of denial. Denial is common in schizophrenia and mania but it is quite unlike the denial found in the neuroses. It ignores reality testing and in this respect can be compared to the forms of denial which occur in childhood. The denial which is encountered in the psychoses is essentially a decathexis of object and realistic self-representations. This decathexis may affect real external objects whose identity the patient denies. Such denial is no different from the decathexis which leads to the kind of "repression" which has already been referred to as occurring in schizophrenia. Both "repression" and denial in psychoses thus consist of a decathexis of self- and object representations. These mechanisms are associated with a loss of the anticathexis (repression proper) which prevents the emergence into consciousness of drive derivatives and the primary process.

In mania the decathexis has the aim of vitiating the danger which would be provoked by the enduring cathexis of the object or self-representation. In this general respect there is no difference from what happens in schizophrenia. In the former, however, the danger usually comprises the dread of object loss or of threats to bodily integrity and self-esteem.

In the latter the danger springs from heightened drive cathexis alone. Psychotic denial makes use of such mechanisms as reversal, displacement and turning in on the self. Denial is not only to be noted in its direct expression but also in delusional content. The content allows the patient to ignore his real predicament and substitute something more agreeable and pleasing to self-esteem. These delusions can be likened to the form of childhood thinking described by A. Freud (1936) as "denial in fantasy."

AFFECTIVE PHENOMENA

Abnormal manifestations of affect are an intrinsic element in a psychotic illness. These phenomena may consist of emotion subjectively experienced, physiological concomitants and behavioral change. They may occur singly, all together or in different combinations. A close examination must be made of the affectivity in psychoses and its relationship to the remainder of the symptomatology, to the underlying conflicts and to the defense organization. In the schizophrenias the affects may be limited in their expression or apparently absent. When there is affective expression it generally provides a better guide to the patient's mental state than the thought content as revealed through speech (A. Freud, 1936).

The affects may be inappropriate with respect to the associated thought content or they may appear with great violence in the absence of an external stimulus. Such subjectively experienced emotions as anxiety, depression and anger are commonplace in the schizophrenias and the paranoid psychoses. In depressive states the emotional reaction (depression of mood) which may include anxiety is accompanied by physiological and behavioral changes. The same is true in mania where the mood (elation) is also expressed somatically and behaviorally.

The affective phenomena which appear in the psychoses are closely related to drive activity. Sometimes this relationship is clearly observable; at other times it can only be inferred from the presence of certain mental contents. This close relationship occurs because affects are, in the main, drive derivatives. In psychosis the affects can be regarded as either a direct outlet of drive cathexes (sexual, aggressive affects) or as a reaction to the activity of these drives (anxiety, guilt, shame, jealousy, etc.). The sudden appearance of angry feelings and sexual affects in cases of psychosis can be understood as the result of a disruption of repression and reaction formation.

Quantitative (economic) consideration must be given a prominent place in any examination of affects in psychosis because of the changes in intensity which characterize their expression. Such considerations are particularly appropriate in the case of anxiety, an affect which is always present in some stage of a psychotic illness. Anxiety no longer performs its signal function as a result of the disorganization of the ego. With repression defective drive representations approach or enter consciousness. The consequence of a failure of repression is that anxiety now follows an "all or none" pattern finding somatic as well as mental outlets. Defenses which are effective in placing the ideational derivatives of the drives outside the individual (externalization, projection) have no influence on anxiety. It is as a result of the absence of repression in psychoses with an acute onset that anxiety reaches the proportions of panic. The intensity of the anxiety is proportional to the intensity of the drive cathexis seeking "discharge" onto external objects.

Affects, being drive derivatives, would be subject to the

influence of defensive operations if their expression resulted in a conflict with the superego or reality. The apparent lack of affect in the schizophrenias must be attributed to repression. In that this repression is by no means stable, under certain conditions it is swept aside by the affective upheaval. Thus patients who are usually withdrawn and without affect become violent as a result of disappointment, or genitally aroused following a course of electroshock treatment. Neither reaction would occur if repression were based on an effective anticathexis. The unexpected expression of affect in such instances proves conclusively that there is no real weakening of affect in schizophrenia.

Depression of mood and sadness are the result of a complex reaction which follows the lack of drive satisfaction (object directed or narcissistic) due to object loss, to the threat of object loss, frustration, disappointment or to a lowering of self-esteem. The appearance of self-reproach is the consequence of the superego reaction to heightened drive cathexis. It follows that depression of mood and sadness may arise in any form of psychosis while there remains a vestige of object cathexis. This object cathexis may relate to a delusional object. For example, a chronic schizophrenic patient became depressed when psychotherapy led to a situation where he found himself confronted with the fact that the longed-for girl friend of his delusional world was a fantasy. The fear of loss led to the depression of mood.

Elation can also be regarded as intimately connected with drive activity. It has been suggested (Lewin, 1950) that this affect initially arises in association with drive gratification. The happy mood in the healthy can be thought of as a repetition of the contented infant's satisfaction at the breast. It is, however, also possible that elation characterizes the completion of all forms of libidinal drive gratification. The elation of the manic patient has been interpreted as being the means whereby anxiety is dispelled from consciousness. Elation differs from anxiety in that it is not the consequence of repressed drive cathexes nor does it perform a signal function. The concept of a "manic defense" which removes depressive fantasies from consciousness finds some support in the fact that anxious and depressed feelings may be interspersed amidst the elation of the manic patient.

The Superego

The state of the superego in psychoses can best be approached by recalling the distinction Freud (1924) made between narcissistic neuroses (melancholia) and the other varieties of alienation. In the former the conflict occurs between ego and the superego while in the latter the disturbance centers on the relationship between id drives and the external world. Although this is a fundamental distinction both categories have in common an instability of the superego.

Two distinct forms of superego pathology occur in the psychoses. The first category consists of all those instances where there is an externalization and dedifferentiation of the superego. In depressive psychoses, to be distinguished from severe depressive states where insight is retained, there is an externalization of the superego which leads to ideas of reference, to misinterpretations and in some instances to auditory hallucinations. The content is always critical and punishing. In the other psychotic states there is likewise an externalization of the superego which may be dedifferentiated into its component objects or their substitutes.

The second type of superego abnormality which occurs in the psychoses is more localized. It may appear alone or in combination with externalization of the superego. The clinical phenomena which follow are of two kinds. First there are those patients usually suffering from schizophrenia or paranoid psychosis who cannot accept responsibility for certain conscious thoughts, emotions or acts. Guilt is avoided by attributing the inspiration for the forbidden idea or emotion to an object. Pressure from the superego is thus avoided. Such a superego must be endowed with pronounced aggressive qualities for its criticism to be so feared. The defense of projection is closely associated with this kind of superego anxiety. The second group of patients make free use of a defense whereby condemned wishes and affects are externalized as before but they do not become conscious. The object onto whom they are externalized becomes the focus of the patient's aggression.

All these forms of superego pathology can be attributed to the effects of regression. The evidence is most compelling in those cases where the superego remains wholly or partly internalized exerting a powerful pressure on the ego to resist the intrusion into consciousness of the drive derivatives. It is well known that prior to full maturation of the superego the child may recognize that certain actions, wishes and feelings are wrong but still cannot acknowledge responsibility for them. There is a tendency for the condemned wishes to be externalized in order to avoid awareness of guilt. When this process is pronounced it leads to the mechanism of identification with the aggressor. Further discussion of this aspect of regression is taken up later in this chapter.

REGRESSION AND FIXATION

The developmental aspects of a neurosis are accounted for in the original profile schema in the section entitled "Assessment of Fixation Points and Regressions." This is a difficult area to cover adequately in a profile of a case of psychosis. The changes which occur in the quality of the drive cathexes in psychosis are the result of regression. This regression follows upon the occurrence of an internal frustration, which promotes a danger situation resulting from the increasing quantities of drive cathexes. These cathexes have failed to find an outlet because of an unaccommodating reality, a fear of the superego or because of object loss. The regression of the libido affects both object relations and the sexual organization. This regression is facilitated by the presence of libidinal fixations which have occurred in the course of development. Additionally fantasies associated with particular fixation points are recathected with libido. The situation in a psychosis differs from that existing in a neurosis in that in the former repression fails to contain the conflict which has resulted from the regression although an attempt is made in this direction through the decathexis of drive and real object representations. The failure of repression allows for the emergence of drive derivatives whose quality has changed as a consequence of the regression of the libido.

The evidence indicating the occurrence of a profound regression in psychosis is obvious enough. It is however more difficult to delineate with accuracy the fixation points to which the libidinal drives have regressed. During the psychoanalytic treatment of a neurosis it is relatively easy to identify the fixations which have affected the sexual organization and object relations. This information becomes available because the patient, acknowledging that he is ill, is prepared to reveal the history of the symptoms and those real and fantasy experiences which provided the basis for the abnormal manifestations. Continuing analytic work also reveals the actual frustrations which provoked the regressions in the first place. In a neurosis fixations may have occurred at the phallic phase with emphasis being placed on passive or exhibitionistic aims. It is equally possible that the fixation may have occurred at any other stage of the sexual development. In the sphere of object relations the situation is similar. The patient's account of his childhood and the repetition of significant relationships in the transference enables the analyst to identify the fixations which arose at the oedipal or preoedipal stages.

The favorable circumstances which are to be found during the treatment of neurosis are absent in the case of psychosis. The patient does not admit to being ill and encouragement to talk about his past or present life is ignored. Questions on these topics are regarded as superfluous and irrelevant. The content of the patient's talk is fixed to a repetition of his delusional ideas or complaints about his having to be in the hospital. Often no communication is possible because of negativism or overactivity. Nevertheless some data become available pointing to the likelihood of a fixation having occurred at a stage of libidinal development either in the sexual organization or in object relations. Thus a patient may express anxieties about masturbation or indicate a preoccupation with delusional ideas which have a homosexual or oral content. Similarly other psychotic manifestations may comprise fantasies which must have arisen in connection with fixations affecting the sexual organization or object relations. Illustrative are the various varieties of oedipal and preoedipal fantasy and merging phenomena.

Regression of the libido to narcissism or autoerotism results in the characteristic symptoms of paranoid psychosis and schizophrenia. The theory implies the presence of fixations at the narcissistic or autoerotic stages of libidinal development. In some cases there is ample evidence, as indicated by the nature of the object relations, that fixations had occurred (Katan, 1954). The problem which arises is not whether libidinal regression occurs as a supplementary defense in psychosis but whether or not the pathological narcissism which emerges is related to a fixation of the developing libido in infancy and childhood or if it is a different kind of narcissism.

The clinical phenomena which can be interpreted as being "products of regression" (Glover, 1949) can be ordered into at least three groups. First, there are the disorders of the sexual organization. These include a direct preoccupation with phallic, anal and oral drive derivatives. The expression of these drive derivatives can be found in the content of the delusions and the hallucinations. While the action of regression can be invoked in many cases where oral and anal drive representations occur this is not so easily determined in those cases where the phallic drive derivatives are the leading manifestation. In these cases there is rarely unequivocal evidence of the patient's having reached the genital phase of libidinal development. Here the most likely possibility is that there has been a fixation at the phallic stage of the sexual organization. In many cases the patient has reached the phallic level of development. During the illness the aims and objects of the drive derivatives may vary between active and passive on the one hand and homo- and heterosexual on the other.

The second category of phenomena which reflect the activity of regression are changes in the relationship with objects. There are the "oedipal-like" attitudes and fantasies, and behavior reminiscent of the preoedipal child as it passes through the oral (need satisfying) and anal phases of the libido. Inability to tolerate the frustration of needs characterizes the former, negativism the latter, to mention only two behavioral manifestations. In the case of the "oedipal" phenomena it is impossible to ascertain with any confidence whether or not these are the outcome of true oedipal conflicts or whether they are what Katan (1954) has described as narcissistic oedipal complexes.

Third are the phenomena which can be regarded as the result of regression of the ego, superego and the ego ideal. In the case of the superego attention has already been drawn to the manner in which regression may lead to the externalization of guilt. It is less easy to designate the externalization of the superego, with the resulting ideas of reference and auditory hallucinations, as due to regression alone. Nevertheless account has to be taken of these clinical phenomena which reveal only too clearly their origins in narcissism, namely those patients who are convinced that others have the power to read their thoughts or arrange the environment in such a way as to test their integrity. Although such patients are self-critical the attribution of magical powers to those about them indicates the activity of a superego which has regained a narcissism, possibly identical to the narcissism of early childhood.

In the case of the ego ideal it is necessary to recall that these formations also have their origins in narcissism. The phenomena encountered are of several kinds. For example the patient may believe that he is omnipotent and omniscient thus reviving nonspecific childhood wishes. Or the content of the delusions may be quite specific consisting of wished-for ambitions belonging to the latency period, puberty or adolescence. Then there are those cases where the ego ideal is externalized and located in a real or fantasy object. In the schema these manifestations are recorded under the heading "Cathexis of Representations of Real and Fantasy Objects." In all these instances the phenomena must be attributed to a form of narcissism, to a hypercathexis of the self.

A case can be made for the view that regression alone plays little part in the genesis of psychotic symptoms. Rather the symptoms can be regarded as the results of a dissolution which affects the drive organizations, the self-representations, the ego, superego and ego ideals. Such a theory would view the alterations in the ego ideal, in the perception of the bodily and mental self as products of a pathological narcissism which is without any continuity with narcissistic phases of development (Schilder, 1928).

This pathological narcissism comprises a cathexis of self-representations with libido which follows instinctual aims and the primary process. All object representations tend to fall under the influence of this narcissism with self- and object representations being hardly distinguishable from each other. Such a hypothesis renders superfluous the theory of regression in object relations to fixations created at the narcissistic phase of development. It does not, however, take account of the fact that patients who come to develop psychoses have made object choices, in the prepsychotic period, on a narcissistic basis. Such object choices are found in patients where there is evidence of a fixation having taken place at the period when self and object were becoming differentiated and when there was an inability to find a satisfying object for the libidinal cathexis. This cathexis then returned to the self and subsequent object choices were modelled on aspects of the self-representations—actual or wished for. Alternatively the narcissistic fixation followed identification with a love object. In such instances introjection of the object caused a return of libidinal cathexis to the self. When the identification was with the mother, as in the case of a young man, object choice in the prepsychotic period was modelled on the basis of this identification. The object choice was derived from self-representations formed from the condensation of the self and object images.

The narcissistic nature of object representations in the prepsychotic period and the presence of narcissistic fixations on which these representations are based gives support to the view that in psychoses part of the regressive process consists of a return of the libido to narcissistic fixations. It is these fixations which provide much of the predisposition to the illness.

Apart from such considerations there is good reason to assume that many symptoms which arise in psychotic states are not the result of regression to fixation points. In the case of such catatonic phenomena as hypertonia of the voluntary musculature, catalepsy and postural persistence, there is a change in the quality of the muscle tone which can hardly be attributed to psychological regression. Muscle groups (upper limb) whose function is that of discrete voluntary movement assume the characteristics of the postural musculature of the lower limb (extensor antigravity muscles). These changes are usually associated with a special state of consciousness which expresses itself in inattention, disinterest and negativism.

Other phenomena can also be understood as the result of the disorganization of the ego and the drives. In the case of the former disorders of the flow of speech (retardation, blocking) and disorders of visual perception (loss of size constancy, etc.) illustrate, while ambitendency and volitional disturbances would be characteristic of the latter. In order to allow for this category of phenomena and give them a place in the schema a section has been included entitled "Results of Drive and Ego-Superego Disorganization."

Conflicts and the Prepsychotic Personality

Evaluation and assessment of the nature and content of the conflicts existing in the patient are particularly important in psychosis both with respect to the prognosis and the possibilities of a psychotherapeutic approach to the illness. While conflicts of an external nature are uncommon in neurosis they assume considerable significance in psychotic states. This is partly because in psychosis the essential conflict is between the id drives and the objects of the environment and because of the extent to which an externalization of wishes, fantasy objects and anxieties takes place. The degree of externalization of conflicts gives some indication of the severity of the disturbance, and indicates how far the patient may gain insight into the detrimental effects of his illness.

It is the internalized conflicts which reveal the essential continuity between the psychosis and the prepsychotic personality. These conflicts may be oedipal, they may arise from death wishes, from passive wishes, from pregenital aims, object loss, etc. The same conflicts are to be found in the prepsychotic period and in the psychosis. In some cases these conflicts find an outlet in neurotic symptoms in the prepsychotic personality. In others they are manifested in inhibitions and specific personality traits. The symptoms of a psychosis only represent a new method of dealing with the conflicts. This new means becomes necessary when a compromise is no longer realizable between the drive derivatives and repression. An evaluation of the internalized conflicts as they appear in the psychosis pave the way for a metapsychological assessment of the prepsychotic personality. Knowledge of conflicts on the one hand, and neurotic symptoms, inhibitions and personality traits on the other provide an insight into the efficacy of repression and other defenses active in the prepsychotic period.

The distribution of libidinal cathexes between self and object, prior to the illness, can be assessed by a scrutiny of the manner in which the patient perceived his self and his preferred forms of interpersonal relationships as and when they occurred. With respect to the self the question to be answered is to what extent it is based on stable identifications or to what extent it has been derived from ego ideal fantasies which are close to the primitive, primary narcissism. Sometimes a recognition can be gained of the quality of the drive derivatives, their aims and objects which underlie the manifest object relations whether real or fantastic. As Katan (1954) has suggested these can be narcissistic in nature. Drive cathexes invest objects which are a barely disguised substitute for the self. The object representation may therefore serve to express passive or active, feminine or masculine wishes. In other cases the object representation is derived from preoedipal phases with drive derivatives having the characteristics of the need-satisfying stage of libidinal development. When such information is available it throws light on the predominant sexual organization existing in the prepsychotic personality.

The final changes effected in this profile relate to the last section—namely "Assessment of Some General Characteristics with a Bearing on Prognosis and Treatment." Criteria which are relevant for estimating a neurotic patient's capacity to engage in analytic therapy are not appropriate for cases of psychosis. The patient with a psychosis usually denies that he is ill. The stability of both ego and superego is doubtful and conflicts are externalized to some extent. Additionally there is rarely the capacity to sustain object cathexes, even when these appear to be present, in the service of a therapeutic alliance. Such object libido as finds expression in transference is unreliable and transient in nature. However this does not mean that a psychotherapeutic approach to the patient is entirely ruled out. It merely indicates that psychoanalytic treatment as employed in the neuroses is usually impossible except in a small number of cases.

CHAPTER 2

The Metapsychological Profile Schema

In psychotic states the combinations of symptoms which can occur are so varied that only occasionally is it possible to identify consistently, recurring patterns of phenomena. In uncomplicated cases of mania and in severe depressions, for example, it is possible to envisage that the clinical phenomena are the result of a primary disorder of affect but this explanation of symptom formation is difficult to sustain in the face of those cases where there is either psychomotor overactivity without elation of mood or the overactivity is accompanied by persecutory delusions. The combination of a disorder of psychomotility either in the direction of overactivity or retardation with a paranoid (persecutory) syndrome is by no means uncommon.

The situation is further complicated in those cases where psychomotor overactivity is gradually replaced by a state characterized by withdrawal, negativism and cataleptic phenomena. The problem has not been solved by the use of such diagnostic terms as paranoid depression, schizo-affective state and mixed manic-depressive psychosis. The same problem is encountered when attempts are made to classify those conditions in which disorders of volition and persecutory delusions play a leading part. More often than not diagnosis has ultimately to be based on the course and outcome of the illness.

With the aid of the Profile Schema all the clinical phenomena which are to be found in cases of psychosis can be examined systematically from a number of different standpoints. Both positive and negative symptoms, to follow the Jacksonian classification (Freeman, 1969a), can be assessed in terms of conflicts, defenses and the regressions which have affected object and drive representations, ego and superego. They can also be assessed according to the fixation points which are cathected by the regression of the libido.

By relating the symptomatology to the state of the libidinal distribution existing between self and object and between the representations of the inner and outer world it becomes possible to view the clinical phenomena from yet another vantage point. The symptoms can then be differentiated on the basis of the extent to which they represent a return to earlier or later stages of libidinal development, thereby permitting comparison with object relations in the healthy infant and child. These symptoms which are caused by a return of primitive forms of libidinal cathexis are distinguished in the Profile from those that are the result of a redistribution of the libido—i.e., the hallucinations and the delusions. At the same time space has been allotted to record the presence of those object and self-cathexes which have not succumbed to the dissolution of healthy mental life.

Profile studies may be made at any point in a psychotic illness—at the onset, when the illness is fully established, when the major symptoms have disappeared, in remission and at relapse. When a series of Profiles are completed on one patient comparisons can be made between the states of the object and self-cathexis, the defense organization, regressions, etc. Profiles made at later stages of the illness amplify and correct the information obtained earlier. For example reports of experiences which are initially regarded as real prove to be the products of psychical reality.

Additionally, Profiles have applicability for those cases where the symptomatology falls within a particular symptom complex or syndrome (catatonic, paranoid etc.) or for those cases where the symptomatology is scattered. A comparison can be made in terms of defenses, regressions, fixations, object and self-cathexis, etc. In the material which will be described later it will be seen that the metapsychological Profile lends itself to an ordering of symptomatology which is quite different from that which is possible by means of the classical descriptive case-taking procedure. Examination of Profiles reveals that symptoms and symptom complexes are but final common paths for the expression of drive representations and the forces opposing them. At the same time in those psychoses where clinical manifestations are apparently dissimilar it can be shown that they hold in common identical conflicts and defenses.

In the profile schema a distinction is made between the "cathexis of real persons," the "cathexis of real object representations" and the "cathexis of fantasy objects." The first concept refers to the patient's attitudes and behavior to others in his immediate environment (current, functioning relationships)—if in hospital, nurses, doctors, ancillary staff and other patients; if at home, relatives and friends. The second concept consists of the endopsychic representation of objects (relatives, friends, etc.) from the present, from the immediate, intermediate and distant past. These object representations may be conscious (as when a patient longs to be home with his wife), preconscious or unconscious. The third concept includes fantasy objects derived from the contemporary life scene or from childhood or adolescent memory and experience. The schema makes provision for the observation that "real persons" may be condensed with "real object representations" (present and past) and with "fantasy object representations."

THE PROFILE SCHEMA

1. REASON FOR REFERRAL

Symptoms, anxieties, abnormal behavior, affective disorders, motility disturbance, breakdowns in functioning, inability to fulfill inherent potentialities, arrests in development leading to faulty ego and superego structuralization, regressions of ego and superego.

2. DESCRIPTION OF THE PATIENT AS DIRECTLY OR INDIRECTLY CONVEYED IN THE INTERVIEW

Personal appearance and behavior, attitudes, affects, etc.

3. FAMILY BACKGROUND (PAST AND PRESENT) AND PERSONAL HISTORY

As provided by patient, relatives, friends, etc.

4. POSSIBLY SIGNIFICANT ENVIRONMENTAL CIRCUMSTANCES

Interviewers as well as patient's evaluation where available.)

(a) in relation to timing of referral.
(b) in relation to overall causation of the disturbances.
(c) in relation to connections between individual and family pathology and their interaction.

5. ASSESSMENT OF THE DRIVES

A. The Libido

(1) *Problems of Libido Distribution*

(a) *Cathexis of the Self.* As the self-representations are not equally affected by the disorder of libidinal distribution an account should be given of those representations which have been involved by the pathological process and those which have not. First, phenomena should be described which reflect a cathexis of the self-representations with drive derivatives which follow the primary process. Does this form of cathexis of the mental self find expression in heightened self-esteem, a pathologically exaggerated self-confidence, sense of power, ideas of omnipotence and omniscience? Does this cathexis so affect the bodily self that there are feelings of great physical strength, sense of well being, an intensification of sensation (e.g., genital, oral), percepts, etc. Is the ego ideal subject to this hypercathexis with wishes and ambitions fulfilled? Is there a merging of self- and object representations? Is there a disturbance of the sense of identity as a consequence of the merging? Is there an externalization of aspects of the bodily and mental self? Is there a tendency to generalize (externalize) thoughts and affects to external objects? Are all the phenomena referred to constant or subject to change? What is the stimulus for the change? Second, are there self-representations based on identifications (secondary) which remain unaffected by the psychosis? An account should be given of them.

Is there a decathexis of the self-representations which finds expression in loss of interest in the self, self-neglect, loss of the sense of well being and self-esteem? Are these phenomena associated with a withdrawal and disinterest in external reality? Is the decathexis of the self or real object representations accompanied by a hypercathexis of the object representations of both past and present? What is the quality of this hypercathexis and the relation to reality testing? Is the loss of the capacity to think, remember, attend and perceive due to a decathexis? Is there a decathexis of the connections between thinking and motility leading to the characteristic splitting between cognition and action? Is there a decathexis of the bodily aspects of the self-representations? Is there a loss of sensation or changes in the body image in the direction of disintegration? Is the sense of identity completely lost?

(b) *Cathexis of Objects*:

i. Cathexis of Real Persons (Current Relationships)

The abnormalities in relating arising from the changes in the quality and quantities (cathexis) of the libidinal drive derivatives should be described. What light do the phenomena throw on the quality of the drive derivatives? Are the drive derivatives instinctual, of primary process type and similar to that obtaining at the need-satisfying level of mental development? Is the patient's interest in the external object wholly or partly dependent on need satisfaction? Is there low frustration tolerance if the need is not met with the consequent expression of aggression? Does lack of satisfaction lead to disinterest in the object? To what extent is the external object an independent entity apart from the patient and his needs? Is there condensation of external objects and representation of other objects, of word representations leading to a lack of correspondence between the external object and its mental representation. This will be expressed in misidentifications, misperceptions and in "aberrant" concepts.

Are the drive derivatives of a more advanced kind reflecting the establishment of object constancy? Is this reflected in a concern for the external object apart from the satisfaction of needs? Is the relationship maintained in the face of the frustration of needs and the expression of aggression? Is there a wish to protect or rescue the object, a concern for its welfare, or is there jealousy and envy of the object? Is there a withdrawal of interest from external objects due to their decathexis? Is this the result of a hypercathexis (introversion) of libidinal cathexis onto object representations of the past or present? Do the clinical phenomena provide information about the quality of the hypercathexis—is reality testing maintained? Is there evidence of disillusionment with the objects together with associated family romance fantasies, twin fantasies, imaginary companions, etc.? Is the object cathexis of the preoedipal, oedipal or postoedipal phases of libidinal development? If the object exists in its own right what part is played by heterosexual cathexis on the one hand and homosexual cathexis on the other hand? Is the patient attracted to objects which serve as substitutes for or extensions of ties with other individuals? Is the cathexis active or passive in aim?

Last, how are external objects experienced by the patient —as loving, reassuring, supporting, advising or persecutory?

ii. Cathexis of Representations of Real and Fantasy Objects

Are the mental representations of current or past real objects subject to a hypercathexis with resultant delusional or hallucinatory phenomena? Are the representations which are cathected with these primitive drive derivatives of a purely fantastic nature? Does the hypercathexis of both kinds of representation result in misidentifications and/or affect bodily and mental sensibility? Details should be provided as to the nature of the misidentifications and of the fantasy (delusional) objects. The modality in which the hallucinations occur should be noted. Do the delusional and hallucinatory phenomena have an "instinctual" content in contrast to the content derived from an externalized and fragmented superego? Is the content aggressive or libidinal? If libidinal, note should be taken of the source, aim and object. The predominating sexual organization and such part instincts as are apparent should be described.

An account should be given of the patient's attitudes to the delusional objects. Is he friendly, hostile or dependent with respect to these objects? Again a description should be given of the attitudes of the delusional objects as perceived by the patient—are they advising, reassuring, critical or persecutory? Do the delusional objects consist of real objects which exist in the present or existed in the past?

Note should be made as to whether or not the delusional objects are intermittent or constant in their expression: are they cathected, decathected and then recathected? If they disappear what circumstances lead to their reappearance? What kind of defenses are associated with the appearance and disappearance of the delusional reality?

(2) *Libidinal Position.* Although details have already been given as to the aims and objects of the libidinal drives in the section on the cathexis of objects, further aspects of their expression are to be referred to here. Note should be made of the levels of sexual organization existing in the patient—both genital and pregenital. If the genital-phallic level has been attained is there evidence of its activity? What are the objects of these drives—are they hetero- or homosex-

ual? If the sexual organization is predominantly pregenital specify whether oral or anal or both, and if both, which libidinal impulses are most prominent. The aims of the pregenital organization should be recorded—are they incorporative, sadistic, retentive, etc.? What part do the component instincts of scopophilia and exhibitionism, sadism and masochism play? Are the aims of the drives predominantly active or passive?

B. *Aggression*

Is there evidence of direct expression of aggression in speech or action? What stimuli lead to the expression of aggression? Is this expression related to frustration of wishes, jealousy and envy or is it a reaction to fear of or actual object loss? What are the consequences of the direct expression of aggression? Are there indications of self-criticism, withdrawal from external reality, fear of aggression from others, catatonic manifestations? Are there other signs of disturbed motility?

What is the quality of the aggression? Has it been altered by the effects of regression? Is the aggression characterized by death wishes or by the sadism associated with the pregenital sexual organizations? Does the aggression find representation in sadistic drives associated with the phallic, anal or oral libido?

Does aggression find an indirect expression only because of the action of defenses set in motion by the danger situation created by the drive? Is the object of the aggression changed by displacement, turning in on the self or identification? Are the aim and object of the aggression altered by projection or by reversal? Is there externalization of the aggression either through generalization to external objects or through attributing responsibility to the real or fantasy object? Is there self-reproach through introjection of the aggression into the superego? Is aggression followed by anxiety for the safety of the object?

What connection exists between the quality of the aggressive drive derivatives and the characteristics of the superego? Does the superego possess features belonging to the pregenital organization of the libido? Does it have oral or anal sadistic features?

6. ASSESSMENT OF EGO AND SUPEREGO

(1) *Ego Functions*

(a) Give details of disorders of thinking as expressed through speech. Is the form of the speech intact? Is there pressure or retardation of speech? Is there an obstruction of speech (blocking of thought), "derailment" or omission in the flow of associations? Is there evidence of perseveration or echo phenomena? Is the content of speech limited to a few themes, compulsively repeated, i.e., is there "distraction of thought"?

Describe where possible the manner in which the primary process has affected verbalization. Are there indications of a fluctuation between normal and abnormal thinking and vice-versa? Does retardation or obstruction of speech give way to fluent verbalization? What is the content of speech when this occurs? What are the conditions under which blocking or retardation becomes manifest? Is the disorder of speech and thinking employed for defensive purposes? Is there evidence of a failure on the patient's part to comprehend the speech of others? When present does this have a defensive aim?

(b) Provide information about those instances where thinking has assumed a magical, omnipotent quality. Describe the operation of the primary process when it influences the thought processes.

(c) Is the patient able to sustain attention for the purposes of ordered thinking and speech and for appropriate reactions to environmental stimuli? Are there signs of distractibility? Does this distractibility emanate from the patient's attempt to understand his experiences or is the external stimulus experienced passively, outside of consciousness, thereby making its appearance in speech only secondarily. Is there a fluctuation between states of inattention and purposive, directed attending? Is the change to normal attention related to the anticipation of the satisfaction of a need or to delusional or hallucinatory experiences.

(d) What is the state of the perceptual functions? Are the modalities adequately differentiated; is there evidence of synesthesia? In the sphere of visual perception is there any disturbance of size, shape or distance constancies? Are percepts experienced more intensely than normal—for example, noise or color. Are percepts experienced concretely? Does the eye or ear have symbolic significance for the patient? Does the patient perceive a physical change in his body? Can he discriminate one individual from another? Are there condensations of visual percepts and memory traces leading to misidentifications? Is there evidence of hallucination in one or more of the sensory modalities?

(e) Note whether there is an obvious defect of short-term or remote memory. Are memories deranged with respect to their temporal sequence? Is there repression of significant life experiences prior to the onset of the illness? Do memories make their appearance in the hallucinations or delusions?

(f) Are there disturbances of voluntary movement (ego control of motility) ? Is the patient able to act and complete an intention or a command? Does motor blocking occur during the course of a voluntary act? Is there evidence of ambitendency? Note the presence of motor perseveration, repetitive movements and echopraxia. Describe any disorders of posture. Note *flexibilitas cerea* if in evidence and postural persistence. Are there periods when voluntary movement occurs normally? What kind of verbal content and affect are associated with the transition from abnormal motility and vice-versa?

Is there motor overactivity? If so what affects and mental content are associated with it? Note the fantasies associated with all varieties of motility disorders.

(2) *Ego Reactions to Danger Situations*

State the extent to which danger is experienced by the ego as coming from the environment. Does this danger arise from fantasy objects which have become condensed with external objects? Does the danger situation arise from "pressure" of the drive derivatives? If so what is their nature? Are they predominantly aggressive or libidinal? What is their content? Is the danger situation created by real or fantasied object loss? How extensive is the role played by the superego in causing the danger situation? Is there overt anxiety as a consequence of these dangers? Is this anxiety then experienced in terms of castration anxiety, separation anxiety, superego anxiety, etc.

(3) *State of Defense Organization*

The extent to which repression has failed in containing the drive representations must be evaluated. Successful repression is based on the operation of an anticathexis which ensures a continued freedom from awareness of the drive derivatives. Thus, where repression has failed, to what extent has projection intervened to influence the source, aim and object of the drive representations, rendering them ego-alien. Is projection accompanied by identification with the aggressor? Is there evidence of externalization in the form of attributing to external objects responsibility and intent for unwanted drive derivatives? Is the externalization part of a merging process of self- and object representations, the aim of which is to annul the danger and anxiety over object loss? Does this primitive form of identification with the lost object compensate for the faulty repression of the painful affect? Is there externalization of aspects of the self-representation as a defense? Does turning in on the self and reversal operate to deflect drive derivatives? Are these mechanisms associated with aggressive or libidinal drive derivatives? What part does denial of external reality play in the defense? Is this denial associated with faulty reality testing? What relationship exists between denial and repression? Are both based on a decathexis? Is reaction formation intact?

In those cases where repression appears to be effective in denying drive representations, memories and ideas access to consciousness as ego-syntonic formations, is this due to repression proper (employment of an anticathexis) or is it a result of a decathexis of the representation, e.g., wishes, thoughts, memories, etc.? Is repression proper or decathexis of internal or external reality motivated by anxiety or the superego? In cases where the ego disorganization is extensive and the superego decathected or externalized, is control of the drives dependent on objects in the environment? Are these real or delusional objects or a condensation of both?

(4) *Affects*

Note should be made of the predominant affects—are they evidenced only in emotion subjectively experienced or do they also find somatic and behavioral expression? Are the affects constantly present or are they episodic? Is there an apparent diminution or loss of affect? When an affect appears is it appropriate to the speech content? Is there loss of control of the affects? What is the patient's reaction to the emergence of strong affects within himself—are they followed by withdrawal, negativism, motility symptoms (catatonic signs) or self-criticism?

Is there depression of mood? Is this accompanied by anxiety? Is the depression of mood associated with psychomotor retardation or with an acceleration of speech and/or motor overactivity? Is self-reproach present or absent? Is the affective state one of apathy and indifference? Where there is elation of mood is there also evidence of depressive thought content such as a sense of hopelessness, loss of interest in life and self-criticism? Is there anxiety associated with the elation? Is there retardation of thought and/or action associated with the elation of mood? What defenses are operating contemporaneously with the expression of affect—is it projection, externalization, identification with the aggressor, denial, etc.?

(5) *Superego*

An assessment must be made of the superego with respect to its relation to the ego on the one hand and the drive derivatives on the other. The stability of the superego must also be assessed. Is there a hypercathexis of the superego with aggression? Does this lead to the ego functions (thinking, remembering, etc.) no longer operating in a smooth, satisfying and effortless manner? Is there self-reproach? Is the aggressive hypercathexis associated with the kind of disturbance of libidinal distribution between self and objects which leads to faulty reality testing, or is it free of this complication? Where there is faulty reality testing is the superego externalized with resultant ideas of being observed and criticized?

Has the superego lost its controlling function over the drive derivatives? Is this due to a decathexis, to regression or dissolution? Do the ego functions completely follow in the wake of the drive derivatives? Is there a dedifferentiation of the superego? Are there signs of regression of the superego? Does the superego have characteristics of the oral or anal-sadistic organizations of the libido? Is the consequence of such regression the appearance of defenses such as projection or identification with the aggressor?

7. ASSESSMENT OF REGRESSIONS AND POSSIBLE FIXATION

The extent of the regressive trend can be assessed from the products of regression which are to be observed within the mass of clinical material. Indications of libidinal regression may be noted in the sphere of object relations and in the predominant sexual organization when compared with the prepsychotic personality. Similarly the clinical phenomena reflect the extent to which regression has affected the ego and superego. At the same time the products of libidinal and ego regression must be distinguished from other positive manifestations of the psychosis which are in part the result of a disorganization of the most advanced levels of the libidinal cathexes (self and object) and of the ego which the patient had achieved prior to the onset of the illness. Sometimes it may be possible to identify the fixation points which occurred in the process of the libidinal development from the nature of the clinical phenomena.

(a) Describe those phenomena which are due to a libidinal regression affecting objects—e.g., note those object relations which are similar to those encountered in infancy and early childhood—where self and object are not completely differentiated; where need satisfaction is predominant; where the capacity to sustain frustration is limited. Provide details of more advanced states of object libidinal development—e.g., relationships with the characteristics of the Oedipus phase. Both elementary and advanced states of object libidinal development may occur in the one case.

(b) Provide details of phenomena which are the result of regression to earlier stages of the sexual organization. Evidences of autoerotic oral, anal and phallic preoccupations, fantasies and interests should be recorded.

(c) Note the presence of phenomena resulting from the regression of ego functions—e.g., certain aspects of thought disorder (magic and concrete thinking), disorders of attention (distractibility), perceptual abnormalities (synesthesias) and "prestages of defense" associated with the early phases of ego development.

(d) Is there evidence of regression of the superego; is there evidence of regression of the ego ideal?

(e) A statement should be given of delusional and hallucinatory content which is representative of specific childhood fantasies (rescue fantasies, fantasies of the imaginary companion, pregnancy fantasies) from any stage of the sexual organization or object libidinal phase.

(f) Describe any indications of possible fixation points in libidinal development from available material.

8. RESULTS OF DRIVE AND EGO DISORGANIZATION

Here a statement should be provided of phenomena which cannot be regarded as resulting from regression. Such phenomena bear no relationship to developmental phases of the libido or the ego. In part they can be attributed to the activity of the primary process.

(a) Detail in turn phenomena reflecting a disorganization of each of the ego functions—e.g., disorders of speech form (blocking); deterioration in conceptual powers with formation of "aberrant" concepts due to condensations and displacements; visual misidentifications and hallucinations; memory defects; disorders of motility (motor blocking, catalepsy, perseveration).

(b) An account should be given of disorders which affect the cathexis of the self. Similarly a description should be provided of phenomena resulting from disorganization of the body ego (e.g., changes in the sexual characteristics of the body, disturbances of voluntary movement).

(c) Provide information about drive disorganization —e.g., ambitendency, automatic obedience, negativism.

9. ASSESSMENT OF CONFLICTS

The assessment of conflicts in psychoses bears directly on the severity of the personality disorganization and the question of prognosis. Attention should therefore be paid to the extent to which conflicts remain internalized and to the degree that internalized conflicts have been externalized.

(a) *External Conflicts:*

As these are quite common in psychosis they should be noted. However they must be distinguished from the externalization of internalized conflicts and the associated object relationship.

(b) *Internalized Conflicts:*

Note should be made of the extent to which conflicts are still internalized.

(c) *Internal Conflicts:*

An account should be given of the degree to which active and passive strivings and, masculine and feminine tendencies remain incompatible with one another.

10. THE PREPSYCHOTIC PERSONALITY

In order to obtain a comprehensive picture of the prepsychotic personality the statements of relatives and friends of the patient are frequently relied upon. The questions which are set out below can sometimes be answered when the following information is sought. Relevant is data about the patient's capacity or incapacity for establishing and enjoying relationships; his sexual life; success or failure in work; ability to enjoy the ordinary pleasures of life; special vulnerabilities; the ability to withstand disappointments; losses, misfortunes, environmental changes, etc.

What was the state of the libidinal distribution between self and objects characterizing the prepsychotic personality? Was there a trend toward the merging of self and object images or undue generalization (externalization) of thoughts and affects? With regard to the self were the representations based on stable identifications or on primitive (narcissistic) fantasies? What was the quality of the drive derivatives; what were their objects and aims? Were the object representations heterosexual or homosexual? If heterosexual did they have a narcissistic basis? Did real objects serve as a vehicle for unwanted aspects of the self or of repudiated drive derivatives? Did real objects act principally as a means of need satisfaction? What was the predominant sexual organization? Were there neurotic symptoms, inhibitions, restrictions and traits of personality characterizing the prepsychotic personality? What internalized conflicts existed? Were they the same as those found during the psychosis? What was the state of the defense organization? Was repression deficient in any way? What other defenses were active? Was there a tendency to externalize unwanted aspects of the self-representations in a nonspecific way? What was the level of intelligence and scholastic achievement?

11. ASSESSMENT OF SOME GENERAL CHARACTERISTICS WITH A BEARING ON PROGNOSIS AND TREATMENT

(a) To what extent is the ego's sphere of influence restricted by withdrawal of cathexes, restitutional symptoms, defenses, etc.?

(b) Are the principal (internalized) conflicts wholly externalized or are they still internalized, at least to some degree?

(c) Are the major defenses, e.g., repression, still intact or is there a direct expression of drive representations, e.g., genital, or pregenital behavior?

(d) Are there areas of established sublimation?

(e) Is the superego still internalized or is it mainly externalized and dedifferentiated?

(f) Does the patient have insight, even transiently, into the fact of being ill?

(g) Is there any capacity for self-observation, self-criticism, ability to think and verbalize?

(h) What is the state of the object cathexes? What is their nature? Is there the possibility of a working transference developing?

(i) Is there sufficient capacity to tolerate anxiety without a further withdrawal of cathexes and further psychotic symptomatology?

PROFILE NO. 1

This Profile is based on material obtained during a five-week period following the patient's admission to hospital.

1. REASON FOR REFERRAL

The patient, a young man of 18, had over a period of three to four weeks become disinterested in his work as a farmer. He was noted to be moody and solitary. One day he became extremely disturbed. His speech was disjointed and he easily became violent. He was found to be adopting strange postures as well as grimacing and laughing to himself. When he spoke it was about vampires, blood, space vehicles and evil spirits. He was frightened and there was some evidence to suggest that he was hearing imaginary voices. At times his attitude became so threatening as to frighten his parents. He was admitted to the Mental Hospital as an emergency.

2. DESCRIPTION OF THE PATIENT AND HISTORY OF THE ILLNESS

Mr. W. was of average height and slight of build. He had very fair hair and was of ruddy complexion. He wore a denture to substitute for two upper front teeth which had been knocked out in an accident some years previously. No sooner was he in the hospital than he attacked a nurse. His whole bearing reflected a potential for violence. He looked angry and his body was held taut. As he was brought into the consulting room he struck a cupboard several times with his fist. When he entered the room he picked up an ashtray and was about to throw it through the window. He laughed and grimaced. He looked at the ceiling and said, "There's that bloody man who wants to break my leg . . . damn him, I don't care." He stared angrily at the admitting doctor and asked him why he was in the hospital. Following this he was unresponsive to questioning and remained silent.

According to the patient's father he had been quite well until a month or two prior to the acute attack. In the autumn of 1969 he had started studies at an Agricultural College, where he was apparently unhappy. He complained that he could neither concentrate nor sleep at night. He left after eight weeks and returned home to work on the farm. He was not upset by having to give up his studies. On the contrary, he felt quite well. He recalled that in the spring of 1970 he was remarkably fit and in excellent spirits. One Sunday at church some girls looked at him. He thought to himself that he must be quite handsome to attract their attention. He even had the thought, at this time, that he was a sufficiently good football player to be employed by an English football club. In late summer of 1970 his brother upset him by talking about homosexuality (see Possibly Significant Environmental Events). Following this he became preoccupied with the fear that he might be a homosexual. This fear was based on his brother's statement that homosexuals recognized each other. His anxiety increased over the next weeks until it culminated in the acute psychotic attack.

3. FAMILY BACKGROUND AND PERSONAL HISTORY

The patient's father was a farmer, a man aged 60. He had suffered two attacks of coronary thrombosis. The first attack occurred when the patient was 12, the second when the patient was 14 years of age. The mother is aged 55 and is healthy. He has two sisters and a brother. The oldest sister is married and in good health. The younger sister, 25 years old, is single and works in a bank. The brother is aged 24 and works on the farm. The patient is the youngest of the family and is six years younger than his brother. There is a history of mental illness in the family. An uncle committed suicide when the patient was 15 years old. Another uncle had been hospitalized on several occasions for mental illness. The patient has always been close to his mother but very fond of his father too. The family is close knit. All were very concerned about the patient's illness. According to the parents he got on well with his siblings.

Mr. W's mother reported that he was a large baby at birth. He walked and talked very quickly. When he started school at five years of age he was inclined to complain of abdominal pain and nausea. He was taken to see the doctor who thought he might have a peptic ulcer. A further complaint at this time was shortness of breath. Both symptoms gradually subsided. At school he had no difficulties with lessons and was considered a bright child. He joined the scouts and went to camp. While there he fainted and was unwell for a few days. His mother recalled that at the age of 11 he was admitted to hospital after having injured his leg. He became considerably upset by the presence of a dying man who was in the adjacent bed. He passed his Eleven Plus examination and started grammar school.

Around 12 or 13 years of age there was a deterioration in his school work and he slipped from third place to the middle of the class. This was the time when his father had a heart attack and when there was some family discord, details of which will be described in the next section. He took G.C.E. when 17 years old and started the Agricultural College in the autumn of 1969. According to the parents the patient was cheerful and a good mixer prior to the illness. Although he did not have much contact with girls, he had several male friends with whom he went to football matches and to a youth club. While still at school he would work with his father on the farm and enjoyed going to the market to buy and sell animals.

4. POSSIBLY SIGNIFICANT ENVIRONMENTAL EVENTS

(a) *In the Years Prior to the Onset of the Illness.* Shortly after starting the Agricultural College two of the students embarked on a program of entering other students' bedrooms at night. This frightened Mr. W. the more so because one of these students had made a homosexual advance to him. According to the patient, the young man in question had two protruding upper front teeth. Each night Mr. W. would barricade his door and could not fall asleep for fear of an intrusion. As mentioned above, shortly before the onset of the illness the patient's brother had talked to him about homosexuality, claiming that homosexuals recognized one another. The patient immediately recalled an experience a year or so earlier when a man tried to seduce him.

(b) *At age 13 to 14.* When Mr. W. was 13 his parents were on bad terms. It was rumored that his father was having an affair with another woman. This upset Mr. W. who recalled being unhappy and depressed. At the time his class at school was studying *Hamlet.* Mr. W. had the fantasy of poisoning his parents and committing suicide. His father had had his first heart attack when the patient was 12.

The patient was frightened and guilty about masturbation. He believed it was causing his blood to become thin, depleting him of energy. He had dreams of a vampire sucking his blood. He believed that the teacher at school could read his mind and knew he was masturbating. He was very self-conscious. This was accentuated by his being teased about his fair hair and red face. He was called "turnip face" by the other children. There were even times when he thought he heard voices talking to him. Gradually all these unpleasant ideas and feelings disappeared but he remained shy particularly with girls.

5. ASSESSMENT OF THE DRIVES:

A. Libido

(1) *Problems of Libido Distribution*

(a) *Cathexis of the Self.* A hypercathexis of the mental self-representations was reflected in ideas of omnipotence. The patient claimed to be a chosen person whose mission it was to help others. He had special powers. He had electricity in his body which detected homosexuals. He could repel evil spirits and remove evil from others. He could cure homosexuality. He could stop people from writing, reading or any action in which they were engaged. He could read minds. There was an externalization of aspects of the mental and bodily self. A scar on his left cheek was also present in everyone else. The scar gave him the power to read minds and the gift of premonition. He had the feeling that the psychiatrist, Dr. T., might be a homosexual. There was a merging of self with objects, the result being that he felt himself influenced by and influencing others. His uncle was subject to depression and peculiar behavior. This caused Mr. W. to behave in the same way. When the uncle was ill so was he; when the uncle recovered he did too. Dr. T. was strong and healthy when he was well, and weaker and ill when he was sickly. His favorite football players played poorly if he felt weak. Mr. W. had observed that his left leg felt weak when he noticed that the dog had a lame left leg.

Certain self-representations were based on identifications.

One discernible identification was with his father, who provided him with various points of connection. Again he identified with Marilyn Monroe, the film actress. Like her he had fair hair, delicate bones and a turned-up nose.

The phenomena resulting from the hypercathexis of the self were not present all the time. After some weeks they gradually disappeared.

b. *Cathexis of Objects:*

i. Cathexis of Real Persons (Current Relationships)

During the first two days in hospital there was no cathexis of real object representations. There was only a cathexis of delusional objects. Shortly afterwards real persons were cathected by both primitive and advanced forms of libidinal drive derivatives. This was to be observed in the patient's thoughts and feelings about Dr. T. He did not always regard him as an entity separate from himself. When Mr. W. experienced a pain or sensation he would indicate that Dr. T. must be having the same experience. Other examples have been given under the concept of merging of self and object. He wished to be like Dr. T. and therefore believed that he had some of his (Dr. T's) physical characteristics. His hair was becoming dark like that of Dr. T. At the same time he acknowledged Dr. T. as a separate person.

The relationship was, after a few weeks, clearly not dependent on need satisfaction. He accepted Dr. T's recommendations and did not show anger or withdrawal if disappointed. He admired and respected Dr. T. He wanted to protect him and save him from evil spirits and homosexuality. The homosexual cathexis of Dr. T. was warded off by his insisting that his liking for him had nothing to do with homosexuality. Similarly he maintained that his love for his father was not homosexual. Heterosexual objects were cathected.

ii. Cathexis of Representations of Real and Fantasy Objects

Many of the fantasies which came to comprise the delusional reality were derived from horror films which the patient appeared to have enjoyed. The cathexis of these fantasies resulted in the belief that certain persons were vampires—e.g., fellow students at the Agricultural College and other patients. He believed a calf was a vampire when he saw blood dripping from its mouth. It was this sight which led to the panic at the onset of the illness. The hypercathexis of these fantasies led to false perceptions. He felt certain persons had protruding teeth like vampires—both males and females. He attacked a male nurse thinking he was a female vampire.

His belief in reincarnation satisfactorily explained his conviction that a patient was really a man who had died when he (the patient) was 12 years old. He had been much affected by this man then and misidentified the patient now. It was his belief that when an evil person died he entered the body of a living being. Several patients were regarded as evil and homosexual. Initially he was afraid that the vampires would suck his blood. He thought his face had become pale as a result of loss of blood. His fear was similar to the one experienced at puberty. He was afraid he would be contaminated by the homosexuality of the delusional objects. Later he believed he could save these individuals from evil, vampirism and homosexuality. He had a dream in which two patients identified by him as homosexuals were engaged in sexual relations. He tried to stop them.

These manifestations were at their height during the first few days after admission. They gradually subsided after a period of some weeks. Fears of being injured and being turned into a homosexual were the first manifestations to disappear.

(2) *Libidinal Position*

At first sight the patient seemed to have reached the phallic phase with active aims directed toward heterosexual objects as evidenced in masturbatory fantasies. However, the feminine identification described above suggested that the object of the genital drive was a narcissistic one, i.e., his own body.

Pregenital, particularly anal drives with passive aims, were present as reflected in his statement that he experienced anal sensations while in the company of Dr. T. Reference to the oral organization of the libido present in this patient will be discussed later (see Regression and Fixations).

B. *Aggression*

This patient was very violent at the time of admission to hospital. He attacked nurses and was threatening in manner. This aggression was activated by anxiety, which arose from the dread of delusional objects. The aggression subsided with the lessening of anxiety. Aggression was further stimulated by the thought that his father was not interested in him. At puberty he had wished his father dead when it was rumored that the father was involved with another woman. Later the death wishes were effectively repressed.

Aggression was projected onto delusional objects—bulls, vampires, etc. One bull in particular frightened the patient. This bull had been bought by his father from a man whom the patient regarded as having an evil face.

6. ASSESSMENT OF EGO AND SUPEREGO:

(1) *Ego Functions*

(a) Speech was always intact in form. The volume of speech was good and there was no evidence of blocking, omission of thoughts, etc.

(b) Reference to the omnipotent thought content has been made.

(c) Attention was good.

(d) Visual perception was disordered in terms of misinterpretations and misidentifications due to condensation of percepts and memory traces.

(e) Memory was intact.

(f) Voluntary movements were periodically subject to sexualization. The patient had a feeling that crossing his legs had a homosexual connotation. He immediately had to adopt a new position. Otherwise movement was quite normal after the initial acute attack when posturing and grimacing occurred.

(2) *Ego Reactions to Danger Situations*

For some weeks Mr. W. experienced the external world as dangerous insofar as it was populated by delusional figures. Reference has already been made to them. The delusional figures were a condensation of real and fantasy objects. Basically the danger situation had three sources. The first was the pressure of the libidinal drive derivatives. The awakening of passive-feminine drive cathexes led to castration anxiety. The castration anxiety not only found expression in oral terms—that is, the fear of the vampire biting and sucking his blood but also in his fear of the bull. This bull was feared because it was thought to be evil. Additionally the patient recalled, after the acute psychotic symptoms had passed, that during time spent with Dr. T. he always experienced an unpleasant sensation in his genitalia. An anxiety dream offered further evidence of castration fear and the causative passive sexual aims—"a man has been hanged, his eyes were staring and then the eyeballs fell out."

Merging with certain objects presented a second source of danger. The patient dreaded his uncle's attacks of illness because of their effect on him. As Mr. W. improved he told Dr. T. he must separate from him to recover. At one point he remembered that immediately prior to the acute attack, he had been raking manure and suddenly became frightened at the thought of being engulfed by it. The patient was fearful of object loss which constituted the third source of danger. Whenever he heard of a death he developed a pain in his chest. He dreaded the thought of his father's death and worried about the latter's earlier heart attacks. When the time came for the patient to be discharged from hospital a mild relapse occurred as a result of separation from Dr. T. This was resolved when he was told that he would be attending the hospital as an outpatient.

(3) *State of the Defense Organization*

Repression failed to contain passive feminine sexual wishes. This led to a preoccupation with "homosexuality." Projection altered the object of these sexual aims with the result that Mr. W. felt persecuted by homosexuals, vampires and evil spirits. For example, evil spirits tried to get at him through the walls of the room. He was afraid of being infected by homosexuals. This was also a failure of repression with respect to oral-sadistic wishes again activated by regression. It should be recalled that the patient was in the habit of indulging in the fantasy of being a vampire, prior to his illness, by protruding his upper denture. The oral-sadistic drives were countered by an externalization of this bodily aspect of the self-representation onto real objects, human, animal and fantasy objects. He dreaded the teeth of these objects. This dread was also compounded of a projection of the oral sadism.

It is of considerable interest that within a few weeks of the onset the clinical phenomena altered. This was due to the fact that the drive derivatives were being dealt with by externalization rather than projection. Although the patient was surrounded by evil he was not affected by it. It is possible that the oral-sadistic fantasies were used defensively to screen the expression of passive genital aims. Repression was effective in denying access to consciousness of death wishes directed against the father. The anxiety which these wishes caused were met with by displacement. The patient feared the bull and not his father.

(4) *Affects*

The predominant affects were anxiety and sadness. Anxiety was outstanding in the first days of the illness but subsided. Mr. W. was saddened by thoughts of death. Thus when he saw a funeral on the television he developed a pain in his chest. He was moved to tears when thinking about the death of his favorite film star. From time to time there were self-reproaches.

(5) *Superego*

There was some evidence to suggest that the superego has been externalized. The patient believed that he was being watched and criticized. As the illness lessened in its intensity the superego apparently was reinternalized. This was evidenced by his self-reproaches—for example, "I'm the black sheep of the family."

7. ASSESSMENT OF REGRESSION AND POSSIBLE FIXATIONS

In this case the libidinal regression led to a psychical situation almost identical with that existing just after puberty.

(a) Regression in the sphere of object relations had two results. It exposed an early stage of self and object integration where a distinction between the self and object representations has not been adequately effected. This facilitated such mechanisms as externalization of drives, generalization of thoughts and feelings, externalization of aspects of the self and merging of self and object images.

A further consequence of regression in object relations was the reappearance of oedipal conflicts. These conflicts related principally to the father. The first concerned death wishes against the father and the second passive feminine aims also directed to the father. These found expression in delusions of vampirism, fear of bulls, etc. No data was available about the patient's drives and conflicts regarding the mother.

(b) With respect to the sexual organization the regression had the effect of causing an abandonment of the narcissistic heterosexuality. This was initially replaced by homosexual wishes with passive aims. It was these drives which led to anxiety and to defense. The regression continued with the exposure of passive feminine wishes. An enhanced anal erotism contributed to these passive aims. Ultimately the regression brought forth an oral-sadistic organization of the libido.

(c) Data indicating a regression of the ego in thinking, perceiving etc. has been described.

(d Attention has been drawn to the externalization of the superego present after the onset of the illness.

(e) Not applicable.

(f) The significant fixations which occurred in development are reflected in the results of regression described above.

8. THE RESULTS OF DRIVE AND EGO DISORGANIZATION

In this case the phenomena which could be most easily attributed to ego disorganization were the misperceptions and misinterpretations which facilitated the development of the delusional reality.

9. ASSESSMENT OF CONFLICTS

(a) External conflicts between the patient and the delusional objects. These conflicts were the result of an externalization of internalized conflicts.

(b) The principal internalized conflicts have been described. They were concerned with passive sexual aims and aggression.

(c) Internal conflicts existed between masculinity and femininity and activity and passivity.

10. THE PREPSYCHOTIC PERSONALITY

The internalized conflicts which were active in the prepsychotic period have been referred to. The patient suffered from a number of neurotic symptoms outstanding among which were a morbid anxiety about his father's health and a tendency to worry about his own physical health—for example, a fear of heart disease, a preoccupation with his appearance and a sensitivity and shyness. He was particularly sensitive about his nose and often wished that he could have the shape of his face changed. He thought his nose was twisted and was concerned that his face always appeared red. There is some evidence that he suffered from an erythrophobia. He thought the combination of his red face and yellow hair made him unsightly. Nevertheless he managed to maintain relationships with other young men. As has been mentioned he was in the habit of going to dances and to football matches. He was a member of a social club. While maintaining that he was physically attracted to girls, at no time had he engaged in a constant relationship. Satisfaction of genital needs was by masturbation. The fantasies were usually of film stars or girls he thought attractive.

The following inferences can be made from the available data. The prepsychotic personality was characterized by a genital sexual organization which superficially appeared to have active aims and a heterosexual object. The patient's statements indicated that the heterosexual object was in fact a narcissistic one. Prior to the illness repression was effective in barring from consciousness awareness of the homosexual interest which initially represented the narcissistic object choice (for example the mutual masturbation at puberty). Passive feminine trends were also repressed but they found an indirect outlet in such symptoms as the abhorrence of his snub nose. This was a compromise formation consisting of his wish for femininity (his nose was similar to that of the film star Marilyn Monroe) and castration anxiety. Repression also kept from consciousness death wishes directed against his father. However these found expression in the symptoms of morbid anxiety regarding the father and fear of contracting heart disease himself. The latter fear arose from an identification with the father. It also allowed the representation of the death wishes and the punishment for them, that is, his developing a heart attack.

11. ASSESSMENT OF SOME GENERAL CHARACTERISTICS, ETC.

The material described shows that at the onset of the attack libidinal cathexes were invested in delusional objects. The internalized conflicts were externalized. Repression was in abeyance. Reality testing was lost. In the ensuing weeks some degree of object cathexis of a more advanced type made its appearance thereby permitting the development of a kind of therapeutic alliance. A father transference appeared. This was disturbed by a partial breakthrough of passive feminine aims.

In this case a working transference may have become a possibility. The danger of a psychotherapeutic approach consisted of the possibility that mounting pressure from the drive derivatives—particularly the feminine tendencies—might lead to a regression and to further psychotic symptoms.

* * *

APPENDIX TO PROFILE NUMBER 1:

In the following pages an account will be given of the course of Mr. W.'s illness during the 16 months which passed after the completion of the profile. During that time the positive symptoms (delusions) disappeared and an increasing degree of normal mental functioning reasserted itself. This continued for about eight to nine months followed by a relapse into an acute psychotic state.

On this second occasion there was a change in the content of the delusions. The second attack lasted for about two months and was followed by a state almost identical to that which was found after the first bout of illness. A profile, to be presented below, was constructed on the basis of the phenomena which appeared in this second attack. Data obtained during the first remission (see below), during the second acute attack and during the subsequent remission gave further support to the hypothesis that it was the recathexis of passive feminine wishes and fantasies pursuant to the abandonment of active genital (heterosexual) aims, in the face of castration fear, which initiated the psychosis with its specific symptomatology.

THE REMISSION AFTER THE FIRST ATTACK

Eight weeks after the onset of the first attack the delusional ideas began to recede. The preoccupation with "homosexuality" and evil spirits continued but without the intensity which had been present earlier. As the patient became less occupied with the delusions he increasingly expressed anxiety and doubts. Interspersed with these utterances were recollections of childhood fears. He said that he had a strong sense of inferiority and found it difficult to mix with others. He lacked confidence, particularly with girls. He worried about his appearance. He knew that these ideas were not new and could trace them back to childhood. As a child he was sensitive, frightened of strangers and the dark. His father's dog had never liked him. He used to wish he had his brother's confidence and self-assurance. Masturbation was a problem at puberty and he feared its effects on his mental and physical health. He was too ashamed to discuss the matter with anyone.

During the next 12 weeks he spent most of his time at home, attending the hospital, daily at first, and then less often. During the first weeks at home he often felt afraid and needed the presence of his parents to ease his anxiety. His anxiety did not spring from delusions but from sources within himself. He found himself clinging to his mother and wanting to be constantly reassured that he would get completely better. At this time he had acquired full insight into the fact that he had been mentally unwell. He would refer to the silly ideas that he had had and wondered how he could have let his imagination get out of control. No longer afraid of being harmed from the outside, he now worried lest there be a "destructive bug" inside himself which would destroy him. This "destructive bug" expressed itself in many different ways—his lack of confidence, lack of interest and ability to work and his loss of pleasure in life, fears of something happening to his parents, doubts about his ability to manage alone if his father died or if his brother left home. At times he felt he might harm his father but this thought was never accompanied by any affect.

About a month after leaving hospital the loss of interest and sense of hopelessness increased in intensity. He began to worry about money, fearing that the farm's income was diminishing. He became agitated when a cow died and then had the thought that the cows were not yielding enough milk. He found himself weeping for no apparent reason and became so depressed in mood that life did not seem worth living. These suicidal ideas were frightening and reminded him of a period in childhood when he had similar preoccupations. He was envious of his brother's good health and was worried lest something happen to him. About this time his brother had three teeth extracted and the patient immediately developed toothache which lasted for some days.

During all this time there was no return of delusional ideas. He did reveal, however, that when in hospital he had not told anyone that he had believed for many years that scientists had been experimenting with him. They had inserted a small instrument into the scar on his cheek and recorded everything about him. He believed they had done this in order to study his mental and physical state because he had an uncle who was mentally ill. He did not then feel this to be a persecution. After leaving the hospital he realized that this series of ideas was just a fantasy. In this connection his earlier delusional ideas about the cows being endowed with human attributes could be traced to a childhood fantasy of talking to the cows and their talking to him.

Gradually he began to regain interest in his surroundings and returned to work on the farm. He went out with one or two friends for a drink or to a dance. His sense of inferiority remained and there were occasions when he worried about his parents' health and that of his brother. About four months after leaving the hospital he claimed that he did not want to attend any longer as an outpatient. It was decided to comply with his request as insistence on his attendance was interpreted by him to mean that he was still unwell, and this in turn caused him considerable anxiety. Quite apart from other signs of instability this disinclination indicated that the remission was by no means complete. During the four-month period of attendance as an outpatient there was no evidence of transference developments other than what has been described earlier. This positive tie had insufficient strength to counter the anxiety generated by attendance at the hospital. Throughout this time the content of these communications consisted almost entirely of anxieties and doubts, beyond which it was impossible to progress.

PROFILE AT RELAPSE

1. REASON FOR REFERRAL and

2. DESCRIPTION OF THE PATIENT, ETC.

Six months after terminating attendance at the hospital as an outpatient Mr. W. contacted the writer and asked for an appointment. He said that he was keeping fairly well and did not have any unusual ideas. However he was worried by the fact that he had started having thoughts about his brother which were disturbing. On the one hand he still felt envious of his brother's stability and self-confidence but on the other hand he was now feeling so much stronger, both physically and mentally, that he feared he might have a bad effect on his brother. This led him to recall how at the onset of the illness he believed that he had special powers and abilities.

Some days later Mr. W.'s parents phoned to say that they were very worried about him. He had become extremely restless and liable to turn aggressive both in speech and action. When seen at the hospital the parents' observations were confirmed. The patient could not sit still; his speech was difficult to follow and showed echopraxia. On the whole he was reasonably friendly. He was now frightened by thoughts of homosexuality and wondered if the writer was a homosexual. He was convinced that the writer was a homosexual, an idea which obviously disturbed him. His brother envied him and wanted him out of the way so that he would inherit the farm. His brother was evil—not only was he a homosexual but he even had sexual desires for their sister.

While talking Mr. W.'s eyes would dart from side to side and he would turn his head this way and that as if listening to something. Later he said that he was hearing a voice which told him not to say too much. He held his body taut as if ready to defend himself or to attack. He looked aggressive and violent from time to time. At a second meeting the next day he was calmer and able to talk more freely. He said that a few days before he had been at church and suddenly thought the clergyman was a homosexual and that all the men in the church were too. He had the conviction that Christ was a homosexual.

3. FAMILY BACKGROUND

As before.

4. POSSIBLY SIGNIFICANT ENVIRONMENTAL CIRCUMSTANCES

In the two weeks before the relapse—that is, immediately before Xmas—Mr. W. had been going out to dances and to parties. He had met several girls who attracted him. However, his lack of confidence prevented him from asking them out or seeking a close emotional and physical contact. In their presence he became sexually excited and would remain in this state for some hours. One night after a dance while on his way home in the car he had stopped and masturbated. During these weeks the conflict over masturbation had been acute and he had resolved to give up the habit. The morning after the incident in the car a friend came to the house. As soon as the patient saw him he became preoccupied with the thought that he (the friend) was a homosexual—that is effeminate and womanly. This was the patient's conception of the term "homosexual." Following this experience he could not rid himself of the idea that he was surrounded by homosexuals.

5. ASSESSMENT OF THE DRIVES

A. *The Libido*

(1) *Problems of Libido Distribution*

(a) *Cathexis of the Self.* As was the case during the first acute attack there was a hypercathexis of self-representations. The patient believed himself to be the focus of great interest. He believed that he had the power to dissipate evil, to draw it from men. This could be accomplished through his eyes which were the same as those of Christ.

When he closed his eyes the world darkened over. As far as his brother was concerned he was envious because he (Mr. W.) was a "chosen person."

Self- and object representations were not clearly differentiated indicating a disorder in the cathexis of the self. He believed that his body, thinking and feeling were affected by anyone with whom he came into contact. On this account he feared proximity to anyone who might be a "homosexual." This explained his reluctance to visit the writer. He became angry if approached by his brother and was convinced that the latter was imitating him all the time. There were occasions when he almost felt mixed up with his brother. He resented this intrusion, questioning why the brother wanted to be the replica of himself. He explained it as due to envy.

Apart from the movement toward generalization of thoughts and feelings to external objects, he automatically followed their actions (echopraxia). Given this dynamic, he did not think it necessary to tell the writer his thoughts because the latter would know them as soon as he (Mr. W.) thought them. He also imputed a sexual significance (homosexual) to movements of the limbs.

Dead people had passed into his body. On this account he was subject to the illnesses from which they had succumbed. At no time did he think that he was losing his sexual identity but he did have fantasies of the writer changing into a woman in front of his eyes.

(b) *Cathexis of Objects:*

i. Cathexis of Real Persons (*Current Relationships*)

Real external objects continued to be cathected by libido which had secondary-process characteristics. This was to be found as follows:

(i) Brother: He feared for his brother who had criminal tendencies. He did not want him to end up in prison. He was concerned about the effect this would have on his father. As his brother knew what he was thinking he was upset lest there be misunderstandings. His brother might look upon him as an enemy.

(ii) The Writer: He was concerned about what was going to happen to the writer. At times he thought the writer was turning into a woman. This was not in any way connected with himself. Apart from distrust he did not like coming to the hospital because this implied that he was mentally ill, hence inferior to his brother.

(iii) Father: He worried about his father's health and the effect his (Mr. W.'s) conflict with his brother would have on the parent. His brother was jealous of the closeness between himself and his father.

(iv) Mother: When frightened or upset he would turn to his mother, apparently finding her reassuring. Sometimes he was angry with her if she took his brother's part.

ii. Cathexis of Representations of Real and Fantasy Objects

In contrast to the first attack there were no delusional objects of a fantasy nature. However real external objects were altered by the externalization of the patient's feminine self-representations. The brother (soft and effeminate) and other young men are illustrative.

(2) *Libidinal Position*

Apart from the references to sexual excitement and masturbation there was no other evidence to indicate a direct preoccupation with other libidinal phases. This of course excludes the material which reflected the presence of passive (feminine) sexual aims.

B. *Aggression*

During the relapse Mr. W. gave free rein to aggression in speech but not in action. He often appeared to be on the verge of making an attack. At home he cursed his brother; his parents were afraid that he might assault him. The aggression was activated by the brother's closeness, his wish to be like the patient and by the latter's distaste for the former. Death wishes were conscious and expressed directly or indirectly in the wish that he (brother) would leave home, get married, etc.

There was an externalization of aggression to the brother. He hoped that the brother would not commit murder. He did not believe the brother would injure him—he was incapable of that. The death wishes were justified on the basis of the idea that the brother would be better dead for his own sake. There was no evidence of other defenses against aggression.

6. EGO AND SUPEREGO

(1) *Ego Functions*

(a-e) At the onset of the attack there was some disorder of speech and thinking, making it difficult to understand what he said. This soon passed. His thinking had a magical, wishful quality as has already been described. Perception and memory were intact but suffered from the impact of the irrational beliefs.

(f) Attention has already been drawn to the echopraxia which appeared at the onset of the attack.

(2) *Ego Reactions to Danger Situations*

Dangers were experienced as coming from three sources. The first, acting as the initiator of the attack, arose from the heightening of active genital aims. This led to castration fear—"you cannot trust women," he said. A dream reported shortly after the relapse had the following content: He was with other men and they were all due to be castrated—the queen was inspecting each man and then sending them off to be castrated. When the patient's turn came she let him escape. The defensive activity in the dream allowed his sleep to remain undisturbed. It is of interest, with respect to this dream, to note that during puberty the patient feared his mother might discover that he masturbated. Specifically he feared she would find him in the middle of the act. The effort to stop the emission would make him ill by causing a blockage of the urethra.

The second source of danger, evidenced during the psychotic attack, was his fear of loss of identity through merging with the brother. He would become a "homosexual" as his brother was—that is, his defense against awareness of his femininity would fail. The third source of danger brought on by the regression from the active genital position, were the passive feminine wishes.

(3) *State of the Defense Organization*

During the psychosis repression no longer held death wishes against the brother in check. Externalization acted against both aggression and the libido. It was the brother who was evil. Aspects of the self-representations—the femininity—were externalized to the brother and to the writer. This, as has been mentioned, facilitated the "repression" of the passive femininity.

Projection played a limited role in the defense. The patient did not feel threatened by his brother nor did he believe that he was hated by him. He was convinced however that the brother was envious and jealous of him. He felt no envy or jealousy of the brother indicating that projection successfully acted against the affective derivatives of the drives.

(4) *Affects*

Anger was the most common emotion observed during the attack. Only after its resolution did anxiety and depression of mood appear.

(5) *Superego*

Apart from hallucinatory experiences the superego remained internalized. On one occasion the patient heard a voice say—"you should share everything with your brother." On rare occasions he felt guilty because he was upsetting his father.

7. Assessment of Regressions and Possible Fixations

Regression had the following consequences:

(a) There was a return to the external conflicts characteristic of the phase of childhood when sibling rivalry is predominant. Here the rivalry related primarily to the father (negative Oedipus complex). The conflict here was internalized (see Assessment of Conflicts) but came to be externalized during the psychosis.

The regression did not lead to the appearance of object relations where need satisfaction was the primary aim.

(b) Anal sensations occasionally experienced indicated a return of the libido to the anal phase.

(c) The fact that externalization was so much in evidence, both in its defensive and nondefensive aspects, as well as faulty self-object discrimination, indicated that the ego had been subject to a very considerable regression.

(d) The regression led to the recathexis of ego-ideal fantasies—e.g., he was Christ, etc.

(e) The wish to be the sole inheritor of the father's property suggests fixations at the oral phase (see "fears of poverty" in Remission). This is complemented by possible fixations at the preoedipal mother relationship. It is known that the patient was very attached to his mother and, in that he was the youngest child by six years, she showed a greater preoccupation with him and more pronounced anxiety about his health. This no doubt predisposed him to feminine identifications and to a hypochondriacal tendency.

8. RESULTS OF DRIVE AND EGO DISORGANIZATION

No data under this head.

9. ASSESSMENT OF CONFLICTS

Internalized conflicts regarding father and brother were externalized as a consequence of the regression. The passive feminine wishes directed to the father were a powerful source of conflict. During the psychosis these passive wishes were externalized and located in the brother. It was the brother who wanted the father for himself. The conflict with the brother led to death wishes which generated further conflict and concern about the brother's fate.

An internal conflict between activity and passivity must be postulated on the basis of the observable phenomena.

10. THE PREPSYCHOTIC PERSONALITY

As before.

11. ASSESSMENT OF SOME GENERAL CHARACTERISTICS, ETC.

The characteristics of this attack suggested a lesser degree of regression than had occurred in the first acute bout of illness. The maintenance of object cathexis following the secondary process allowed the patient to respond to the support and reassurance of his parents and thereby served as a counterforce to the psychotic reality. The ego was not entirely submerged in the id.

The defense organization was more effective in containing anxiety than in the first attack. Reality was subject to less distortion. Nevertheless the tendency to externalize both libidinal wishes (passivity) and the feminine self-representations onto the writer made, during the acute phase, a therapeutic alliance virtually impossible.

THE PHASE OF PARTIAL REMISSION

Gradually the anger and resentment against the brother subsided. The patient was ashamed of his earlier feelings and became somewhat self-critical. He attributed his behavior to overimagination. Coincidentally there was a return of the anxieties and doubts which had been present following the first acute attack. He was afraid of something happening to his brother and worried about who would then manage the farm. Once again he felt inadequate compared with his brother, and the sense of inferiority and lack of confidence returned. He was easily moved to tears and would turn to his mother for reassurance. A major fear was poverty if anything should go wrong on the farm. He did not want to go out.

Homosexuality no longer played a major part in his thinking but fears in this respect were easily aroused. If, for example, he was sitting in the company of another man and he felt the slightest sensation or movement of his penis he would immediately fear that this was a sign that he was a homosexual. He also had several dreams with a homosexual content which caused him considerable anxiety. Consciously he had no homosexual interest. Although unable to establish contact in reality with girls, he masturbated with heterosexual fantasies. He disliked talking about sexual matters because they provoked a feeling of disgust.

Such childhood memories as appeared pointed to an everconstant castration fear. Recollections of his distaste for the idea of being a girl instead of a boy were awakened after dreaming of seeing a girl with a penis. He remembered having believed that only boys would be strong enough to work on a farm and that if he had been a girl this would not have been possible for him.

Although repression was restored in this period of partial remission the aggressive and libidinal (passive) drives remained cathected. It was these cathexes which were the cause of the everpresent anxiety about his brother, family and homosexuality. The lack of interest and energy about which he complained could be understood as due to the high expenditure of anticathexis necessary for the maintenance of the ego and repression.

CHAPTER 3

Disorders of Libido Distribution in Psychoses: Cathexis of Objects – Real and Delusional

The redistribution of libido which occurs at the onset of a psychosis comprises an attempt to dissipate a danger situation. There is a withdrawal of cathexis from object and drive representations and a hypercathexis of the self. This does not cause psychotic forms of relating either with real or delusional objects. The attempt at repression only leads to a withdrawal from real persons and a preoccupation with the self. It is when repression does not succeed that psychotic phenomena appear. This results from regression which, substituting for repression, aims to dispel the original danger. There is a change in the quality of the libido with self, object and drive representations becoming subject to the primary process. For purposes of description the libidinal cathexis of objects and of the self must be treated separately. It must be emphasized however that many psychotic phenomena can be described and assessed equally well in terms of either object or self-cathexis.

In psychotic states the libidinal drive cathexes and their representations have aims and objects no less significant than those which exist in the healthy and in neurotic states.

One difference lies in the nature of the object and its representation. In psychosis this may be a real person (present functioning relationships), the representation of a real person (current or past), a fantasy object or some aspect of the self. This object may be in receipt of the most powerful cathexis as is shown by the strength of the attachment to the object or by the reactions which the object engenders.

Primitive Forms of Object Libido

The presence of primitive forms of object libido can be inferred in a wide variety of psychotic states. Extreme withdrawal, negativism, psychomotor overactivity and retardation, elation, depression of mood and anxiety are some of the leading clinical manifestations. Diagnoses of acute and chronic schizophrenia, mania, mixed manic-depressive states may be allotted to these cases. In spite of the many formal differences between cases there are numerous similarities which point to the common underlying form of mental activity.

In cases categorized as chronic schizophrenia there is an absence of interest in others and no affective manifestations. These patients have little spontaneous speech and what there is is disorganized. They are changeable in their attitudes. One day they may be friendly and speak a few words; on another day there is total negativism. Recognition of persons is also variable. An individual recognized at one time is later seen as a stranger or is confused with someone else. They will evince complete disinterest in a topic of conversation. Irrelevant answers to questions are the rule. In speech there is a distortion of verbal ideas and a perseverative tendency. The immediate environment is confused with memories of other places so that some degree of disorientation is common.

A patient may have doubts about his identity. This is sometimes accompanied by a merging of self and object with the result that the patient attributes his thoughts and feelings to another and believes that each is aware of the other's inner experience.

When patients of this kind are seen regularly over a period of months a different picture emerges. They may express an interest in the psychiatrist even though they remain unable to acknowledge his role as a hospital doctor. Interest is poorly sustained and there are days when the patient will remain silent and indifferent. Nevertheless there are a number of indications which point to the presence of attachment. Occasionally the patient will become animated and show pleasure at the interest taken in him. He will occasionally inquire after the psychiatrist if an interview has to be cancelled. Characteristic is an unpredictable response to events. At times a break in meetings will evoke no response either when it is announced or upon resumption. At other times there will be a complete withdrawal or an outburst of anger.

Patients are most likely to persevere with interviews if they are afforded the satisfaction of a need. In one case the patient may want cigarettes; in another, he may wish an interest to be taken in his delusional ideas. The relationship with the psychiatrist is at stake because the patient has little capacity for disappointment or frustration. An inevitable interruption may end the interviews. They may also be disrupted if the patient feels that the psychiatrist cannot supply what is wished for. At such times affects are likely to make an appearance. Anger is freely expressed, and consistent with this spontaneity, there is accompanying speech which is both relevant and appropriate. Alternatively there may be a further withdrawal with negativism. Sometimes there is depression of mood. Apart from these brief periods of dramatic drive and affect expression the patient will be known to engage in frequent masturbation, in genital exhibitionism and other forms of autoerotic activity.

Although patients turn away from new relationships they nevertheless manifest strong attachment behavior. This is pronounced in those who have spent many years in hospital. The attachment may be to a senior nurse who has been with the patient since his admission, or it may be to the institution itself. Illustrative is the case of a patient who had been the inmate of a hospital for many years. He inherited a large sum of money and was given the chance of being transferred to a private hospital where his material conditions would have been better. This notwithstanding, he refused to leave. In this case there was a strong bond between patient and nurse. The patient's only contact with others was through this nurse and it was only he who understood the patient's peculiar form of speech. Similar behavior is found in chronically ill patients who have been kept at home. Inquiry from those who have cared for these patients reveals that there is rarely any overt sign of attachment apart from those occasions when there is need. In many of these cases it is impossible to obtain knowledge of the patient's inner life. The observer has to fall back on such information as he can obtain about the symptoms at the onset of the illness, what he can find out from nurses and relatives and such details of delusions and hallucinations as the patient is prepared to describe.

The tendency to relate to an external object on the basis of need, the difficulty in maintaining an identity between an external object and its mental representation with resultant misidentification and faulty recognition, disorders of word formation and syntax, fusion of self- and object representations and confusion of memories are also found in the other diagnostic groups. In illness diagnosed as mania or mixed manic depressions with elation of mood, psychomotor overactivity or retardation there is the same tendency for the patient to regard another individual solely as a means of need satisfaction. If demands are not met immediately there is an outburst of aggression. Misidentifications are common and the patient has difficulty in maintaining the recognition of an object. For example, a young woman of 20 fell ill with a maniclike condition. She was elated in mood and overactive. The illness followed a disappointment in love. She had met the writer on many occasions and had been told his name and occupation. The following is an excerpt from an interview:

> I don't know what I'm here for . . . because I haven't a troubled mind . . . what is your line of work, it could be an electrician, reporter, doctor, taximan. . . . You're like George (ex-boyfriend) . . . an electrician . . . why do doctors tickle your feet George . . . you're George." [She laughed and giggled at this point.] "You could be a man or a woman . . . a woman dressed up . . . maybe the women in the ward are men.

This kind of material could as easily be found in a case of acute or chronic schizophrenia. The following is illustrative. The patient was a single woman of 28 who had been ill for several years. "You'll be having the weekend off . . . you'll be away . . . will you be in Dundee? I was thinking you must be a traveller when I saw your brief case . . . travellers used to come to the shop . . . they used to come to my uncle's shop." The only difference between the two cases is the presence of psychomotor overactivity and elation in the former and withdrawal and psychomotor restriction in the latter. Both revealed a lack of stability of the object representations.

The clinical data permit certain assumptions about the

nature of the mental processes behind the expressions. All the phenomena which have been described result from the action of the primary process. The mental representation of real objects, of the self, of percepts, words and memories are condensed with other representations leading to the confusion of persons, memories, etc. Judgment and reality testing are deficient.

Where the activity of the primary process is most evident libidinal drives have instinctual aims. These aims comprise the need for the immediate satisfaction of bodily needs—oral, genital, etc. In psychoses of acute onset and in cases of chronic schizophrenia which have suffered an acute exacerbation, there are misidentifications, disorders of word form an intense if labile affectivity. In both categories of cases the libidinal drive derivatives are turned towards real or fantasy objects. The chronic schizophrenic patient who ordinarily ignores the real object or misidentifies him will show signs of sexual excitement or destructive behavior. The heightened eroticism will be accompanied by grandiose delusions either concerning the body or personal attributes. At such a time the clinical picture will be identical to that found in a psychosis of acute onset. These observations indicate that the disinterest, inattention and negativism which usually characterizes the behavior of the chronic schizophrenic patient results from the cathexis of the object representations which comprise the delusional reality. This will vary in its degree of complexity or fragmentation. The cathexis of real external objects will only arise when there is a need. This will occur, as has already been described, on the basis of hunger or some other need or wish. It will also occur in an acute exacerbation of the illness as has been referred to above.

In Profile Number 2 (see page 107) the disturbance of

interpersonal relationships is described in terms of the changes which affected the quality and distribution of libido between self and objects.

More Advanced Forms of Object Libido

In the group of conditions now to be described the primary process has partly been replaced by the secondary process. Object cathexes do not have predominantly instinctual aims. The activity of the secondary process ensures a reality-oriented cognition (a reality ego) and some control over the quality and intensity of the drive derivatives (defensive ego). This is reflected in the fact that there are many patients suffering from psychoses who still retain a good contact with reality. They initially welcome a friendly approach and respond to it. They are glad of an opportunity to speak about their experiences. Speech form is good and there are no misidentifications. In all these respects such patients differ from those described above. Interest in the psychiatrist or nurse is sustained, the patient looking to the therapist as someone who can assist in bringing about an understanding and resolution of his anxiety and unpleasant experiences. Thus the external object, in this case psychiatrist or nurse, and its mental representation remain securely linked. There is no ambiguity or doubt regarding identification. Soon however new developments occur which alter the patient's attitude.

In some cases the psychiatrist is perceived in a new light. For example, a young man suffering from delusional ideas of various kinds came to believe that the writer had changed in appearance. This was the result of malevolent influences which were affecting both. He identified the writer correctly but perceived him as half man and half woman. The patient was worried that the change in the writer was his fault. At no time was the interest and concern dependent on the writer's capacity to provide the satisfaction of a need.

Another reaction is provided by patients who gradually come to regard the psychiatrist as someone who has the power to help contain instinctual behavior. While the relationship is in a sense dependent on the satisfaction of a need, the need arises from anxiety and guilt.

Case 1

A young man of 23 developed a psychotic illness during which he came to believe that his left incisor tooth was the cause of his disturbing thoughts and emotions. He could not free his mind from the sensations emanating from the tooth. They made him feel violent and he was afraid that if they continued he might commit murder. The content of interviews was concentrated on his wish to have the tooth extracted. No other subject could elicit the slightest interest, his attachment to the writer being solely dependent on whether or not he would arrange to have the tooth removed.

Case 2

In this case, the patient, a woman of 21, was aware of a loss of control of feeling and drive. She felt that she could exert no control over smoking, masturbation or urination. She knew that she sexualized every relationship whether heterosexual or homosexual. She pleaded for some means to restore control and she looked to the writer to provide this. Here again the viability of the treatment relationship depended on the real object's capacity to satisfy the patient's need to abolish the danger situation.

A further group of cases comprises those in whom there

is a continuing transition of clinical phenomena. Symptoms resulting from the action of primitive object libido and the primary process alternate with cognition and drive characteristic of the secondary process.

Case 3

This woman patient of 24 was inattentive, negativistic and, at times, outright aggressive. She experienced auditory hallucinations and had many delusional ideas. Her interest in doctors and nurses was activated exclusively by her need of them. When she wanted something such as a trip to the hairdresser or a visit home she would become quite lively. In her withdrawn state her speech was indistinct and difficult to follow because of grammatical faults and disturbances of word form. She masturbated continuously. She misidentified external objects and merged the self with them. Periodically this mental state would be replaced by normal, comprehensible speech, an interest in both herself and her surroundings as well as a return of control over sexual expression and aggression. Object and self-representations were no longer fused nor was there evidence of misidentification. These changes were accompanied by an improvement in her attitude to other persons. She was willing to help them when necessary and be of general assistance to the nursing staff. Disappointments were tolerated without aggression or withdrawal. However, a return to the first state would take place after a matter of weeks or months.

A willingness to talk affords an opportunity to learn something about the patient's thoughts and feelings. Often the circumstances under which the patient lived facilitated the emergence of the symptomatology. A case in point is provided by the young man (Case 1) who complained of his tooth. It became apparent that he did not get on with his parents. He hated his father to whom he referred as "the worst man in the world." The patient claimed that his father was a hypocrite who went to church every Sunday but sinned the rest of the week. The patient was convinced that his father had committed a serious crime—robbery or murder—and was now covering up the traces of his misdeeds. His father was a jealous man, envying the patient his youth. His main intent was to provoke the patient and work him into a rage. The patient was suspicious of his mother as well. He maintained that she was sly and deceitful. She pretended to care for him but in subtle ways she managed to upset him. There were times when he felt so enraged that he feared he might bite her. In spite of all these thoughts he hated being in the hospital and wanted to go home.

The young woman (Case 2) who was frightened by her lack of control was conscious of sexual feelings for her father with whom she shared living quarters. The female patient (Case 3) who passed from one mental state to another was very attached to her father. She entertained pregnancy fantasies within the context of that relationship. Thus she said: "I was sure I was having a baby when Daddy was bringing me back to hospital in the car." A male patient of 22 years of age believed, following his father's death, that his mother was trying to kill him. He denied the fact of his father's death, maintaining that he had seen him in the street.

Jealousy and envy are affects frequently found in these cases. They are to be observed in the patient's interactions with other patients, nurses and doctors as well as with their parents and siblings. As in the case cited above it is not uncommon for patients to become aware of genital sensations with an incestuous content. More commonly these affects and thoughts are repressed, finding indirect expression in the content of delusional ideas. Although masturbatory conflicts are commonplace in these cases the genital drives rarely find an outlet with external objects in the period prior to the onset of the illness. Sometimes the illness follows an attempt to establish a heterosexual relationship or is the consequence of a casual sexual encounter. Often a wished-for relationship is sustained in thought for years but is never actualized.

In the cases belonging to this second group there is sufficient libidinal cathexis accompanying the secondary process to allow the establishment of relationships at the level of object constancy. The future of such relationships is entirely dependent on the patient's ability to utilize the external object as a means of controlling the instinctual cathexes which act as a threat. In cases of the first group the libidinal cathexis, under the influence of the primary process, creates a purely need-satisfying relationship with external objects.

Attempts to establish the kind of therapeutic alliance necessary for psychoanalytic treatment fail in both groups of patients but for different reasons. In the former there is failure because of the patient's disinterest and withdrawal. In the latter the dread of libidinal arousal leads the patient to attempt to shape the treatment in accordance with his need for control over drive and affect. The treatment situation can become a source of instinctual arousal which would obviously end the therapy. In some cases it is possible to observe in the transference the emergence of instinctual aims. It is these transference reactions which the patient fears. Interpretation does not lead to relief of anxiety as will occur in a case of anxiety hysteria.

The psychotic patient can no longer distinguish between the analyst as a real person and his transference representation. Thus the external object and the representation become an equal source of danger. This occurred in the case to be described in profile No. 2 (see page 107) where the writer was misidentified as the patient's father. The object representation had become the focus of libidinal drives with instinctual aims. The libidinal drive derivatives found expression in a trancelike orgastic state which occurred during the clinical interviews. The heightening of the instinctual drives brings about a distortion of cognition as an effect of the primary process. Auditory and visual percepts are misinterpreted, memory traces are revived as hallucinations and delusional ideas are intensified. All impede the patient in his effort to sustain the therapeutic alliance. It is under such circumstances that the patient may transiently revert to a state similar to that found in the first group of cases where the primary process determines the content of the clinical phenomena.

The cases described have been differentiated into two groups on the basis of the quality of the libidinal drives existing at any one moment of time. In the second group the nature of the object libido was such as to permit the temporary establishment of real relationships and the continuation of such relationships as had existed. Even in these cases an alteration in the quality of the libido with a return to a more primitive drive constellation can result in the disruption of object ties and a further loss of reality testing. This sequence of events is not inevitable in all cases of psychosis. There is yet a third group of patients who are capable of establishing and maintaining a therapeutic relationship. These cases have frequently been described in the analytic literature. Here the libidinal drive derivatives continue to follow the secondary process. Preconscious representations retain their cathexis allowing the patient to maintain a realistic appraisal of the object. Interest, concern and attachment having become separated from instinctual aims can be used for the purposes of therapy.

There is no absolute barrier separating any of the three clinical groups described. A patient may pass successively through phases of illness each of which bears the characteristics of one of the three groups. The illness may begin with instinctual libido dominating mental life, thereby preventing the emergence of a realistic object relationship in thought or in fact. Later in the course of the illness, when the primary process phenomena have disappeared, the patient may be able to relate for periods of time without the intrusion of libidinal drives which have direct instinctual aims. Further development may lead to a condition similar to that of patients in the third category of illness. While such transitions occur many patients remain arrested at the earlier stages and do not proceed to a state where an analytic form of psychotherapy becomes possible.

Freud (1914) proposed that in a psychotic illness the clinical phenomena can be classified under three headings. First, those which represent the illness process itself, namely the withdrawal of libidinal cathexes from object representations. Second, manifestations which result from the attempt on the part of the withdrawn cathexes to find new objects and third, phenomena belonging to the residual healthy mental function. Patients who belong to the third category are those for whom there is the greatest residue of healthy mental life. Healthy mental life in this context implies the presence of secondary process drives continuing their investment of the preconscious representations. While capable of reverting to their instinctual state, this will only occur under certain conditions.

Reference has already been made to the experiences of those who treat psychotic patients. Working transferences may develop in certain cases, even though the patient may be delusional and hallucinated. From a descriptive standpoint these delusions and hallucinations are similar to those which occur in cases where there is no possibility of a working transference. This observation points to the fact that the decisive factor effecting prognosis is not the presence of the accessory symptoms, delusions and hallucinations (Freud's second class of phenomena), but the distribution and quality of the object libido.

CATHEXIS OF DELUSIONAL OBJECTS

Patients suffering from psychoses develop in varying degrees unreal forms of object relationship which come to dominate their mental lives. It is only when the illness is established that a clear picture is obtained of the objects which comprise this psychotic reality. Where the illness is of recent origin the psychotic reality will consist of representations of those who were involved in the circumstances leading to the outbreak of symptoms. Illustrative is the woman who hears the voice of her former lover who now acts as a persecutor. Alternatively she may accuse the lover of forcing her to experience genital sensations.

It is in cases where the illness has been present for some time that the psychotic reality reaches its full development. In most instances the delusional objects are comprised of individuals who were once emotionally important to the patient. The delusional objects can be divided into those toward whom the patient is consciously attached and those by whom the patient feels persecuted. While both kinds of object may coexist one variety usually predominates. In some cases the belief is held that doctors, lawyers, relatives or an unknown authority prevents them from being united with the longed-for love object. In others unwanted sexual thoughts (homosexual, heterosexual) and feelings are attributed to unknown persecutors who use secret techniques to carry out their purposes.

The degree of interest which these patients show in real persons varies. It may depend on whether the individual concerned is willing to listen to an account of the delusional reality. Common to all cases is an intensity of involvement with the delusional objects irrespective of whether they are wished for or thought of as persecutors. These objects representations become the recipients of libidinal cathexes in the same way that the object representations of the healthy person or the psychoneurotic patient are cathected. This is most apparent where the patient is dependent on the delusional object or has loving and affectionate feelings toward it. Delusional objects of this kind are idealized and bereft of genital or aggressive associations. The object may be a person from the patient's youth or early adult life about whom the patient had wishful fantasies. Usually there was no close contact with the person in reality. It is equally possible for the delusional object to be a figure from childhood, as in the case of the patient who hallucinated the voice of her schoolmaster.

Examination of delusional objects which are a source of annoyance and persecution to the patient reveals that they fall into at least three classes. First there are the real persons who were originally the object of libidinal cathexes which had instinctual aims. Disappointment resulted in a change from love to hate, with projection altering the direction of the drive derivatives. Second are those patients who, unable to tolerate the awareness of genital drives, attribute them to nonspecific persecutors. Third are those delusional objects which have a superego significance. These objects, which are comprised of parents or parental substitutes, manifest a critical attitude to the patient.

In many cases the content of the psychotic reality, with the exception of the idealized figures, is almost wholly taken up with genital fantasies. This content is repudiated by the patient, the delusional objects being designated as the instigators of these affects and sensations. The extent of the patient's anxiety and guilt regarding the underlying instinctual drives is reflected in the need to create idealized delusional objects which act as a counter to the persecutors. Just as some patients will seek out a real object to help contain the instinctual drives the idealized delusional object is employed for the same purpose. In such instances there is a real dread of losing the delusional object. In one instance a patient became very anxious when she did not hear the voice of her delusional object for a period of days. The conflict between the instinctual elements, and the forces antagonistic to them, can come to be represented in a clash between different delusional objects. Here the patient's conflict is externalized and represented in the psychotic reality. The purpose is the repudiation of responsibility or interest in instinctual expression.

At first sight it appears as if many psychotic patients still retain the capacity for object cathexis as reflected in their delusional object relations. However, a more in-depth understanding of the patient reveals that these objects have a wholly narcissistic basis. The object representations arise from different aspects of the self-representations—both actual and wished for. Many patients are delusionally preoccupied with a member of the opposite sex whose attentions please or annoy them. These persons were attractive to the patient in the prepsychotic period. They were chosen on a narcissistic basis representing some wished-for attribute—for example, masculinity in the case of the female patient or femininity in the case of the male patient. The subsequent delusional object representation thus has its origins in the cathexis of self-representation. It is this which prevents the patient from directing a libidinal cathexis to the real object when, for example, he is given the opportunity to engage in psychoanalytic or psychotherapeutic treatment. If such patients actually commence therapy the narcissistic nature of their libidinal cathexes becomes immediately apparent. The representation of the psychiatrist is also determined by the patient's self-representations. When the patient is favorably inclined to the psychiatrist the latter is endowed with omniscience, omnipotence and other positive attributes. This is most evident in cases of mania. If regarded in a hostile way the psychiatrist inherits all those aspects of the self-representations—physical and mental—which the patient repudiates.

Economic Aspects of Object Relations

In the course of this account of the clinical phenomena some attempts at explanation have already been made. Now it is time to enquire more closely into the nature of the mental changes which lead to the pathology of interpersonal relationships. This means that attention will be concentrated on those phenomena which prevent the initiation of relationships or lead to their disruption. Withdrawal and negativism, the sudden emergence of affect, the appearance of delusional ideas and hallucinations, the development of a coherent psychotic reality are manifestations which require explanation. This task can be undertaken by scrutinizing all the clinical data from the dynamic and economic standpoints.

In all the conditions described a conflict exists between

the libidinal wishes on the one side and a fear of the consequences of their fulfillment on the other. In the case of schizophrenic illnesses the content of the symptoms invariably points to such a conflict as do the circumstances which attended the onset of the illness. Additional support for the hypothesis that such patients dread the consequences of the expression of drive derivatives is provided first, by the reactions of patients when efforts are made to begin psychotherapy and second, by their behavior in their daily interactions with doctors and nurses. Psychotherapists, doctors and nurses are accused of provoking genital, anal and oral sensations and inevitably become the objects of the patient's aggression.

The conflict between the libidinal drives seeking immediate outlets and the forces opposed to them is represented in the symptoms of withdrawal, negativism and ambitendency. It also makes its appearance in the distractibility of thought which occurs in states of psychomotor overactivity. Psychomotor retardation is yet another form through which the conflict finds a representation. All these phenomena as well as many cognitive abnormalities (speech disorders, misidentifications, defects in short-term memory) serve as a defense against any external stimulation which might lead to libidinal arousal with its painful consequences. There are however occasions when the measures designed to protect the patient and object fail. This is common in the overactive states but less frequent in schizophrenic disorders.

Delusions and hallucinations are also the product of conflict. In all cases of psychosis whether at onset, relapse or in chronicity the emergence of these phenomena is dependent on the means employed to deal with the conflict. The defensive measures are an integral aspect of the dynamic situation. In the case of paranoid ideas it is projection and externalization which are responsible. The hallucinatory mechanism deflects the instinctual drives from the action pathways to a perceptual mode of expression. Attention has already been drawn to the likelihood that the construction of a psychotic reality has the purpose of vitiating the effects of conflict. Where there is psychomotor overactivity the externalization of unwanted libidinal drives leads to the patient accusing others of thoughts and feelings he harbors himself. Externalization is supplemented by denial with the patient refusing to believe that certain events have occurred or that he has been responsible for them.

The dynamic interpretation provides an explanation of why the clinical phenomena develop their particular form and content. It enables the establishment of a connection between internalized conflicts which existed at the time of the onset of the illness and the symptomatology. In addition it offers an understanding of the purpose of the symptoms. By itself however the dynamic approach fails to explain why symptoms emerge at a particular point in time, why they vary in intensity and why there can be an involvement with delusional and real objects no less strong than is to be found in the mentally healthy. These questions can only be answered by turning to the economic aspects of mental life.

Reference has already been made to the hypothesis that in psychoses there is a change in the quality of the libido. The extent of this change varies from patient to patient and within each patient. It was proposed that the libido is most affected in those states which are characterized by extreme withdrawal or by psychomotor overactivity. The change in quality takes the form of a reversion of the libidinal cathexes to their earlier instinctual state. A danger situation is created by the qualitative change and by an increase in quantity. The danger is one of a traumatic situation provoked by the heightening of instinctual cathexes. Freud

(1926) defined a traumatic situation as one in which the individual finds himself in a state of helplessness—"the danger situation is a recognized, remembered and expected situation of helplessness" (Freud, 1926).

The questions raised above can be answered on the basis of the trauma hypothesis. As has been mentioned withdrawn schizophrenic patients do not become affectively disturbed or express delusional ideas or hallucinations except within the context of an interpersonal situation, the details of which will vary in the individual case. Affects, delusional ideas and hallucinations appear coincident with the activation of libidinal drives which have an instinctual quality. An example is provided by a young female patient suffering from chronic schizophrenia (case 3). During an interview with the writer she complained that her hand had been squeezed while she was lying in bed. This tactile hallucination was accompanied by genital sensations which the patient blamed on persecutors. It became apparent that this hallucination was a revived memory of her hand being pressed during lovemaking. Hallucinations provide an outlet for libidinal drives through the cathexis of memory traces of previous acts of satisfaction. In this case libidinal arousal led to anxiety. Hallucinations are, as Katan (1960) has suggested, a means of cathectic discharge no different from the dream hallucination. The instinctual cathexes expressed through delusional ideas and hallucination offset the danger of a traumatic situation.

Other means of reducing the "level" of the cathexes are also available. In withdrawn patients constant masturbation, other autoerotic activities, mannerisms, tics and speech peculiarities serve as outlets for libidinal drive cathexes. The trauma-avoidance hypothesis also provides an explanation for why patients with chronic illness develop what appears to be an intense attachment to a nurse, relative or even to the institution. The object is the vehicle whereby a trauma, of the kind that initiated the illness in the first place, can be avoided. In this regard the patient can be compared to the infant who requires the mother to provide the satisfaction of needs and in so doing reduces the "level" of instinctual cathexis. As with the infant, the patient transfers the anxiety regarding a possible trauma to the situation in which it may arise, to a time when the object is no longer available, that is to the danger of object loss (Freud, 1926).

In those cases of psychosis where there is no sign of withdrawal or negativism it is likely that the libido is more evenly distributed between that which follows the secondary processes and that which has reverted to the instinctual state. These patients can participate in relationships more easily and their appreciation of reality is better. Their conscious dread of loss of control shows that they are aware of an impending traumatic situation. The constant search for an object which will impose a control over the instinctual libido reflects this dread. When such an object attachment is formed separation anxiety is always present. Object loss frequently acts as a precipitant of psychotic illness. Jacobson (1967) has underlined the fact that an object relationship can serve as a barrier against the development of a psychosis.

In those cases where the psychotic reality was the leading manifestation the involvement with the delusional objects was intense and enduring. The quality of the libido varied with respect to the different delusional objects comprising the psychotic reality. On the one hand there were the idealized objects who were loved and respected. Objects which had been cast in a superego mold served the same function as those real objects which had helped patients avoid traumatic situations. On the other hand there were those delusional objects toward whom were directed the instinctual cathexes which gave rise to conflict and danger situations.

The foregoing economic considerations offer a sound explanation as to why so few patients suffering from psychoses are amenable to psychoanalytic treatment. These patients rarely have sufficient libido chanelled along secondary process lines to establish a therapeutic alliance. This requires a cathexis of objects which is sound enough to maintain the treatment situation even when it is disturbed by the activation of drive derivatives which provoke danger situations and anxiety. Even those patients who seem to recognize that they are ill do not consciously regard the therapy as a means of understanding the illness and bringing about a resolution of the symptoms. They view the psychiatrist as one who can help establish a control over needs and affects which they are incapable of containing themselves. Soon they may come to fear him as the cause of libidinal overstimulation.

In neuroses psychoanalytic treatment opens up therapeutic possibilities by the revival of real and fantasied childhood relationships through the medium of the transference. The reexperiencing of formerly repressed drive derivatives has a beneficial effect in that the expenditure of anticathexis in repression is no longer necessary. In psychotic illness the patient dreads a further access of instinctual derivatives which would occur contemporaneously with the revival of childhood object relations in the transference. The result is a strenuous resistance against the development of transferences. Typically, the patient abandons the treatment or there may be anxiety and agitation with the emergence of further psychotic symptoms. The reaction of the chronic schizophrenic patient to attempts at psychoanalytic treatment consists of a general decathexis of preconscious representations. The analyst can be ignored or confused with someone else;

speech becomes unintelligible. In states characterized by psychomotor overactivity a similar decathexis occurs but this is less extensive or consistent. The patient's distraction of thought offers him protection against whatever he perceives as having threatening verbal content.

Although psychoanalysis and interpretative psychotherapy have only a limited role to play in the treatment of the psychoses, psychotherapeutic measures based on an understanding of the dynamics and economics of the individual case can be introduced for the patient's benefit. Experience has demonstrated that the need for an object can be exploited in such a way as to assist in the remission of symptoms.

Finally a reference must be made to the way in which the economic interpretation can throw light on the problem of reality testing (see Chapter 6). Pathological forms of interpersonal relationship proceed hand-in-hand with varying degrees of disorganization of reality testing. Two factors appear to be decisive for its disruption. First, the preconscious representation of objects lose their libidinal cathexis. This cathexis being noninstinctual conforms to the principles of the secondary process. The movement of cathexis is reflected in the symptoms of withdrawal, perplexity and distractibility of thought. Second, the libidinal cathexes which have regained their instinctual quality have a significant impact. The preconscious representations are now acted upon by the primary process. This explains such symptoms as special forms of thought content, misidentifications, etc. Apart from the dream it is only in cases of functional and organic psychosis that a first-hand view can be obtained of the way in which a preconscious representation can lose its cathexis and then be acted upon by the primary process. Failure to recognize a real object and a subsequent misidentification of that object are the resultant phenomena. They reflect the process which Freud (1900) described when discussing the economics of repression and its effects—"From the moment at which the repressed thoughts are strongly cathected by the unconscious wishful impulse and, on the other hand, abandoned by the preconscious cathexis, they become subject to the primary psychical process . . ." (Freud, 1900).

In those states showing clinical improvement it may be inferred that there is a restoration of drive cathexes which are of secondary-process type to the preconscious representations. As the instinctual drive cathexes recede reality testing becomes more effective. Regarded from this standpoint reality testing is dependent on the distribution of the libido, its quality and the state of the preconscious representation. This hypothesis is in accord with the knowledge that in the healthy child reality testing passes through a series of stages prior to its full development and that these early stages are characterized by forms of object relationship which are primarily concerned with the obtaining of instinctual satisfactions.

PROFILE NO. 2

The patient who is the subject of this Profile was 31 years of age, married with three children. She already had had two attacks of mental illness prior to her admission to Holywell Hospital on 31 May 1970. No information was available about her first period of hospitalization at the age of 19. The data concerning her second breakdown in 1968 at the age of 29 will be given below (see Reason for Referral). The material on which this Profile is based was obtained between 2 June 1970 and 7 August 1970.

1. REASON FOR REFERRAL AND HISTORY OF THE ILLNESS

Mrs. A. was admitted to hospital as an emergency because she had become impossible to manage at home. She had become progressively disinterested in her domestic duties and eventually incapable of completing simple tasks. For example, she would put potatoes on to boil but let the pan run dry. She neglected the children. Her behavior was unpredictable. On one occasion she threw a knife at her husband, on another she attacked him viciously, pulling out handfuls of his hair. The main topic of her conversation consisted of her belief that her neighbors were against her. She said that she was unhappy in the housing estate where she lived and that her children were bullied by other children, the parents of whom made no effort to impose controls. Her husband noted that she was in the habit of talking to herself and at such times was totally unresponsive. He also reported that for some weeks she had been very "depressed."

It appears that Mrs. A. fell ill at the age of 19 following a disappointment in love. She was admitted to a mental hospital where she remained for about six months. Subsequently she made a complete recovery. In 1968 she became depressed in mood and sleepless. She attributed this to her unsatisfactory living conditions. At that time her husband and three children were living in an isolated part of the country in a house which had poor facilities and had been condemned as uninhabitable. Her general practitioner had prescribed tranquilizers but these had had no effect. In June 1968 she said that the boyfriend who had disappointed her when she was 19 was coming to her house every night. There was no truth in this assertion.

When she was admitted to the mental hospital in June 1968 she was able to give a reasonable account of her problems and in the following manner tried to explain why the man had been coming to her house. She explained to the admitting doctor that when she was 16 she had become friendly with a young man about whom she came to have expectations. They were very close for three years and intended to marry. When he broke off the relationship she became ill. No details of the symptoms are available. After recovery she met her husband whom she married at the age of 22. Recently her sister-in-law had told her hairdresser that the patient was ill again with her "nerves." According to the patient the hairdresser passed on this information to her former boyfriend. The result was that every night he came to her house to torment her. She knew he was outside the house because she heard his voice. She had not seen him. She was angry with her husband for not going out and chasing him away. She phoned the police on two occasions and complained. She had the idea that her ex-boyfriend was also having a breakdown himself and that it was he who should be a patient in the hospital. She was of the opinion that the ex-boyfriend, who was now married, blamed her for the fact that his second child had been deformed at birth. She said (August 1968): "He is trying to make me ill because of this child. I think he mustn't be right in the head following me about but I don't know what's to be done." Later she made explicit her fear that the man was trying to put her out of her mind.

During her stay in hospital which lasted from July to September 1968 it was observed that she appeared mixed up in her thinking and "confused." Often she would not reply to questions or she would mutter phrases which could not be heard. She would look around her with a puzzled expression indicating a certain perplexity. At no time were hallucinatory phenomena detected. She did say however that she suspected people were trying to make her think things—particularly, that the doctor in charge of her case was forcing her to believe that she was in love with him. She was treated by means of electroshock therapy.

This treatment led to an improvement in her mental state. She talked more freely, claiming that she had had the idea that the doctor was keen on her. Now she knew it was a lot of nonsense. She passed the same judgment on her ideas about the ex-boyfriend. During the remainder of her stay in hospital it was noted that she seemed to be without drive or energy. She was apathetic and indifferent to everything except the prospects of going home. This preoccupied her to the exclusion of everything else. It was decided that she had suffered from a schizophrenic illness which was now in a state of almost full remission.

From the end of 1968 until the end of 1969 she was seen every two to three months as an outpatient. At no time did she present symptoms which could be described as psychotic. Arrangements were made with the local authority and accommodation was provided in a new housing estate. She and her family moved from their isolated country house in June 1969. It was noted at that time that there was considerable friction between the patient and her husband. She said "I don't love him enough to have any more children by him." Toward the end of the year she began to complain about her neighbors and again of her husband—he was "nasty and ignorant." She did not appear for appointments made in January and February 1970.

Information obtained from a social worker revealed that at the beginning of the illness in June 1968 the patient had had the idea that her husband and her mother were having a love affair. She suspected this when, one day, her husband prevented her mother from falling in a faint. The mother suffered from congestive heart failure. The social worker learned that a few weeks prior to the onset of the patient's symptoms the husband had informed the patient that he was going to leave his post and join a construction firm in Africa. The patient was to remain in Northern Ireland and he would send her money.

2. DESCRIPTION OF THE PATIENT

Mrs. A. was a woman of average build and height. Her dress and hair were untidy. She had a pretty but expressionless face. She appeared neither depressed nor anxious. Although cooperative there was a trace of suspiciousness in her attitude. Occasionally her train of thought would cease but she explained that this was because she was thinking of what to say. She explained that she became very upset if neighbors criticized her children. She said, "I have been feeling out of sorts and I can't cope with my housework . . . my mother tells me one thing and my husband another and it confuses me, for example my husband tells me to keep the children away from the other children and my mother thinks they should mix." She complained that her husband would not take her out. She would have liked to go out for a drink or to a dance. She admitted to throwing "something" at her husband but she explained that she was angry with him because he treated her badly. Later when telling about discord with neighbors she revealed that a neighbor disliked her because the woman believed that the patient was attracted to her husband.

In the next few days it was observed that Mrs. A. was most reluctant to speak and when she did the rate of speech was markedly retarded. She would begin to speak and then stop. She was inclined to sit staring directly ahead into space.

On several occasions she acted impulsively, running out of the ward and making as if to attack another patient. One morning while still in bed she threw back the bed-clothes as the writer approached and exposed her pubic region. "Why did you do that?" she was asked. She ignored the question. At an interview later she replied as follows to the same inquiry: "It's this place . . . it's dirty." She would say no more, keeping her forefingers over her mouth. After some minutes she began to laugh but did not speak. Later she said, "I'll sing you a song" and then suddenly added "I can't stand filth and dirt in here . . . you have treated me like dirt."

The following data are also illustrative of her mental state within the first two days after admission to hospital. She sat motionless staring in front of her. Her eyes filled with tears. She was asked what was upsetting her. She replied, "love . . . I love him . . . I need him . . . I need him to hold me . . . I am dead without him." While talking in this manner her eyes rolled upwards until only the sclera could be observed. It seemed as if she were momentarily in a trance state. It was impossible to know exactly to whom she had been referring. Following this she became completely inaccessible. It is important to add that she did not acknowledge that she was ill or in need of hospitalization. She said that it was her husband who was unwell. She wanted to return to her children.

3. FAMILY BACKGROUND (PAST AND PRESENT)

Both the patient's parents were alive. Her father was about 60 years of age. He had been a French-polisher but had to give up work on account of ill health due principally to alcoholism. Her mother was about the same age and suffered from heart disease. Mrs. A. has a brother, two to three years younger than herself. There is no family history of mental illness.

The patient was born in the North of Ireland and lived there until she was 12 years of age. At that time the family had to sell their home on account of debt which had been incurred as a consequence of the father's alcoholism. The family moved to the South of Ireland. Mrs. A. was very unhappy at having to leave her home, school and friends. She did not settle well in her new home and no longer did well at school. Two years later, when she was 14, the family returned to the North of Ireland. Mrs. A. resented her father from that time on, believing that he had ruined the family and her chances of education through his irresponsibility.

Mrs. A. had been an attractive, good looking child. To use her words, "My mother put me on a pedestal." Relations between the parents deteriorated prior to the move to the South and in subsequent years. Mrs. A. was very close to her mother and ignored her father to the extent that it was possible. She left school at 15 and worked as a shop assistant until she married. As will be mentioned later, she was anxious to have further education but her mother was unwilling to allow this. She married in 1961 to a man a year or so older than herself. He was a fitter by trade. There were three children from the marriage, a boy of eight and girls of six and five years of age respectively. During her stay in hospital Mrs. A. said that her mother never wanted her to marry her husband and was antagonistic to him. Apparently Mrs. A. had a suitor who was more acceptable to her mother but the patient found this man too quiet and reserved. Further details about the patient's feelings about her parents will be given later.

4. POSSIBLY SIGNIFICANT ENVIRONMENTAL CIRCUMSTANCES

It is difficult to establish with certainty whether Mrs. A. fully recovered after her discharge from hospital in 1968. The outpatient notes extending from December 1968 until December 1969 indicate that while significant symptoms were absent she was extremely unhappy and depressed in mood. She continually complained about living in a housing estate and her inability to get on with her neighbors. She criticized her husband, blaming him for not taking her out and not being understanding. She worried excessively about the children. There was a short time when she was convinced that he was interested in other women. As mentioned above she was frequently in a conflict of loyalty between her mother and her husband. A further significant factor was persistent sexual frustration due to the husband's practice of coitus interruptus.

No information was available about possible childhood predisposing factors.

5. ASSESSMENT OF THE DRIVES

A. *The Libido*

(1) *Problems of Libido Distribution*

(a) *Cathexis of the Self.* At one point in the illness there was a hypercathexis of the self-representations which found expression in a belief in her omnipotence: "I don't want to destroy the world . . . I am the world." The ego-ideal formations were also subject to a hypercathexis. This led to the wishful delusion that she was a princess—"I am a bastard princess." The fantasies which provided the basis for this delusional idea will be described later under Section 7. A further expression of the hypercathexis, this time of the bodily self, was her belief that she was pregnant. On several occasions she expressed ideas which pointed to the trend toward the fusion of self- and object representations. For example she said to the writer: "I want to work with you." When asked why, she replied, "because we are one."

For the most part Mrs. A. neglected her appearance. She was disinclined to wash or keep herself clean. This decathexis of the bodily self was paralleled by a decathexis of real persons, resulting in a withdrawal. Information obtained from the nursing staff indicated that the cathexis was directed to certain object representations which, as will be noted below, influenced the patient's capacity to make a correct judgment of her perceptions. The quality of the hypercathexis which was turned to these object representations had primary-process quality (see below).

(b) *Cathexis of Objects:*

i. Cathexis of Real Persons (Current Relationships)

The quality of the cathexis which was invested in real persons was often instinctual and followed the primary process. This resulted in a condensation of the perception of the external object and the representation of another object, a phenomenon which was to be observed in her communications with the writer. After minutes of silence during the course of an interview Mrs. A. said "I love you . . . you are my father." At another time she stated "I love you . . . I want you to . . . I want you to make love to me. . . ." This time she confused the writer with a man she had fallen in love with while a patient in the hospital in 1968. The writer himself was also the object of these libidinal cathexes. The libidinal arousal was always associated with an upturning of the eyes as has been described above. On another occasion she said to the male nurse in charge of the ward "I am in love." "With whom?" she was asked. "You," she replied. At another time she asked the same nurse, "Who is that man walking down the ward?" (there was no man there). "What man?" the nurse asked. "It's John McC . . . he is my lover."

Disinterest in the real external object occurred immediately if there was no response. There was a decathexis of the object and further communication was impossible. It appeared as if in this phase of the illness the external object had reality only as long as it was a possible means of instinctual satisfaction. In the case of the patient's husband frustration of her wishes led to anger. She accused him of making her ill because he had not been able to satisfy her sexually. He had employed coitus interruptus as a contraceptive method. She said that she wanted to marry someone else. She was forever wanting to go to dances and meet men—"I want to have a good time." She found it difficult to contain her genital needs as was instanced by some of her remarks—"dancing relieves my feelings."

There were occasions when Mrs. A. was able to identify the writer correctly and give him an account of the thoughts and feelings she had had when she had misidentified him with others, as well as when she had been withdrawn and in a negativistic state. She explained that she could not come to interviews or speak to the writer because he looked like her father and she was afraid of him—"I'm frightened because you look like my father and he wants to make love to me." She based this statement on the way her father kept staring at her and looking at her legs. She said that she avoided him and was afraid to be alone with him. She added, "My father wanted to make love to me from the moment I was born." It is necessary to add that she occasionally regarded the writer as hostile and persecuting, forcing her to his will—"You try to overpower me." In this respect many of her attitudes to the writer could be regarded as transferences—for example, she said "my husband forces himself on me." Like her husband the writer was considered to be domineering, forcing her to have sexual feelings and to have coitus; he was seen as selfish like her father. This material illustrated the patient's tendency to withdraw cathexis from external objects and hypercathect representations of objects with resultant loss of reality testing.

Much of the patient's communications revealed a disappointment and disillusionment with real persons—husband, father and mother. She expressed the following delusional ideas based on a family romance fantasy. She said that she was not her father's daughter. He did not behave like a father (sexual interest in her, for example). He was selfish. He destroyed their home and her confidence in herself. "I am not sure if my mother is my real mother." When asked why she thought this she replied—"because . . . she's attractive . . . she buys me clothes that don't suit me . . . my mother did not treat me like a mother . . . I wanted to be educated, not go with boys . . . she has ruined my life." Attention has already been drawn to her delusion of being a princess.

ii. Cathexis of Representations of Real and Fantasy Objects

The disinterest in external reality, self-preoccupation and the occasional utterance indicated that a hypercathexis of representations of real objects from the past had occurred. The cathexis followed the primary process, reality testing having been suspended. Data has already been presented showing that there was a libidinal hypercathexis of the representation of the father, a former boyfriend and other men who were attractive to the patient. They, along with the writer and a male nurse, formed the basis for misidentifications.

There was also hypercathexis of object representations and memories of the hospitalization in 1968. She referred to the hospital as "a sex place." She believed that when she was given electrical treatment in that hospital the doctors had had intercourse with her while she was under the anesthetic. She also had sexual fantasies about one of the doctors who attended to her. She was afraid of having electroshock therapy and yet on one occasion asked to have it. She gave the impression that she had enjoyed a relationship with a man while in the hospital in 1968. Later when in a more stable state of mind she insisted that she had never been unfaithful to her husband.

(2) *Libidinal Position*

Throughout the period of study the patient gave the impression of being in a state of genital arousal—sometimes as has been described this was manifest, at other times latent, its presence only being betrayed by a chance remark. Mrs. A. appeared to have reached the phallic-genital level of libidinal development. Active aims predominated. Reference has already been made to the difficulty she experienced in containing her genital needs. Shortly after admission to hospital she exhibited herself as has been mentioned above. There was much to suggest that dancing was a masturbatory substitute. On two occasions she was found with male patients—on one occasion there was some question as to whether or not coitus occurred.

B. *Aggression*

(a) Mrs. A. was aggressive in action and speech. She attacked her husband on several occasions. Her silence shortly after her admission to hospital had an aggressive quality. She said the ward was dirty. Illustrative of some of her statements with aggressive content was the following, "I hate you; you are destroying everything." The criticisms of her parents have already been detailed.

(b) Aggression appeared to be connected with the genital-phallic level.

(c) Aggression was always directed toward external objects, never toward the self or the ego via the superego. There was never any attempt to injure herself nor was there any sign of self-criticism or self-reproach.

(d) Aggression was activated by frustration of wishes. When her husband refused to take her out she became aggressive. She blamed him for not satisfying her sexually. He had refused to buy condoms and had practiced coitus interruptus. She said that he was too mean to buy condoms and as a result he had made her ill.

(e) The only discernible defense against aggression was externalization in the form of generalization. She feared neighbors with whom she herself had been angry.

6. ASSESSMENT OF EGO AND SUPEREGO

Ego Functions

(a) Speech was slow and showed evidences of blocking —for example, "years ago . . . I . . . loved a boy called. . . ." She did not complete the sentence. Answers to questions were often irrelevant and inappropriate For example she said in reply to the question, "Why did you say your mother is not your real mother?"—"Because she is going to die, she has thrombosis." Repeating the question elicited the following —"My sister-in-law goes out with another man. . . ." Often it was difficult to understand what she said because connecting thoughts were omitted as in the following instance—"He would not buy me a wedding dress. . . . I don't want to live with him any more." She continued, "I wanted to buy a wedding dress. He wouldn't let me and took me to see a bad film." A reference to the wedding dress was part of a memory from the time before they married. They had been out for the evening and went to see "Lady Chatterly's Lover." She had not wanted to go to the movies and would have preferred to look at the shops where wedding dresses were sold.

At other times her speech was easily communicated and understood. This improvement followed the disappearance of the withdrawal and disinterest in external reality.

(b) In those instances where the patient misidentified the writer as her father, boyfriend from adolescence or other men, her thinking was omnipotent—the libidinal drives resulted in a perceptual distortion in consequence of the action of the primary process (condensation). Here there was the revival in perception of a memory with which a drive expectancy was associated.

(c) An account has already been given of the period of withdrawal which prevented her from attending or concentrating on what was said to her. She became attentive, during such phases of withdrawal, when there was a libidinal arousal.

(d) Perceptual functions were intact except for the tendency to misidentify.

There was no definite evidence of hallucinations.

(e) Memory function was intact except for some slight "confusion" when in the withdrawn state.

(f) While withdrawn the patient tended to be motionless. At other times she was slow in her movements. During the first two weeks in hospital there were periods when she was negativistic, uncooperative and inattentive.

Ego Reactions to Danger Situations

Danger situations arose from both libidinal and the aggressive drives. The superego did not create a danger situation in this case. Mrs. A. feared object loss as a punishment for the satisfaction of libidinal and aggressive drives. Details have been provided of the contents of these drive representations.

State of the Defense Organizations

During the illness repression failed to contain the representations of both libidinal and aggressive drives. This led to the patient's becoming acutely aware of the derivatives—thoughts and affects. Aggressive actions occurred and possibly libidinal acts as well. A number of defenses were employed in order to contain the libidinal drive derivatives. Condensation and displacement were used defensively in the case of the cathexis directed to the writer. The object of the cathexis was thus altered and misidentification resulted. It was her father, lover, etc. who was consciously believed to be the object of her libidinal cathexis. Projection resulted in her belief that her father had sexual feelings about her. More prominent was the defense of externalization. She attributed to the writer responsibility for her genital urges. Thus her statement: "You make me feel in love with you and make me want to have intercourse." She accused the writer of making her change her feelings toward her husband. It is likely that she generalized her genital feelings to the writer as well. Similarly she externalized her own genital wishes onto her husband—"He is more sexually inclined than I am" or "He thinks that I am interested in other men." She externalized to the husband her own wishes for extramarital relationships and accused him of going out with women. There was no truth in this. She externalized her wish for a relationship with a neighbor's husband by saying that the neighbor accused her of that intention.

Externalization was associated with aggression but not always defensively. Mrs. A. generalized her aggressive feelings to neighbors. They disliked her and were against her. A further example of this tendency to generalize was a statement made about the time of her admission to the hospital which possibly referred to the writer—"I hate you . . . you are destroying everything."

Affects

This patient complained of depression of mood at the beginning of her period of hospitalization. Her husband stated that she had been depressed. However, during the greater part of her stay in hospital she did not give the impression of being depressed. Nor did she manifest signs of anxiety. A certain gaiety made its appearance in the form of general amusement or in laughter. Illustrative of this mood was her remark, "Would you like me to sing a song" or "I'm happy." As has been mentioned Mrs. A. was either immobile or her movements were slow when these affects made their appearance.

Superego

The superego appeared to be unresponsive to the activity of drive derivatives during the period described by this profile. Such defenses as were initiated could be characterized as due to "objective anxiety" rather than "superego anxiety."

7. ASSESSMENT OF REGRESSIONS AND POSSIBLE FIXATIONS

(a) The content of the patient's speech suggested that a libidinal regression in the sphere of object relations had occurred to fixation points located in the preoedipal and oedipal phases of development. The tendency to generalize wishes and affects to external objects and the occasional merging of self and object representations indicated a regression to a fixation point in the phase prior to self-object differentiation. The preoedipal fixation was also revealed in the ambivalent attitude to the mother and husband. Both were frustrating and demanding and did not allow her the satisfaction of her own needs. A regression to this preoedipal period is suggested further by the fear of object loss and by the fear of loss of love. The fixation at the oedipal period was reflected in the family romance fantasy, the reactive aggression against the father and the disillusionment in him.

(b) There was some evidence of a fixation of the libidinal drives at the phallic level. There was also some evidence of homosexual conflict which found an outlet in her delusional ideas about her neighbors. The phallic nature of the patient's sexuality is supported first, by the active character of the patient's sexual organization and second by the fact that as a child she engaged in sexual games with her brother. It is likely that she was the instigator of these games; possibly she herself had been "seduced" by other children at a previous time.

(c) Reference has already been made to the omnipotent thinking.

8. RESULTS OF DRIVE AND EGO DISORGANIZATION

The disorder of speech and perception can be regarded as a result of ego disorganization as can the slowing of movement.

9. ASSESSMENT OF CONFLICTS

(a) Mrs. A. was in conflict with a number of external objects—for example, husband and mother. These conflicts had an aggressive content.

(b) The principal internalized conflict revolved around the wish for libidinal satisfaction with fear of loss of love (object loss).

(c) No evidence available regarding internal conflicts.

10. THE PREPSYCHOTIC PERSONALITY

In the period prior to 1968 when Mrs. A. was apparently well there was a consistent cathexis of husband, children, parents and other persons. Ego functions were intact and the sexual organization had genital-phallic characteristics. In the year or so before the illness reappeared there was a frustration of genital libido due to the husband practicing coitus interruptus as a means of contraception. This frustration led to disturbances in the relationship with the husband as a consequence of reactive aggression in the face of this disappointment. In general, the patient's expectations of the husband were an outgrowth of the relationship she had had with her mother. In childhood and adolescence Mrs. A.'s mother had met her demands for love, support and material necessities. The husband's inability to meet her needs for companionship, support and entertainment as well as those arising from the genital libido resulted in either aggressive speech and action or depression of mood.

In the prepsychotic period Mrs. A. complained of loneliness, her husband being away from early in the morning until late at night. Living in the country far from other people aggravated the separation anxiety which had been a leading feature of Mrs. A.'s personality ever since childhood. As a child Mrs. A. dreaded being separated from her mother and when alone feared that some harm may have befallen the mother. This expected punishment for death wishes was also present in adult life when she had identical fears about the husband when he was away at work. Much of her separation anxiety can be understood as arising from the unsettled home conditions due to father's alcoholism and the move to the South of Ireland.

Before the outbreak of symptoms in 1968 the defense organization was effective in maintaining the repression of the unsatisfied genital libido. These unsatisfied needs provoked a regression of the libido. There was a recathexis of oedipal wishes with the libidinal drives directed to the father. This was possible because of the fixation which had occurred during development at the phallic level of the sexual organization and at the oedipal phase of object relations —both promoted or enhanced by childhood sexual play and clitoral masturbation. Although these regressed oedipal drives remained in repression during the prepsychotic period their intensity was such as to lead to special defensive maneuvers. They found an indirect outlet in an inhibition in Mrs. A.'s relations with her father. Additionally the phallic sexuality heightened by regression resulted in the wish for extramarital relations. The ensuing conflict (fear of loss, etc.) was resolved by externalization of the drive. She believed her husband was having "affairs" and about to leave her. She also generalized her infidelity wishes to other women. This was pronounced after she moved to the housing estate.

Mrs. A. was reluctant to be in her father's company, particularly by herself. She had, as has already been mentioned, the idea that he scrutinized her body and legs in a "sexual" way. Repression was thus aided by projection. Only when repression failed and there was a change in the quality of the libido did projection lead to the delusion that she was being tortured (sexually) by her former lover. Later, when the psychotic attack reached its height, the regression led to the exposure of the previously repressed oedipal wishes for the father.

11. ASSESSMENT OF SOME GENERAL CHARACTERISTICS, ETC.

In the withdrawn period it was impossible to establish useful contact with the patient. Such object cathexis as occurred was directed to the representation of objects from the past and was basically of a primary process nature. When Mrs. A. was in a more integrated state it was clear that an internalized conflict over libidinal expression existed. At that time there was some evidence of a cathexis of external objects—with cathexis following the secondary process. Upon restoration of the ego a defense organization was recognizable with the realization of the fact of having been ill. Although there was a cathexis of external objects a workable transference was impossible because of the patient's resistance to any idea of continued treatment. This resistance probably arose from anxiety lest the object cathexis regain its instinctual quality.

CHAPTER 4

Disorders of Libido Distribution in Psychoses: Cathexis of the Self

The abnormalities of interpersonal relationships which occur in psychotic states are always accompanied by changes in the perception of the self. There is no change specific for any one diagnostic category and identical phenomena may be found in different kinds of psychosis.

Clinical Phenomena

The disorders of perception of the self can be described as follows. There are those manifestations which reflect a deficiency in the sense of autonomy of the self. Under normal circumstances the healthy individual not only feels in command of his feelings, percepts and thoughts but he also discerns himself as an entity separate from other entities. Common to nearly all psychotic states is the feeling of being exposed to the attentions, curiosity and criticism of other individuals. All events appear to have a specific self-reference. This may mystify the patient and give rise to a feeling of perplexity. The autonomy of the self may be further disturbed by the impression that thoughts and feelings have passed into the control of those who are unfriendly to the patient. Action as well as thought and feeling are no longer felt as the product of an act of will. Certain conscious mental contents and behavior are experienced as arising automatically at the instigation of a known or unknown persecutor. These ideas of influence and the pathological egocentrism are to be found in cases which have quite different formal characteristics. They are to be encountered in patients who are withdrawn or show psychomotor retardation, in those who are mentally and physically overactive, in those who are depressed in mood and in those who are elated.

No matter the nature of the illness the patient suffering from a psychosis believes that all external events relate directly to himself. This pathological egocentrism is therefore a nonspecific symptom and cannot be used as an aid to diagnosis. It does however indicate that a shift in attention and interest has taken place from external reality and real persons to the self. It is the occurrence of this pathological egocentrism which gives a foundation to the theory that in psychoses a dramatic change has occurred in the "normal" distribution of libido between self and objects.

There is yet another category of disorder of the autonomy of the self, which in contrast to that already described, is not necessarily painful or distressing. The impression gained from statements made is that the distinction which is normally made between self and object is in abeyance. Percepts, thoughts and feelings are felt as shared. In some instances this identity extends to bodily experience. The individual with whom the merging occurs is often someone who is emotionally significant to the patient. An example of the "sharing" of mental experience is provided by the patient who believes that her mind and that of a former lover are one. Both are aware of each other's feelings, thoughts, wishes and memories. Each can read the other's mind.

Illustrative of the fusion of bodily experience are those patients who state that they experience the sensations of other individuals. A female patient, for example, complained of being tormented by genital sensations. These sensations, she said, came from male genitals which were located within her own genitalia. She could not distinguish between her own sensations and those of the unknown men. When they masturbated she was affected. There are few cases of psychosis which do not manifest this tendency toward a fusion of different aspects of self- and object images (representations) and once again this phenomenon occurs independently of the formal characteristics of the particular illness. This fusion is most apparent in those cases where the patient believes that his whole being has been taken over by another individual. A case in point is that of a man who was unable to distinguish between his own physical and mental experience and that of another man who, he believed, had insinuated himself into his body. In other cases the patient recognizes that he is free from such a fusion but insists that when he speaks or acts the behavior is that of another person.

Closely related to those disorders of the autonomy of the self which manifest themselves in a fusion of self- and object images are the phenomena of denial of personal identity and changes in identity. The sense of personal identity may be affected in a number of different ways. The capacity to use the first person in speech may be partially or permanently lost. The patient may be unable to sustain the concept of "I" and change to the third person to provide a description of thoughts, feelings, memories, etc. This phenomenon is quite common in cases of chronic schizophrenia. In other psychotic states a doubt may be expressed about identity. Sometimes this doubt is accompanied by the queried assumption of an aspect of another individual's identity. Here there is evidence of faulty self-object discrimination with fusion of self- and object images. A patient was heard to say—"I have lived with those other people for so long . . . now they are all part of me and I am part of them."

Quite frequently patients are found who deny their name and occupation or assume new ones. The changes may be transient or permanent. In some instances there is a denial of all or part of their previous life experiences. There may be the assumption of a new name which they refuse to relinquish. The new identity may be part of a delusional complex but it is not always so. The patient may select an ordinary everyday name. Transient changes in name and occupation are more commonly encountered in acute psychotic states although they may also be found in chronic conditions. In some cases of chronic psychosis the patient's identity and occupation alters in accordance with whomever they may be in contact. The patient assumes the name and occupation of that person. If the person is a doctor the patient is a doctor, if a nurse then he is a nurse and so on. These tendencies are most common in patients who display some degree of psychomotor overactivity. They are commonplace therefore in acute psychotic reactions. They are pronounced in cases of mania but may also appear in other psychotic conditions where the illness is punctuated by phases of psychomotor overactivity.

The sense of self may be disrupted by abnormalities affecting the representations of the body. The representations of anatomical sexuality may be disturbed in such a way as to lead the patient to believe that he is undergoing a change of sexual identity. Male patients may complain that they are only partially male, having become half man and half woman. In the case of female patients there may be similar ideas with the belief that they are changing sex. In all cases these ideas are accompanied by the conviction that others have been similarly affected. Sometimes the change is attributed to malevolent influences, sometimes not. Anxiety about the change only occurs when it is regarded as a form of persecution. Another group of disturbances of the representations of the body consists of unusual changes affecting the head, trunk and limbs. The head may be experienced as bigger or smaller, the limbs as lengthened or shortened and the chest as losing its breadth and depth.

In describing the disorders of object relations which may occur in psychoses attention has already been directed to the fact that a patient's perception of real persons can be determined by the manner in which he perceives himself. The facial expression and appearance of the other person is described as if it were the patient himself. Similarly mental and physical experiences are attributed to the other person. Examples have already been given of patients who endow the external object with their own omnipotent ideas, sense of physical strength and well being, etc. In other cases what is attributed to the other person is an awareness of abnormal bodily experiences and changes in sexual identity. All these manifestations can be regarded as due to a loss of the capacity to discriminate self from object.

Yet another group of disorders of the self is characterized by the phenomena arising out of heightened self-esteem on the one hand and lowered self-esteem on the other. In both there is faulty judgment such that the self-evaluation is taken as correct. The self-inflation or self-depreciation may eventually acquire a delusional intensity. Grandiose and wish-fulfilling delusions may be accompanied by psychomotor overactivity and elation of mood as in mania. This is not invariable and these expressions of a pathologically exaggerated self-esteem may occur in association with increased motor activity but without elation. Again delusions of this kind may appear in patients who are usually in a withdrawn state exhibiting some degree of psychomotor inhibition.

Lowered self-esteem usually occurs together with signs of psychomotor retardation and depression of mood. However there are cases where the lowered self-esteem and depression of mood are accompanied by an overactivity of thought. Thinking may follow the sound of a word rather than its meaning and there may be a flight of ideas. The lowered self-esteem may not only find expression through self-criticism but also through a concrete mode of thought.

Enhancement or depreciation of the self may occur in combination with one or more of the other disturbances in perception of the self which have been described. Most frequently increased self-esteem and delusions of omnipotence are found in association with a fusion of self- and object representations and the presence of psychomotor overactivity.

Dynamic Aspects

The disorders of the self which have been described can be related to a conflict between libidinal drives on the one hand and defenses on the other. The purpose of the defenses is to deflect the drive derivatives from their aims and thus annul the anxiety which brought them into operation. The phenomena which are most easily understood from the dynamic standpoint consist of the so-called passivity feelings (ideas, feelings, sensations, movements being influenced against the will), certain forms of delusion which have an omnipotent and omniscient content and the denial of identity and past experiences.

The loss of the "ego quality" of sensations, ideas, affects, intentions and actions can be regarded as resulting from the attribution to others of these unwanted conscious mental contents. From the descriptive standpoint patients can be differentiated according to whether or not they experience the affective element of the drive representation be they libidinal or aggressive. In one category of case the patient is aware of sexual (genital or pregenital) or aggressive affects but believes that the stimulus and intent come from outside himself. In the other category of case the patient is unaware of such affects but believes that others are hostile, unfriendly, entertain various ideas about them and may wish to do them an injury. The patient experiences mental tension and anxiety which finds some form or other of ideational expression. For example the woman described in Profile 2 believed that her unpleasant bodily and mental sensations were caused by a former lover who was determined to "torture the life out of her."

In the first group there is repression of the active aims of the drives and by means of externalization the stimulus and intent are attributed to a "persecutor." The affect belonging to the drive is not repressed and enters consciousness. In the second group of cases the active aims and the affect associated with the drive remain unconscious due to the action of projection. Projection not only results in an externalization of stimulus and intent but maintains the "repression" of the drive derivatives. In the case of the woman who believed that she was being tortured projection of unsatisfied genital libido allowed her to remain guilt-free. The two categories of case referred to above can therefore be differentiated both descriptively and dynamically. Externalization and projection lead to different clinical presentations and the choice of mechanism appears to be in part dependent on the extent of regression which has effected the libido and the ego (see Chapter 8).

It is often revealed that grandiose and omnipotent fantasies which assume a delusional quality are a means of denying reality judgments about the self which are no longer acceptable. These mechanisms of denial, reversal and "repression" are to be found in patients categorized as suffering from schizophrenia and mania. Chronic schizophrenic patients are found in whom the grandiose delusion serves the purpose of avoiding recognition of the situation in which the patient finds himself. A case in point is the patient who believes that the hospital is indebted to him because of important services which he rendered to it in the past. A young woman patient suffering from an illness characterized by psychomotor overactivity insisted that she was a doctor and that her husband was ill. The change of place with the husband serves the same purpose as the delusion of the patient suffering from chronic schizophrenia. Denial of identity and the refusal to acknowledge relatives, friends and everything that belongs to the past life springs from the action of "repression." This has as its aim the removal of all the affects with a painful, anxiety or guilt-provoking quality.

A defensive process may also be inferred in many of the cases which manifest the phenomena which follow the merging of self and object representations. One case has already been referred to where there was a merging of the bodily aspects of self and object representations. This merging of representations may be confined only to the mental aspects as in the case of patients who believe that self and object have identical experiences. In many of these cases the phenomena follow object loss. The merging is a form of identification. It is however a form of identification quite unlike that which leads to the growth of the ego and the personality (secondary identification). It is a form of complete or total identification and is comparable to the primary identification which occurs in infancy as the first kind of object relationship. Illustrative is a young woman who complained of blurred vision and a squint. She was deluded and overactive. These complaints were the symptoms of a young man the patient had nursed in an ophthalmic hospital and with whom she fell in love.

Object loss is a common stimulus for the merging of self and object representations and occurs in different forms of mental illness. The phenomena may appear at the onset of an illness or when it has reached a chronic stage. There may be accompanying psychomotor overactivity, delusions of a persecutory type and negativism with catatonic signs.

Case 4

A patient who had been ill for many years with chronic schizophrenia presented the following manifestations resulting from the merging of bodily aspects of self- and object representations. As in the case of the young female patient just referred to the merging had the defensive aim of annulling the pain of object loss. The patient had fallen ill when he could no longer sustain the fantasy that a girl he both admired and loved would marry him. During the illness which lasted for many years he was preoccupied with thoughts about her. At one point, when he was struggling against awareness of depressive affects, he expressed thoughts which indicated that there was a merging between the representations of the self and of the love object. On two separate occasions he said—". . . the hospital is no place for U—" (the girl friend) and "It's wrong for U to be kept in a ward with men."

The mode of presentation of the phenomena resulting from the merging of self- and object representations after object loss is materially influenced by the predominating drive derivatives—libidinal or aggressive—and the defenses employed against them. It is a fact of observation that some patients regard the merging experience as a form of persecution. In others there is no sign of distress apart from the longing for the lost object and the ensuing depression of mood. In both groups of patients the lost object with whom the merging occurs is recognized as a distinct and separate entity from the self.

Case 5

An example of the type of patient who experiences the fusion of self with object as a persecution is provided by the case of an unmarried female patient, aged 27, whose illness manifested itself subsequent to the realization that an admired man had no real interest in her. She was convinced that he knew everything that she was thinking and similarly she was aware of all his thoughts, wishes and emotions. Their behavior and mental states were identical. She even believed that he was also a patient in the hospital and had an illness of a nervous nature. A leading feature of the psychosis was the hallucination of the man's voice. She heard this in her head and considered it, in conjunction with the other experiences, as torture which he inflicted upon her. She hated the formerly loved object on this account. In those cases where persecutory feelings are absent the predominant affects are varying degrees of elation, anxiety and depression. In some there may be psychomotor overactivity.

It is predominantly in states of psychomotor overactivity that the transient fusions of self- and object representations occur. In these cases it is evident that the merging phenomena follow on the libidinal cathexis of an object representation.

Case 6

A female patient who was elated and overactive complained of genital frustration due to her husband's impotence. She claimed that she was Mr. A.—a male nurse. She denied her own identity vigorously. Dressing in a white coat, she played the part of nurse with the other patients. She said that she found Mr. A. very attractive. The self had become the object providing a substitute form of drive gratification. The merging, in this instance, had no immediate defensive aim as occurs in those cases where there is object loss. In the case quoted the cathexis was heterosexual but it may just as well have been homosexual. When heterosexual or homosexual cathexes provoke a danger situation and lead to anxiety projection may result in the patient's accusing others of making homosexual or heterosexual advances to him.

Case 7

A patient developed an acute psychotic state during psychotherapy. In this episode the stimulus for the merging of representations was a libidinal cathexis whose object was the therapist. The patient, a single woman of 29, had already suffered from a psychotic attack some years previously. She had sought psychotherapy on account of depressive symptoms. After some months of treatment she revealed that she had been hearing the therapist's voice when at home. This was usually comforting and reassuring. At the same time she had the feeling of no longer being a separate entity nor could she resist being influenced by what others said and did. The psychotic episode had its full development when she announced that on the previous night, in bed, she felt the therapist's body next to hers and she believed that they had engaged in coitus. She experienced his body as hers and hers as his. All thoughts and feelings were shared. During the course of the night she believed she was observed by hidden cameras. She then felt that she had been forced into this compromising situation so that she might be discredited. The genital arousal had been forced on her.

The descriptive distinction which is made between patients who present the merging experiences against a background of psychomotor overactivity and those who manifest the phenomena in association with persecutory ideas, negativism and catatonic signs is understandable on the basis of whether or not there is a reaction of anxiety and guilt to the drive derivatives whose activity provoked a danger situation. The merging provides the means of expression for drive derivatives (the libidinal cathexes) which previously had no outlet. If this causes anxiety the projection and attribution of responsibility leads to the experience of persecution as in the case described above. Persecutory ideas based on externalization occur in states of psychomotor overactivity but they are usually transient. The fusion of self- and object representations occurring in these states, which are a means for the representation and expression of libidinal aims, may assume a defensive function insofar as it protects the patient from awareness of his illness and denies his vulnerable emotional state. This is most obvious when the psychomotor overactivity follows object loss.

ECONOMIC ASPECTS

The dynamic explanation holds good for many, but not all of the disorders of self-awareness and perception of the self. It is unable, for example, to shed light on the origins of conscious mental contents which are employed for the purposes of defense. This is true also for heightened self-esteem, elation of mood and delusions with an omnipotent and omniscient content. The dynamic approach cannot easily account for the disturbances of bodily awareness and the bisexual fantasies which reach delusional intensity. In some of these cases of disturbance of sexual identity it may be suggested that the delusions arise from a merging of self and object bodily representations following object loss. In many patients, however, there is no such loss either in reality or in fantasy. Even when delusions with a bisexual content can be traced to a conflict situation the problem still remains as to why the fantasy made its appearance when it did and how it found delusional expression.

The dynamic theory of grandiose delusions, omnipotence of thought and sense of omniscience proposes that these phenomena are the result of the operation of the mechanisms of denial and reversal. This theory is weakened by the fact that denial and reversal by themselves do not ordinarily lead to the kind of faulty reality testing which gives rise to psychotic phenomena. Denial leads to some distortion of judgment but this is strictly confined in both the psychoneurotic patient and in the healthy adult. There are times when it even has an adaptive function. Only in the child, where reality testing has not yet achieved its full maturity, do reversal and denial lead to fantasies not unlike the delusions found in the psychotic patient (A. Freud, 1936).

When grandiose delusions are examined from the developmental as well as the descriptive standpoint it becomes apparent that they are based on fantasies which were active in the patient's early childhood, in puberty or in adolescence. These fantasies may be part of the ego ideal as in the case of redeemer fantasies or fantasies concerning literary, artistic or scientific aspirations. The fantasies may be based on repressed libidinal drives associated with either the oedipal or preoedipal period. The nature of the fantasies will depend on a number of factors specific to the individual case but it will be decisively influenced by the predominating instinctual aims. It may be possible therefore to find pregnancy fantasies in the male (the delusion of having given birth to children) and active, masculine fantasies in the female (delusions whose content is analogous to rescue fantasies in the male). The dynamic theory cannot explain why these fantasies which have remained latent in the mind recur in the illness in the form of delusions.

Heightened self-esteem, sensations of great physical strength and elation of mood are equally difficult to account for solely on the basis of the dynamic explanation. This does no more than point to the stimulus for the appearance of these manifestations. It is clear that some new development in the psychic economy must be invoked in order to provide a satisfactory explanation of the delusions, omniscience and heightened self-esteem. It is of interest that Freud (1922), on the basis of clinical observations, pointed out that in the case of patients suffering from persecutory delusions there was the possibility that these delusions are not newly created at the onset of the illness but are actually present as fantasies for a long time prior to the outbreak of the symptoms. He went on to emphasize that the qualitative factor—the presence of fantasies or "neurotic formations" is of less practical significance for the appearance of the clinical manifestations than the quantitative factor. This quantitative factor consists of the extent to which the fantasies become cathected with libido. A striking example will be described (see Case 13) in which the delusion arose on the basis of a fantasy of an "imaginary companion."

The conversion of a preexisting fantasy into a delusion

is most clearly seen in the persecutory delusions of female patients regarding former lovers. The revival of the fantasy in consciousness can only be explained on the basis of a re-cathexis of the fantasy. Conflict follows when the genital libido provokes a danger situation. The dynamic interpretation cannot account for the intensity of attachment to the delusional object, why the delusion substitutes for the patient's relationship with real persons and why it should disappear in certain cases. It only disappears when the libidinal cathexes are able to find their way back to the real persons with whom the patient had a relationship prior to the illness. The delusion remains when the patient was without such a relationship in the days before the psychotic attack.

The economic concept is concerned with the intensities of the drive derivatives and the changes which may affect their quality. Its use supplements the dynamic explanation of symptom formation with its emphasis on conflict and defense. The clinical phenomena can be conceptualized in terms of the quantity and quality of the libidinal drive which invest the self and its representations. The transformation of grandiose, wish-fulfilling, omnipotent, bisexual and other fantasies into delusions presupposes changes in the distribution and quality of the libidinal cathexes. The effect of this redistribution is the enhancement of narcissism. There is a change in the direction of the cathexes from objects to the self and to the object fantasies based on the self. Projection and identification increase the quantities of "ego" libido by returning instinctual cathexes to the self.

The narcissistic organization which is present in psychoses is shown by the pathological egocentrism with its ideas of reference, misinterpretation of visual and auditory percepts and feelings of passivity. It is to be seen in the egotism, self-love and indifference to real persons (see Profile Number 3).

Under certain circumstances the narcissism is hidden behind self-reproaches or it is externalized. The extent of the pathological egocentrism is determined by the degree to which object cathexes have been abandoned in favor of cathexis of the self. Where the self-cathexis is limited the egocentrism will be confined to ideas of reference and object attachments will remain, but where the self-cathexis is extensive there will be a wholesale withdrawal of cathexis from object representations with the development of a complex psychotic reality. Many of these delusional object relations will, as has already been mentioned in the last chapter, be narcissistic in nature.

The role of the economic factor in symptom formation can be illustrated by returning to the case of the young nurse referred to earlier. Complaining of squint and of blurred vision, she demanded dark glasses. She told everyone that she was going to be married. She said she was pregnant and frequently complained of abdominal pain. During interviews with the writer she said that she had fallen in love with a young man. He had promised to marry her and they had had coitus. He gave her up and it was this experience which initiated the illness. She wanted to know why she was in a mental hospital and denied that there was anything wrong with her. She had not given up thoughts of her lover, saying—"I wonder if I'll ever see my darling again . . . there's always a chance I might." Her behavior and utterances were often erotic in character. She said—"You don't mind if I'm a wee bit forward. . . ." At this she touched the writer's hand, saying—"once bitten, twice shy." On another occasion she announced—"You are a fascinating man; I can't help what I feel inside" and later—"I'm fed up because I haven't got a man." In this state of genital arousal she was frequently hallucinated. She heard her former lover's voice and she had visual hallucinations of men. She reported—"I saw a man in the ward last night when I was in bed."

At the onset of this illness it may be assumed that there was a withdrawal of cathexis from real objects. These drives, once regaining their instinctual quality, became concentrated on the self. This hypercathexis of the self facilitated the revival of previously unconscious pregnancy fantasies and of memories of words spoken by her lover. The appearance of this narcissistic state permitted these fantasies and memories to be felt as real experiences. It is important to note that the hallucinatory phenomena became manifest at moments of instinctual arousal—at times when there was an increase in the quantities of the instinctual cathexes. In this case the merging of self and object representations had a restitutional function insofar as it restored the object psychically. The accompanying change in direction of the cathexes, from external object to self, had the effect of heightening the narcissistic condition.

The appearance of grandiose and omnipotent thoughts similarly results from an investment of the self with primitive drive cathexes. Observations made on patients who, after a period during which the illness is quiescent, suddenly claim exceptional powers and talents suggest that these ideas follow a withdrawal of cathexis from external objects. The cathexis which is withdrawn returns to the self and having regained its instinctual state invests fantasies which until this time had been in a preconscious or unconscious state. The stimulus for such a redistribution of cathexis is usually frustration, disappointment or object loss. In such instances the patient becomes aggressive, expresses omnipotent thoughts and becomes refractory to influence.

Case 8

An example of this development is provided by a young married woman whose illness followed the birth of her first child. There was pronounced psychomotor overactivity. At the time of admission to hospital she claimed special powers and contended that it was her husband who was ill. It later transpired that what she meant by this was that her husband was impotent and had only once been capable of coitus. She said she was a doctor and could cure all the patients by hypnotism. She wore a white coat and recommended treatment for the other patients. These delusional ideas gradually subsided and the illness appeared to be about to remit. However a week or so later her husband refused to take her home for a few days leave. Reacting violently to this disappointment, she threatened to divorce her husband and criticized him on many counts. The omnipotent ideas returned with great intensity. She claimed to be the most brilliant doctor in the world, indicating that she had a special gift which allowed her to influence others as she wished. In this acute psychotic state cathexis was withdrawn from the husband and real external objects and returned to the self. The resulting delusional ideas, based on the hypercathexis of wishful fantasies, offered the patient an emotional compensation for her disappointment and frustration.

The analytic treatment of patients suffering from neuroses and sexual deviations has frequently demonstrated that omnipotent and wishful fantasies of the type described here have their origin in unsatisfactory childhood object relations. Self-love replaces object love and serves as a defense against the mental pain incurred by loss and disappointment. The narcissistic fixations which arise occur when individuals are subjected, in early childhood, to injury to their developing object libido. In one case separation from the mother and interference with bodily functions led to depression and feelings of helplessness. These affects were only lessened by the development of omnipotent fantasies in which the patient controlled others and subjected them to his will. Masturbatory fantasies had this kind of content—erections provided a sense of strength. The penis was personified, regarded as an object and then made subject to the patient's control. The part which reversal and denial played in the construction of these fantasies is quite apparent. The heightened narcissism—the self-love—acted as a defense against the dangers provoked by disappointment and object loss. This was so in adult life as well as in childhood. At no time did these fantasies find a delusional expression although the narcissism from which they sprang had a far-reaching effect on the patient's personality, his sexual development and his capacity to relate to others in a satisfying way.

The narcissistic reaction to the frustration of object-directed libidinal drives can, in childhood, take other forms. In some cases disappointment in the response of the love objects may lead the child to find a substitute object in a dog or other animal. This choice may lead to an identification which is lived out in fantasy. In other cases the child creates an imaginary companion (Nagera, 1969). The narcissistic quality of these developments is especially apparent when the sex of the animal or companion is the same as that of the child or the one wished for as, for example, in the case of the little girl with two younger brothers whose imaginary companion was a boy.

The disturbances of the self which occur in the psychoses can be attributed to the effects of a special form of pathological narcissism. This narcissism is different from that which is discerned in cases of neurosis and sexual deviation. The difference is most apparent when account is taken of the way in which the different categories of patient reacted to the emergence of a specific danger situation. In the face of the threat of object loss, of bodily damage, when object loss or genital frustration occurs the psychotic patient abandons the cathexis of the real objects and proceeds to cathect the representation of the lost object, a delusional object or the self.

In some cases, depending on the extent of the regression, there may be a merging of self- and object representations. This results in the patient identifying with the object, either temporarily or permanently. In other cases there is a hypercathexis of fantasies. This has a restitutional function and obviates the pain of object loss. The psychotic patient denies the loss insisting that the object is near at hand. The psychoneurotic patient may also react to object loss by withdrawing cathexis from real objects and cathecting the representation of the lost object. Here the hypercathected object representation remains in repression, thereby leading to self-preoccupation and a loss of interest in external objects. Sometimes symptoms, apart from depression of mood, may appear or some new character trait may emerge as a consequence of the identification with the lost object. In the absence of regression of the libido and the accompanying failure of repression the object representation does not make an appearance and thus there is no break with reality.

The variety of disorders of the self which occur in psychoses reflects the different ways in which the pathological narcissism finds expression. The phenomena comprise a spectrum at one end of which is to be found the hypersensitivity and egocentrism which provide the basis for the misinterpretation of environmental experience. Concomitant manifestations are ideas of being influenced, both mentally and physically, and alterations in bodily sensibility. All these experiences are painful and distressing to the patient. The other end of the spectrum includes such manifestations as grandiosity, omnipotence and inflated self-esteem.

At first sight the phenomena arising from the psychotic narcissism appear to be in the service of defense. This explanation, applicable to patients who present an omnipotence which frees them from dependency, the threat or fact of bodily injury or effect of object loss, cannot be so easily applied to those who feel persecuted and oppressed. Whatever the truth may be concerning the defensive functions of a psychotic narcissism there can be no doubt that the sequence of events which ultimately leads to its establishment is initiated by anxiety provoked by a danger situation (see Profile Number 3). In this respect psychotic narcissism is the outcome of a defense.

PROFILE NO. 3

This profile is based on a study of an unmarried man of 21 years of age. The data on which it is based was gathered over a period of five weeks and was obtained from psychiatric social work reports as well as from interviews with the writer.

1. REASON FOR REFERRAL AND HISTORY OF THE ILLNESS

Mr. E. was seen initially at home at the request of his general practitioner. The day previously he informed his parents that there were men in the garden who wanted to kill him. He was very frightened and aggressive. He walked about with an antique sword which had been in the house for many years. He told the general practitioner, and the writer subsequently, that he had heard men talking outside the house, mostly repeating his own thoughts and referring to incidents in his life which no one could know about except himself. He also observed that his hands moved without any intention on his part to carry out an act.

He told the general practitioner and the writer that he had been off work until six weeks previously. In April 1970 he had been at a dance where he became involved in a fight which, he insisted, was not at his instigation. In response to the provocation he struggled successfully with several men until he slipped and fell. He was then kicked on the head and sustained an eye injury. He attributed his freedom from more extensive injury to the fact that he was proficient in judo—a sport which he had diligently followed for several years.

The eye injury was serious and required a prolonged period of hospitalization for its treatment. The result of the injury was a visual defect resulting from damage to the retina. He no longer had central vision. He found that he was rather nervous after leaving the hospital and reluctant to go out. Prior to the injury he had worked for an insurance company collecting premiums on policies. In that this position was not permanent, he had to find alternative employment. He obtained a clerical post and was placed in an office with other employees.

During the first few weeks he did not notice anything untoward. Later however he observed that one of the women appeared to be taking considerable interest in him. He had heard that she had an illegitimate child. About this time he told his father, who thought he was joking, that his colleagues in the office regarded him as the best-dressed man there as well as being the most handsome. Shortly afterwards he announced that this girl in the office wanted to marry him—in point of fact, during the entire episode, there had never been any conversation between Mr. E. and this girl. He said that the girl's father was so keen on the marriage that once it was settled he (Mr. E.) would receive £10,000. Everyone in the office said that he was absolutely the right person for the girl. Mr. E.'s father told the writer that at this time he was concerned about his son because he noticed that he seemed rather excited, overactive and elated in his mood.

Five days or so before the acute episode a colleague at the office asked Mr. E. to join him for lunch. At the restaurant Mr. E. noticed that two men were sitting at a table nearby. Immediately he thought that they were relatives of the girl who had come to "look him over." Feeling uneasy, it occurred to him that his colleague had asked him to lunch so that these "relatives" could listen in on their conversation. Mr. E. suddenly realized that his colleague was asking questions in order to draw him out and reveal his views and opinions. Later that day his anxiety increased and he explained that this was due to the fear that his colleague was a spy posted to keep him under surveillance.

Over the next few days these frightening thoughts increased in number until he came to the conclusion that the girl in the office had only pretended to be in love with him in order to lure him into a trap. Her aim was to lead him to the men he had fought with in the dance hall who would then kill him. Over that weekend he remained constantly on watch from inside the house in case these men should arrive. On the night before being seen by the writer he was so afraid of being attacked that he slept in the same bed as his father.

2. DESCRIPTION OF THE PATIENT

Mr. E. was in bed when seen initially. He was unshaven and wore dark glasses. Although quite friendly in manner, he was, according to his father, extremely suspicious, irritable and easily given to outbursts of rage. The father emphasized that his son was very strong, fit and potentially dangerous in view of his proficiency in judo. Much of the data described above which had been obtained at this first meeting, was presented in a coherent and intelligible manner. Apart from the persecutory ideas and the hallucinatory experiences which were described, Mr. E. showed that he had an inflated idea of his importance and a general tendency to overvalue himself. He said that everyone in the town knew him because of the fight which had led to his eye injury. He had observed for several weeks that when out walking in the town everyone had looked at him. Apparently, he had quite enjoyed this notoriety. Only later, after the lunch with the colleague, did he realize that some of the people who looked at him were in fact watching him with dangerous intent.

Seven days later at an outpatient clinic Mr. E. presented himself as a tall slim young man who obviously was concerned about his appearance. On this occasion he said he was very frightened of his father but had kept this fear secret. He thought his father might drug him and then drown him. It was because of this fear that he had agreed to be admitted to the mental hospital after the first consultation. He actually arrived at the hospital but did not stay because in his opinion it was too depressing. The fear of his father receded in the face of the greater fear presented by the mental hospital.

In subsequent interviews Mr. E. appeared to be under some degree of pressure and it was reported that he was restless and overactive. It was significant that at no time did he spontaneously refer to his sexual life beyond saying that it was necessary to have regular exercise every day to get rid of excess energy.

3. FAMILY BACKGROUND AND PERSONAL HISTORY (PAST AND PRESENT)

Mr. E. is an only child, his parents aged 52 and 53 were married in 1942. The father is a skilled craftsman who has been consistently employed. For several years he has suffered with a peptic ulcer and about three years ago had an operation for this condition. The operation has not been a success. Mr. E.'s mother had been in good health until three years ago when she underwent a cholecystectomy. The father told the psychiatric social worker, with whom he had several interviews, that his wife had little interest in the son and that she found his illness a great burden. These assertions have not been borne out by the attitudes of the mother or her behavior with him. Mr. E. has been closer to his father and since the onset of the illness the latter has taken the leading part in its management.

Relations between the parents have never been very satisfactory. The father has, in his interviews with the psychiatric social worker, criticized his wife freely, finding her unattractive physically. Coitus has not taken place for many years. Mr. E.'s mother spent a lot of her time gardening or working about the house. According to Mr. E. his parents have never been on good terms. He stated that when he was a small boy, and until the age of about eight, his father drank to excess and he was very afraid of him. At the same time he complained that his mother was domineering and indifferent to his needs. Her irritability frightened him as well. It was her indifference that led him to turn to his father.

Mr. E. attended a grammar school from the age of five until he was 16. He left after obtaining a number of O level passes in the G.C.E. While at school he was a member of different societies. He was fond of gymnastics and it was at school that he developed his interest in judo. His mother states that he was a neat child who abhorred dirt and untidiness. He was quite independent and not unduly tied to her. He had several hobbies including stamp and coin collecting. These interests continued after he left school. In the father's eyes Mr. E. is without ambition. He would have preferred that his son had remained at school and entered a profession. In his opinion his son was lazy and would not apply himself to studies or take the opportunities which he (the father) was denied by his own father.

In spite of his father's disappointment in him Mr. E. obtained great satisfaction from the belief that he was physically superior to other boys and even to adults. This belief was strengthened by his excellent performance in such activities as weight lifting and judo. A further source of emotional satisfaction was motorcycling. He had owned a cycle from the age of 17 and had considerable interest in the mechanical aspects of the machine as well as in riding it. Money has always meant a lot to Mr. E. From the time he started to work as an insurance agent he saved most of his salary with the result that when he fell ill he had accumulated quite a sizeable sum in the bank. Most of his activities have been solitary—collecting coins and stamps, reading, etc. He has not had any regular boyfriends. His only social activity would be to go to a dance once during the week. He was never known to have a girlfriend. There is a history of pubertal masturbation which was the cause of guilt feelings and anxiety about his bodily health.

4. POSSIBLY SIGNIFICANT ENVIRONMENTAL CIRCUMSTANCES

The injury to the eye was the main significant event prior to the onset of the illness. This was followed by minor nervous symptom disorders which consisted of a disinclination to leave the house and a reluctance to meet people. It was the commencement of work involving daily contact with others which preceded the onset of the positive symptoms (delusions, hallucinations, etc.).

The patient's early history suggests that the predisposition to the illness was in part caused by the instability which characterized the parental relationship.

5. ASSESSMENT OF THE DRIVES

A. *The Libido*

(1) *Problems of Libido Distribution*

(a) *Cathexis of the Self.* The acute phase of the illness was initiated as a consequence of a hypercathexis of the self-representations. The resulting phenomena have been described. This overvaluation of the self continued after the subsidence of the persecutory delusions. The patient claimed: "I am as well known as the Lord Mayor"—"I am as light as a feather and strong as a bull." He enjoyed the movements of his body and obtained great pleasure from looking at himself, admiring himself and parading in front of others. This self-love indicated that the self-directed libido followed instinctual aims.

Hypercathexis of the self resulted in the delusion that pleasurable wishes had become facts—"a beautiful girl called to see me." He also believed that he was to be given a large sum of money. There was a generalization of his own self-admiration to others, e.g., they admired him, etc.

The persecutory phase resulted from a further redistribution of the libidinal cathexes. The self-cathexis gave way to the cathexis of delusional objects and self-representations became the focus of aggression. In this state there was an externalization of ego functions (thinking, memory) resulting in auditory phenomena whereby Mr. E. heard unknown persons voicing his thoughts and describing past events in his life.

(b) *Cathexis of Objects:*

i. Cathexis of Real Persons (Current Relationships):

The libidinal cathexis of real persons had not reverted to that state characterized by need satisfaction alone. Real objects (father, mother, the girl at the office) were cathected by drive derivatives whose expression was more appropriate to the period of the Oedipus complex. Mr. E. entertained fantasies of being destroyed by his father (see above). He had entered into a rivalry with him (see prepsychotic personality) believing that his father was jealous of his strength. Although Mr. E. said that he hated his father the wish to be protected and loved was also present—it should be recalled that Mr. E. slept with his father at the height of the "persecutory anxiety."

The most striking feature of Mr. E.'s attitudes about his mother was the absence of tender or protective feelings toward her. He was only able to express criticism of her in much the same way as he was preoccupied with the shortcomings of his father. However the preoccupation with and attachment to inanimate objects (coins, stamps, money) suggests that the cathexis was derived from that originally directed to the mother.

ii. Cathexis of Representations of Real and Fantasy Objects:

The object representations which constituted the delusional reality were of an entirely fantastic nature except for the woman colleague. Mr. E. initially thought that she wanted him but later he came to fear her. He feared the fantasy objects which were derived from the men he fought with at the dance-hall. These objects were represented in the auditory modality. He heard voices. There was a displacement from the fantasy objects to real persons who looked at him in a threatening manner. The delusional objects were cathected by drive derivatives which ordinarily belonged (unconsciously) with real persons (father, mother). This oedipal complex found representations in the delusional reality (girl = mother; persecutors = father) following on the alteration of the direction and aims of the drive cathexes by projection (see Ego-Defense).

(2) *Libidinal Position*

In the prepersecutory phase of the illness Mr. E.'s belief in his attractiveness to women reflected the predominance of passive sexual aims vaguely associated with the genital organization of the libido. Outstanding were the exhibitionistic tendencies which were given free expression in action and fantasy. Body and penis were equated. It may be assumed from the passive aims (the wish to be looked at) with respect to the body as a whole that similar aims were associated with the penis. There was an absence of active genital aims directed to heterosexual objects. In the persecutory phase the pleasure in being looked at was converted into anxiety at being looked at.

B. *Aggression*

Mr. E. was very aggressive on various occasions but this did not translate well into action. The aggression was reactive to the anxiety which sprang from the delusional reality.

When the persecutory ideas subsided Mr. E. was able to speak about his hatred which he periodically felt toward his father.

During the persecutory period projection may have fostered a situation in which death wishes formerly directed toward the father were now redirected against the self by the persecutors. No other defenses against aggression were noted.

6. ASSESSMENT OF EGO AND SUPEREGO

Ego Functions (a) - (e)

Speech was intact, lacking in any formal defects. Reference has already been made to the periodic omnipotent nature of thinking. Attention, memory and perceptual functions were within normal limits with the exception of those occasions when auditory hallucinations occurred. Motility was not affected except at the onset of the persecutory phase when Mr. E. experienced a movement of his arms which was not consciously initiated.

Ego Reactions to Danger Situations

In the period prior to returning to work Mr. E. regarded the social environment as frightening. He preferred to remain at home rather than go out. This anxiety was associated with the partial loss of vision. The anxiety had its origin in the fear of being attacked and injured by those with whom he had fought in the dance-hall. In the "grandiose" phase this anxiety disappeared only to return in the persecutory phase when the patient believed he was to be killed or injured either by the persecutors or by his father. Persecutors and father were condensed. The most likely source of the danger were passive libidinal drives which had been activated by the injury. Mr. E. was now less than masculine—the injury having promoted his feminine identifications. The specific nature of the anxiety was castration anxiety (body-penis).

State of the Defense Organization

Repression remained effective during the immediate prepsychotic period. The passive femininity referred to above remained in repression, finding expression solely in anxiety which was ultimately contained through his confinement to the house. Return to work and contact with others (men and women) threatened the repression. This led to a withdrawal of cathexis from real persons and its concentration on the self (the "grandiose" phase). The redistribution of libido from object to self served as a defense in that it allowed Mr. E. to dispel the awareness of a bodily defect and substitute a more agreeable reality (that he was admired). This defense did not succeed, eventually being replaced by projection. Initially the projection resulted in an externalization of heterosexual wishes (the girl wanted to marry him) but this was followed by the thought that her father wanted him (passive feminine wishes) and eventually by the fear of the persecutors.

Projection was the principal defense in the persecutory phase leading to the delusional ideas. It is perhaps important to note as has been mentioned above that projection also acted against acknowledgment of heterosexual wishes—for example, women were interested in *him*. At no time did he express the idea that he was attracted to women; nor was he ever conscious of a passive femininity in himself. Externalization (externalization of aspects of the self or attribution of cause) played no part in the defense.

Affects

Anxiety was the principal affect expressed during the illness, except for the period characterized by inflated self-regard.

Superego

The clinical phenomena offered little material on which to base a statement as to the status of the superego during the illness. There was never any sign of guilt feelings. There is a suggestion that the superego may have been partially externalized in the persecutory phase. While micturating Mr. E. accidentally wet himself—a voice said, "you've wet yourself" and the patient felt humiliated.

7. ASSESSMENT OF REGRESSIONS AND POSSIBLE FIXATIONS

The content of the delusional ideas provided some indication of the extent of the regressions which occurred and the fixations which had affected the libido in the course of development. The clinical phenomena did not reflect a rapid or extensive regression affecting drives, ego and superego.

(a) The persecutory delusion pointed to the likelihood that regression had led to the cathexis of passive oedipal wishes. This in turn resulted in castration anxiety expressed through fear of bodily injury.

(b) The sexual organization in the persecutory phase was characterized by passive aims. Even when the exhibitionistic wishes were uppermost, as in the "grandiose" period, they were predominately passive in nature. This exhibitionistic component of sexuality which was so pronounced can hardly be regarded as a result of the occurrence of regression as part of the psychotic process. It is quite likely (see prepsychotic personality) that this libidinal position was that obtaining prior to the onset of the illness even though it did not find conscious expression.

(c) The ego remained virtually intact with projection acting in place of repression.

(d) There was no evidence of superego regression.

(e) No specific childhood fantasies appeared in the delusions apart from those referred to. It is quite likely however that in early childhood the patient had anxieties based on passive oedipal fantasies.

(f) The clinical evidence suggests that a fixation had been present at the phase of the negative Oedipus complex. This reduced the cathexis of active sexual aims. This passive orientation of the libido (inverted Oedipus complex) was overshadowed in the "grandiose" phase by the cathexis of exhibitionistic wishes. There was also evidence of fixations having occurred at the anal phase and seeking expression in such interests as coin collecting and a preoccupation with money. As has been mentioned above this cathexis of material possessions was, no doubt, in part a displacement from the mother relationship.

8. RESULTS OF DRIVE AND EGO DISORGANIZATION

The only possible expression of ego disorganization in Mr. E.'s case was the occurrence of hallucinations the content of which consisted of hearing his own thoughts and accounts of past memories.

9. ASSESSMENT OF CONFLICTS

(a) The external conflicts which appeared in this case were the result of externalization of internalized conflicts (see b).

(b) The conflict between passive sexual wishes and

castration fear was externalized, resulting in persecutory delusions. The persecutors in a sense represented the feared passive wishes. There was, in the initial stages of the psychosis, no conflict over the exhibitionistic impulses—later conflict made its appearance and the exhibitionism was replaced by an anxiety whenever he felt someone was looking at him.

(c) Conflicts existed between activity and passivity and heterosexuality and homosexuality.

10. THE PREPSYCHOTIC PERSONALITY

In the prepsychotic period the libidinal distribution was such as to lead to an overvaluation of the self (an enhanced narcissism). This was reflected in an undue preoccupation with the body. At the same time there was anxiety regarding injury or disease of the body. As a boy the patient could not emulate his father as a boxer because he feared injury. The interest in judo had as its aim the defense of the body. Basically this anxiety was castration anxiety—body and penis being equated.

Heterosexual development was minimal. the libido having reached the phallic phase but having become arrested at an exhibitionistic organization. It is likely that the libido had at one time achieved cathexis of active aims but the danger of castration had brought about a regression to a passive phallic exhibitionism which was displaced to the body. The father's behavior and attitudes, during the patient's childhood, promoted passive wishes on the one hand and castration fear on the other. Cathexis was withdrawn from the active oedipal position leaving the earlier passive attachment to the mother libidinized.

Mr. E. always wanted to be admired by his father. However his latent aggression and passive wishes prevented him from achieving the ambitions his father had set for him. Passive-feminine and homosexual tendencies had an outlet in the judo where close bodily contact with other men was acceptable and aggression could be channeled in a controlled environment.

11. ASSESSMENT OF SOME GENERAL CHARACTERISTICS, ETC.

In the acute phases of the illness (grandiose and persecutory) the withdrawal of libidinal cathexis, the creation of a restitutional complex and the externalization of conflicts made it quite impossible to communicate with the patient. There was no insight into the fact of mental illness. When the persecutory delusions lost their intensity Mr. E. was willing to discuss his experiences but it became clear that, although no longer oppressed, he believed in their reality. Additionally some signs of the earlier grandiosity had returned. The concentration of cathexis on the self precluded the development of a therapeutic alliance at that time. The ambivalent attitude to the father was so pronounced that it is doubtful if that relationship would be sufficient to provide the basis for such an alliance. Further observation of the patient would be necessary to determine whether or not systematic psychotherapy could be initiated or would prove profitable in this case.

CHAPTER 5

The Role and Expression of the Aggressive Drives in Psychoses

Aggressive acts, thoughts and affects are commonplace in psychotic states. They may be directed against others or against the self. Such occurrences are more easily identifiable as the expression of the aggressive drives than are the contents of delusions and hallucinations which may loosely be described as persecutory. There are many such manifestations which the patient describes as hostile to himself. There are experiences of being observed, of being spied upon, followed and criticized unjustly. There are the somatic and mental feelings of passivity. There are the experiences of being unnecessarily bothered, imposed upon and interfered with by known or unknown persons or agencies. Last there are influences at work which the patient regards as damaging and destructive to both body and mind.

The Mode of Expression of Aggression

In psychoses aggression may appear directly in act, thought and affect. This occurs at least under three different conditions. First when the patient is in a state of morbid anxiety (see Profile No. 1), second when he feels oppressed by the presence or actions of another person, real or imagined (see Profile No. 3), and third when he is subject to a frustration imposed by the environment (see Profile No. 2). States of morbid anxiety are frequent at the onset of a psychosis and at certain times during the course of a chronic illness. Usually this anxiety occurs when a condensation has taken place between real objects and delusional objects which are regarded as dangerous to the self. Illustrative is a young male patient who believed that the nurses and other patients were hermaphroditic creatures about to attack him. A young woman who had been ill with a schizophrenic illness for some years periodically struck out at other patients when she believed that they were in fact magical figures intent on doing her harm. Patients become angry and violent when they believe that a person known to them in the present or in the past continues to interfere in their affairs or will not leave them alone. This person is imagined as being nearby, appearing at night or using his influence with those near the patient. Frustration of wishes or needs as an immediate cause of aggressive acts and affects is to be found at the onset of psychoses characterized by psychomotor overactivity. It can also be observed in cases of chronic schizophrenia which are characterized by withdrawal, inattention and disinterest. The frustration may be due to the inability to satisfy oral or genital needs or it may arise because there is no possibility of accommodating some aspect of the patient's delusional reality.

In many cases the aggressive drives do not reach consciousness as affects or wishes. They find representation in the belief of an omnipotent destructiveness. The patient fears that this power will cause untold damage to those around him. In one case the patient refuses to look at another person because the glance may be lethal. In another he must not breathe because that will result in someone's death.

One patient believed that he had to be isolated from everyone or else all would be killed. A similar significance may be given to voluntary movements thereby rendering the patient immobile. In one particular case already referred to the patient attributed his outbursts of anger to a canine tooth. He wanted the tooth removed to stop the expression of aggression.

A further indirect manifestation of the aggressive drives in psychoses is through the content of delusions and hallucinations. These phenomena are characterized by contents of different kinds. The patient fears that his body and mind will be destroyed in numerous ways. In some cases he believes that he is to be preyed upon by birds or animal-like creatures. Sometimes he fears that a bite or an injection will spread a poisonous substance throughout his body. Patients will claim that another person or body has invaded their bodies and consequently act in accordance with the invader's properties. Frequently the patients respond with suicidal thoughts in order to liberate themselves from the foreign creature which now dominates their actions, thoughts and feelings. In other cases the persecution takes the form of poison gases to which the patient is exposed at night while he is asleep. Other patients complain that their bodies and minds are being gradually destroyed by electricity. As part of the general destructive aim, these delusions may also contain the idea that the genitalia are being constantly stimulated.

Another indirect expression of aggression in psychoses is to be found in the prolonged states of withdrawal and in the catatonic phenomena which are so common in longstanding cases of schizophrenia. Patients who present such manifestations are easily roused to anger and to violent acts. It is not uncommon for such occurrences to appear, apparently spontaneously, and without any overt stimulus. Usually however there has been an excitatory cause which precipitates the aggressive outbursts although this can only be discerned when the patient has been observed in his environment for a considerable length of time. These patients do not welcome the attentions of others. They readily show their resentment and antagonism when an attempt is made to strike up a relationship with them. Their first reaction is generally an intensification of the withdrawal; their second, anger or violence. This aggression may not be directed against the individual concerned but toward another person or inanimate object which acts as a substitute.

THE CONFLICT OVER AGGRESSION

I

The direct expression of aggression in psychoses is less common than its indirect representation in delusions, hallucinations and motility disorders. This suggests that the arousal of aggressive drive derivatives is more likely to result in conflict than find an outlet in speech or action. Even when there are aggressive acts or affects in the acute stages of an illness or during the chronic stage they are typically followed by manifestations resulting from a reaction to the drive expression. For example a patient suffering from mania may resort to violence when his instructions are not carried out. Shortly afterwards when he is no longer angry he will accuse others of being aggressive or become self-reproachful. Psychomotor overactivity may be gradually replaced by retardation. Similarly a patient will return to his original state of withdrawal after an outburst of rage. The conflict generated by heightened aggression can also be observed in those cases where the psychosis is characterized by persecutory delusions centering on a lost love object. In these cases, usually single women between 30 and 40 years of age, the love object may have existed either in fact, in that there was a real love relationship, or it may have only had a fantasy existence. In these cases the patient reacts to the loss of the love object by reconstituting a delusional relationship. The love object then intrudes into the patient's privacy, influences her thinking, causes her to experience genital sensations against her will, upsets her memory and tries to drive her insane. All this is explained by the patient as resulting from hatred—a hatred caused by her rejection of the former lover. The patient in turn hates the persecutor and constantly attempts to get rid of him. Such anger is interpreted by the patient as purely reactive to her predicament.

A conflict resulting from an increase in the intensity of the aggressive drives can also be postulated in those patients who complain that destructive attacks are being made on their minds and bodies. These patients claim that they do not experience aggression except insofar as they wish to remove the external source of danger. The conflict may find an alternative expression. The patient, instead of believing that he is the target for the destructive attacks, considers himself immune although still surrounded by hostile influences. In all the instances cited the internal conflict is resolved by the fact that the aggressive drive derivatives are located outside the individual patient.

Conflicts over aggression are a constant finding in manic depressions. As a result, the drive derivatives are expressed only indirectly in the form of self-reproaches, depression of mood, anxiety and psychomotor retardation, except when there is a suicidal or a homicidal attempt.

II

The conflicts which have been described occur during the psychosis. In nearly every case the heightening of the aggressive drive cathexes which led to the conflict was due to disappointment, jealousy, frustration or object loss in fact or in fantasy. These conflicts were the source of symptoms and their activity insured the continuance of the clinical phenomena. However this does not imply that there were no other conflicts over aggression present during the illness or in the prepsychotic period. Recognition of such conflicts becomes possible under two conditions. The first is when the patient can cooperate in psychotherapy with the resulting emergence of thoughts, affects and memories. This allows an insight into the conflicts characterizing the prepsychotic personality. The second is when the illness has passed into a state of partial remission with the appearance of neurotic-like symptoms.

Once the conflicts which existed prior to the illness are discovered an explanation of the patient's reaction to disappointment, loss, etc., becomes possible. An opportunity is afforded to gain insight into important conflicts of puberty and childhood. In some cases unequivocal evidence becomes available as to a conflict over death wishes directed against a parent or sibling, which typically arise within the context of an oedipal situation. In other cases death wishes appear because of frustrations imposed by fate or by the parents. The onset of a psychosis is coincidental with a heightening of the death wishes and a change in the quality of the underlying aggressive drive derivatives.

Case 9

These considerations can be illustrated by reference to a patient, Mrs. B., whose illness consisted of the experiencing of auditory hallucinations. The patient was a married woman of 34 with two children. She had been married for about 15 years. According to Mrs. B. the voice, which was in her head, was intent on making her miserable and unhappy. She was instructed to act in ways contrary to her natural inclinations. For example, she was told to be unkind to her husband, to strike him, throw his dinner which she had prepared to the floor, or throw tea over a newly painted wall. She was ordered to sit still and not speak or to run out of the house and go for a walk. It was this apparently incomprehensible behavior which led to her being taken to her general practitioner. The voice criticized her, commented on her appearance and recounted painful memories of childhood. She hated the voice because it seemed to have control over her. She was frightened when it said she should kill herself. In spite of all this she did not acknowledge that she was ill.

Initially Mrs. B. claimed that the hallucinations had started shortly after she had discovered that her husband had secured a bank loan for her sister whom she disliked and distrusted. She was very upset because she had earlier obtained a promise from her husband that he would have no contact whatsoever with her sister. According to Mrs. B. her sister was an immoral woman who used men for her own ends. She believed that her sister had been and was determined to ruin her marriage. Mrs. B. was convinced that both her mother and her sister disliked her because she did not approve of the way they behaved. Gradually Mrs. B. revealed that the auditory hallucinations had been present for a number of years but she had managed to ignore them or prevent them from affecting her behavior. The content of the hallucinations was not always entirely critical. For example when she had been overweight the voice told her she was fat and ugly and that she should diet. She proceeded to do so and lost several stone in weight.

Mrs. B. explained that the voice had originally presented itself when she realized that her husband was not really interested in her. She suspected that her sister had enticed him away and was convinced that he no longer loved her, regarding her solely as someone to provide for his needs and look after the children. She was bitterly disillusioned as she looked to her husband as the one person in her life who had loved and cared for her. It was impossible for her to dismiss the idea that he was more interested in her sister than in herself. Thus she was led to ask him to promise not to have any contact with her whatsoever. Despite her attempts to dismiss unhappy thoughts from her mind the voice constantly reminded her of them. It would recall every word or action of her husband that showed his lack of love and concern. When she discovered that he had not kept his promise she became depressed in mood and utterly miserable. From this time onwards the voice continually made critical remarks about her husband, telling her that he was not to be trusted, never to be forgiven, that she should annoy and upset him in every way possible. These ideas frightened her to the point where she came to fear that she might make him ill, drive him mad or cause him an injury.

Mrs. B. was the youngest of three children. As a small child, according to her report, she had been very close to her mother. This relationship apparently ceased when the patient was about five or six years of age. In the patient's opinion this termination occurred because her mother became interested in her sister and in other activities outside the home. Mrs. B. developed an imaginary companion (Nagera, 1969) which was a consolation in her loneliness. It was her habit to play games and talk with this imaginary friend. She remembered being very much afraid of being left alone and was frightened by the dark. Her sister used to frighten her with stories about a neighbor who had hanged himself. In the winter mornings when everyone had left for work and she was alone in the house the imaginary companion would tell her not to be afraid. There were however times when the "friend" would say things which were aggressive and destructive as, for example, "bang your head against the wall."

During this period of Mrs. B.'s childhood, her family life was very unhappy. Her parents did not get on and there was considerable strife. Her mother was in the habit of going out with other men and as the sister grew up she accompanied her mother. The patient condemned both mother and sister for this behavior, resolving that her own life would be faultless. She felt that she was an outsider, ignored and ignoring the rest of the family. The only exception was her brother. Her father had no time for her either. She recalled feeling neglected and lonely. Later she referred to herself as "Second Hand Rose." Until the age of 16 she had no friends. It was only with the development of friendships which began to develop at this age that the imaginary companion disappeared, there no longer being any need for it.

When she met her husband she believed that at last her life would be happy and that she now had someone in whose life she would be first. When she suffered disillusionment with him she returned to her earlier preoccupation with the imaginary companion. She realized the connection between the two events. However she noticed that the companion had changed insofar as it had become domineering and controlling. At times she equated it with the bad part of herself. As the years passed she gradually forgot that the voice was originally that of the imaginary companion of her childhood and adolescence.

In this case a conflict came to life when the patient was

threatened by loss of love. There was an intensification of aggressive drives toward the husband which led to anxiety and guilt. This conflict was a repetition of a similar conflict of childhood relating to the mother. Both mother and husband were regarded as evil, deceitful and wicked. The voice expressed aggression which could be disowned by the patient. In childhood the imaginary companion had absorbed the libidinal cathexes withdrawn from the mother. In adult life it acted as a vehicle for aggression as it had no doubt done, on occasions, in childhood.

DEFENSE AGAINST AGGRESSION

In psychoses the form of certain symptoms and signs is due directly to the action of specific defenses against the emergence into consciousness of aggressive drive derivatives. These mechanisms are substitutes for repression. They do not have the stability of that mechanism which can be attributed to the maintenance of an anticathexis. It is not only repression which is disorganized in the psychoses. Reaction formations are also severely impaired. In psychoses which have an acute onset both repression and reaction formation suffer. They are no longer adequate to contain the libidinal and aggressive drive derivatives. Hence the patient cannot restrain aggression. Violence is common and there is a loss of all those traits of character which depend on the integrity of reaction formations. The restoration of repression and reaction formations occurs contemporaneously with the recovery of reality testing and the disappearance of the symptoms of the psychosis.

Permanent damage to the mechanisms of repression and reaction formation is found in cases of chronic schizophrenia. It is the malfunction of these defenses, particularly the reaction formations, which leads to the alterations in personality characteristic of the long-standing case of schizophrenia. Prior to the start of the illness the patient was regarded as agreeable in manner, modest in behavior, inoffensive, gentle, concerned with his appearance, perhaps too malleable and always clean and tidy. All such traits disappear as the illness continues over an extended period of time. The patient becomes arrogant, unpleasant in manner, unresponsive, irritable and easily roused to anger and violence, given to shouting obscenities, dirty in habits, utterly indifferent to the feeling and reactions of others and given to autoerotic practices. These changes cannot wholly be attributed to the effects of prolonged hospitalization as they are to be found in patients who have remained at home throughout the illness as well. It is in these cases of chronic schizophrenia that aggression is free from the controls of the anticathexis and can be evoked by the slightest stimulus. Indeed there is considerable evidence to suggest that aggressive behavior is employed defensively to prevent the development of interpersonal relations which may provoke libidinal arousal. As has been mentioned previously the defensive decathexis of object representations is employed to obviate this danger.

Many of the subjective experiences which patients describe during their illnesses can be explained as due to the way in which aggressive drive derivatives are influenced by the different forms of externalization and by projection. As the clinical examples have shown some patients experience aggressive affects and have aggressive intent. Other patients are not conscious of such mental contents. There are patients who believe that they are being incited to aggression against their wishes. Additionally there are patients who become aggressive although there is no correspondence in time with the aggression they feel is directed to themselves.

That form of externalization which manifests itself as attribution of responsibility explains why some patients ascribe their experiencing of aggression to a delusional object, a hallucinatory voice or to some real object. This particular defense is to be found in recent cases of psychoses which present psychomotor overactivity, those in whom there are persecutory delusions and auditory hallucinations. It is also active in chronic schizophrenia and in illnesses sometimes described as chronic mania. The other form of externalization in which thoughts and affects are generalized, the patient being aware of aggression in himself and the object simultaneously, is less common perhaps because it is less easily observed. Most often the patient experiences aggression as directed against himself after he has felt anger and an urge to aggressive action. This state is to be found in all the conditions referred to. For convenience it could be described as due to a defensive use of generalization.

In those cases where the patient is not aware of aggressive affect, and believes that he is its object, the action of projection must be inferred. Patients whose aggression is influenced by projection experience auditory hallucinations the contents of which consist of expressions of hate or painful affects and sensations. It is important to recall that the auditory hallucinations comprise memories of words spoken at some time in the patient's past. The projection mechanism thus contributes to the process of restitution—to the recathexis of a lost reality—and acts as a means of defense as well. Projection must also be operative in those patients who feel that they are being provoked to aggressive affect and action. This may, as in the case just described (case 9), be based on auditory hallucinations.

There are cases of psychoses where there is a change of the mechanism, from projection to externalization, which occurs in the process of influencing the aggressive drive derivatives. Initially projection is employed to alter the object of the drives and their direction. At a later stage both object and direction are altered by the appearance of externalization. The patient no longer feels himslf to be the object of the drive and the source of the drive within himself continues to be denied. In such cases the action of externalization must be presumed even though, as has been mentioned, the aggressive drive derivatives are prevented from reaching consciousness. Such instances of a transition from projection to externalization and vice versa indicates that the closest connection exists between the two mental mechanisms.

There are two other defenses which act against aggressive drive derivatives. The first is displacement; the second turning in on the self. Displacement is encountered in psychoses as frequently as it is in neuroses and in the mentally healthy. It is to be found early in the course of a psychotherapy. Aggressive affect is displaced from the therapist to an animate or inanimate object. A patient attacked a male nurse after a psychotherapeutic session when he was told about an impending break in the daily interview. Another patient smashed a window. He said later "God told me to break the window in order to save Mr. X.'s (another patient) life." Displacement occurs in all varieties of psychoses and at any phase of a particular illness.

Aggression turned on the self is by no means uncommon in psychoses—both in the acute stage and in chronicity. As in the case of displacement it is a defense which alters the object of the drive. It is ineffective in containing the expression of aggression. Patients may be observed who although already angry and potentially violent attempt to injure themselves. A patient was observed to repeatedly burn his hands with a lit cigarette. The responsibility for this action was also attributed to someone else—"I didn't do that," he said. Reference must also be made, even if briefly, to the phenomena of negativism, catalepsy and hypertonia of the limb musculature as a method of restricting the aggressive drives.

None of the phenomena described thus far, resulting from the operation of defenses, are comparable to psychoneurotic symptoms which represent compromises between drive derivatives on the one hand and the ego and superego on the other hand. However symptoms which do have this structure are to be found in the psychoses. They are symptoms which were present in the prepsychotic period and continue into the psychosis itself. These symptoms arise from the danger created by aggressive drive derivatives, and often have death wishes as their content. As in hysteria the symptom expresses the fulfillment of a wish together with the punishment for it. Identification is the defense mechanism which counters the death wishes by altering their direction and their object.

THE ROLE OF AGGRESSION IN SYMPTOM FORMATION

A discussion of the role of aggression in psychoses must take into account the fact that the derivatives of this instinctual drive are often combined with those of the libido. It is therefore not simply a matter of identifying the activity of aggression in psychoses, as expressed for example in death wishes, but also of detecting the presence of those stages of the pregenital organization whose aim is no less one of destruction of the object. As regression of the sexual organization to pregenital aims and objects is a frequent occurrence in psychoses it follows that the content of delusional fantasies will have a destructive content.

The onset of many psychoses is provoked by aggression. These are the cases where the manifest precipitant consists of disappointments, real or threatened object loss and the frustration of genital needs. Jealousy and envy often play a part in leading up to the aggressive crisis. The aggressive drive derivatives initiate a danger situation. There is a threat to the safety of the love object. This danger cannot be overcome by repression. The result is an alteration both in the quality and distribution of the libidinal drive derivatives and a concomitant regression of the sexual organization. Pregenital drives are recathected with libido. Oral, anal, and phallic sadistic fantasies provide a fresh danger situation on account of their inherent destructive nature. They lead to the action of defenses as was described above. The sequence of events resulting in the onset of a psychosis is well illustrated in the following case history.

Case 10

The patient was a 50-year-old married woman. She was admitted to the mental hospital because she complained that she was being followed, that all her movements were observed and that her house was entered and searched whenever she was out. She believed that some people whom she may have unwittingly antagonized were the instigators of this persecution. She had no proof of these assertions. After a few weeks and treatment with drugs the irrational ideas disappeared and she was discharged. Four months later she had to be readmitted to the hospital with identical complaints. On this occasion a psychotherapeutic treatment was undertaken and as a result information became available which led to an understanding of the illness.

The illness started when her only child—a son, 22 years

old—decided to leave home and take up an occupation of which the patient strongly disapproved. Relations with her husband were unsatisfactory from her point of view. She had no difficulty in expressing her anger against him if he did not comply with her wishes. There was evidence of genital frustration. Sometimes she would become violent and throw plates or any other object within reach at him. Some months prior to the onset of the illness she may have been responsible for an accident her husband met with in which he fell from his motor scooter and injured his head. This caused her considerable guilt.

The patient's early childhood had been very unsettled. The family moved frequently. When she was seven years of age her father abandoned her mother, her older brother and herself. At first she stayed with relatives but was then moved to an orphanage. At about the age of 12 she went to live with her grandmother who was given to excessive drinking. At 14 years of age her brother joined the Army and she never saw him again. When 11 years old she was seduced by a grocer for whom she did errands. This stimulation continued over a period of time. Her early life was therefore characterized by numerous traumatic events, disappointments and separations.

The patient's relapse, four months after the initial attack, occurred when she was told by her son that he was engaged to be married. It was learned that in the year prior to the outbreak of the illness the patient had been unfaithful to her husband. As has been mentioned this was attributed to a lack of sexual satisfaction in the marital relationship.

At the time of the relapse the patient believed that her son was dead. The death wishes which had led to this delusional idea had returned to consciousness. When the son left home against her wishes the patient had wished him dead. If she could not have him, no one could. Knowledge of his engagement had accentuated this thought and the belief that he was dead was intensified. During psychotherapy many destructive fantasies became manifest, relating to the writer as well as to other patients. These were sadistic fantasies mostly associated with the phallic organization of the libido. They appeared in consciousness in their projected and externalized form. She complained that she was being interfered with sexually at night and that her genitalia were damaged. Another delusion involved her being taken from her bed in a drugged state, led into the hospital grounds and sexually assaulted by an unknown man older than herself. She based her accusations on the observation of some slight vaginal bleeding, for which there was no apparent physical basis. In addition to this delusion she accused the writer of putting a substance into her food which allowed him to control her mind and body. He could alter her sensibilities so that she lost bodily sensations and memory. The predominant theme throughout was that she was being forced, principally by the writer, to experience thoughts, affects and sensations against her will. Inevitably there were outbursts of rage and an occasional act of violence.

In this case the aggression which was provoked by object loss led to a danger situation. Repression failed to contain the drive derivatives. A series of regressive movements affected the libidinal drives, altering not only their distribution and quality with an outcome in faulty reality testing, but bringing about a recathexis of sadistic fantasies belonging to the phallic organization. Experiences of puberty and possibly those of childhood offered the necessary fixation points. The delusional ideas provided the vehicle for the expression of the recathected fantasies which originally must have been connected with masturbation and ideas about coitus. The seduction which occurred at puberty had its revival in the delusion of being assaulted. The conflict between the wish for and the fear of a repetition of the traumatic experiences resulted in a further danger situation which led to projection. Much of the repetition could be attributed to the transference activated by the psychotherapy. It was the frustration of the libidinal drive derivatives, some of which may be assumed to have had active sadistic aims, which led to the aggression against the writer and other patients.

In other cases of psychoses, as has already been described, the destructive content of the delusional phenomena suggests that oral and anal-sadistic fantasies are revived by the libidinal regression. The action of projection has the effect of substituting passive for active aims, the patient then coming to fear being attacked orally or anally. In a similar way scoptophilic and exhibitionistic tendencies may become associated with sadistic aims so that the patient comes to fear the consequences of looking or being looked at. In some cases of psychoses, as in the case just described, it is possible to trace the regression from the most advanced level of the libido achieved by the patient to the fantasies based on fixation points which were established in childhood and puberty. This cannot be accomplished in every case because the libidinal cathexes are almost entirely invested in the restitutional phenomena (the psychotic reality). The patient has neither the interest nor capacity to recall either in memory or by repetition in action the experiences and fantasies which led to the decisive libidinal fixations.

AGGRESSION AND THE SUPEREGO

In the case of the 50-year-old woman (case 10) several of the symptoms which appeared at the onset of the illness and at the relapse may be understood as having resulted from the externalization of the superego. The patient believed herself to be under observation. She imagined that she was being followed and that her house was being searched in her absence. There was a sense of guilt which revealed itself in the idea that these "occurrences" were due to her having unwittingly offended someone or other at some past time. In all such cases the patient regards the persistent surveillance and the interference as a persecution. It is undeserved and often no explanation is forthcoming. An aggressive if not destructive intent is attributed to those unknown persons who follow the patient, spy on him and give him no rest. There may or may not be auditory hallucinations which are critical and condemning.

The aggressive tendencies which are reflected in the superego attitudes can only be explained on the basis of a patient's own aggressive drives which have to be repudiated. The quality of the aggression emanating from the externalized superego appears to depend upon the extent of libidinal regression effecting the sexual organization. Where there is a regression of the sexual organization to pregenital levels, for example to oral sadism, the superego is then characterized by a sadism which has the qualities of that instinctual phase. It is peremptory, impatient and demanding. The sadism also finds an outlet in the experience of a relentless pursuit by a ruthless enemy. Where there is an anal component the patient will complain that his house and possessions are messed up and destroyed by his persecutors. It is abnormal phenomena of this kind which reveal so clearly the instinctual roots of the superego.

As has been described the aggressive conflict in these cases is met by externalization and projection of drive derivatives. A patient said to a psychiatrist "I can feel you hating me."

The patient either finds the world full of hatred or experiences the hatred as directed against himself. When there are auditory hallucinations they consist of insults, obscene words and direct expressions of hate for the patient. It is sometimes difficult in the individual case to distinguish between persecutory delusions and hallucinations due to an externalized superego and those due to a projection of drive derivatives. The destructive nature of these psychotic phenomena whether due to externalization of the superego or to projection of id drives follows from the extent to which regression has affected the sexual organization In some cases of psychosis the persecutory phenomena are due simply to an externalization of the superego. These are the cases in which a paranoid illness alternates with a depressive one. In other cases the persecutory manifestations result only from projection of the drive derivatives. However there are those cases where there has been an extensive regression of the libido, rapid or gradual, in the spheres of object relations (that is, to a form of primary identification) and the sexual organization, quite apart from the alteration in quality and distribution of the cathexes, resulting in symptoms which arise from both the externalization of the superego and from the projection of the drives.

CONCLUDING REMARKS

The clinical illustrations support the theory that in some cases of psychosis an increase in the intensity of the aggressive cathexes is the principal factor leading to the sequence of events which ends in symptom formation. This change in the magnitude of aggressive drives was seen to be a reaction to disturbances of libidinal economics and as such, secondary in nature. In every case, the aggression appears to follow a frustration of one kind or another. It is the danger of a traumatic situation developing from the accumulation of libidinal cathexes which results in the aggressive response.

In certain cases aggression was seen to have a direct expression in speech and action. In other cases a defensive process ensued by way of regression. This regression affected the quality of the libidinal cathexes and the sexual organization. From this point on the aggressive drive derivatives no longer found representation in preconscious or unconscious death wishes and actual or potential affects of hate and rage. Instead they were expressed through the sadism which is an integral part of the various pregenital sexual organizations. This sadism then resulted in a new danger and in the action of externalization and projection. The defenses created the form which the symptoms assumed while the repudiated sadistic drives provided the content.

The frequency with which overt aggression occurs in psychoses and the extent to which destructive content is to be found in delusions and hallucinations has resulted in theories which afford aggression a primary role in the formation of the symptomatology. In particular delusions and hallucinations with a persecutory content have been used as a starting point for the construction of such theories. The retention of delusional objects over so many years, however, can only be explained on the assumption of their having an underlying libidinal basis. The hatred for delusional objects arises because of the frustration suffered by the patient. This situation is to be encountered in almost every case where delusions and hallucinations have a persecutory content.

Phenomena observed in cases of psychoses have been used to provide support for the theory that in the infant object relationships are primarily influenced by the aggressive instincts. The assumption is made that in psychoses there is a regression to such infantile modes of mental activity. It is questionable whether it is legitimate to utilize pathological phenomena to create or support a theory of infantile mental development. If it is legitimate to proceed in this way the clinical phenomena favor the hypothesis that the infant's first objects, both real and endopsychic, are used as sources of libidinal satisfaction. Aggressive and destructive trends arise when these libidinal needs are frustrated.

CHAPTER 6

The Ego Organization and Reality Testing in Psychoses

The cognitive functions, defense and certain aspects of personality are brought together under the concept of the ego. The ego is a subsystem of the self. It is an organization, the purpose of which is to provide those conditions which will ensure an optimal adjustment to the psychosocial environment. This is achieved by correlating the perception of the material reality with its mental representation on the one hand and by making those adjustments which are necessary to accommodate the demands of the drive representations and the superego on the other. In the healthy person, the ego function of attending, thinking, perceiving, memory and control over motility are activated by drives which have lost their instinctual quality. These drives thus follow the secondary process. Much ego activity proceeds preconsciously and does not require the intervention of consciousness. The automatic character of many purposive acts which have adaptive aims testifies to the highly integrated nature of the ego organization. This is also reflected in its defensive functions which are entirely unconscious.

Hartmann's (1958) theory of a "conflict-free ego sphere" has drawn attention to the possibility that the ego functions are relatively independent of the instinctual drives. This independence is present from the beginning and throughout their development. Hereditary influences play an important part in their maturation and ultimate form. Only secondarily do the cognitive functions become involved with conflicts provoked by the drives. The theory of autonomous ego development has brought psychoanalysis into close contact with genetic psychology. According to its leading proponents (Piaget, Werner, etc.) mental processes in infancy are undifferentiated. There is no inhibitory influence preventing the spread of a stimulus from the perceptual to the motor apparatus. This inhibition develops gradually and is the mechanism which Freud referred to as characteristic of the secondary process. Sensory experiences are seen as lacking discrimination between the different sensory modalities. Hearing, vision and sensation are not differentiated, hence the synesthesias frequently observed in children.

Symptoms and behavioral abnormalities due to regression and disorganization of the ego functions are commonplace in psychoses. Conceptual thinking may be replaced by infantile forms of abstract thought as occurs in the "pars pro toto" phenomenon. Aberrant concepts due to the action of condensation of word representations are frequently found. Concrete thinking is another instance of the disorder which affects this particular ego function. Quite apart from hallucinatory phenomena there are a number of disorders of visual, auditory and tactile perception. Size, shape and distance constancies in visual perception may be deranged. The mechanisms which integrate perception and motility may also be disorganized. The result is that motility is automatically influenced by auditory, visual and kinesthetic percepts. This can lead to catatonic phenomena (Chapman, Freeman and McGhie, 1959; Chapman, 1966). The connections which exist between conceptual thinking and motility may be so upset that a patient's ability to respond appropriately to verbal communication becomes impossible. In the sphere of motility there is a loss of control over the spontaneous repetitive tendency which is an inherent quality of primitive motility patterns. This is manifested in repetitive forms of perseveration in speech, action, writing and drawing. Disorders of memory function find expression in defects of recall and in a condensation of past memory traces.

Many but not all of these manifestations are akin to the expression of cognitive functions in childhood. The egocentrism and the disorders of consciousness which occur in psychoses can also be regarded in the same way. The disorders of consciousness comprise the loss in varying degrees of self-awareness and of volition. The patient can no longer voluntarily attend to mental contents or to aspects of external reality. Thoughts, speech and action cannot be initiated or restricted by an act of will. All these manifestations can be attributed to regression and disorganization of the ego. Concurrent with alterations in function is the loss of the ability to discriminate clearly between percepts and thoughts and between the self and external objects. There is also a deterioration of repression and reaction formation.

Psychotic states can be differentiated on the basis of the degree to which the ego is deranged in its functions. These derangements due to regression or dissolution are extensive in illnesses which have a sudden onset. They are less apparent when the onset is gradual. A distinction must be made here between those cases where there is a well-organized delusional reality and those in which there is no such manifestation. In the former the cognitive functions will show a minimal impairment. In the latter the cognitive functions may be impaired along the lines already described. This is found in certain forms of schizophrenia. The extent of the ego disorganization in a recent case offers no assistance in the assessment of the possible course of the illness. A far-reaching ego regression may resolve as quickly as it appeared while a more limited defect may remain.

Disorganization of ego functions is also to be observed in organic mental states. They can be studied in detail in that group of disorders generally referred to as diffuse cerebral degenerations. All the defects of cognition which have been described for the functional psychoses are to be found in these organic mental states (Freeman, 1969b). There is a similar withdrawal from external reality and a preoccupation with the self. Both repression and reaction formations can be disturbed to the extent that there is a free expression of drive derivatives and the appearance of pregenital tendencies.

ECONOMIC ASPECTS OF EGO DISORGANIZATION

When there is an extensive disorganization of the ego there is always a contemporaneous alteration in the distribution of the libido between self and objects. In cases of acute onset the emergence of primitive ego functions is paralleled by the appearance of abnormal modes of relating and attitudes to the self. This interrelationship is to be seen in the following case.

Case 11

The patient, a single man of 26, was admitted to hospital because of a strange behavior and acute anxiety. His speech was disjointed. He appeared to be confused and perplexed. He did not know where he was or who he was. He had no recollection of the previous day when he was brought to the hospital. His short-term memory was deficient. He did not recognize the writer even though he had seen him before on several occasions. When asked if he knew what the writer's occupation was he replied, "You are all." Later this was followed by "I am all . . . I am he." He was clearly experiencing sensations, affects and thoughts but could not describe them. After a silence he exclaimed "I am red hot." He continually tapped his feet on the floor and showed signs of other repetitive motility patterns as well. He did not know his name, remember where he lived or what his occupation was. With help he recalled his first name.

On another occasion his speech was plentiful but incoherent. One theme after another was taken up and dropped. There was no apparent connection between phrases and sentences. He claimed that parents and siblings were dead, which was untrue. A voice said to him "curse God" and "F— God." He turned his head this way and that while relating these experiences as if to show how he tried to protect his ears from the voices. He believed that something was passing into his feet and causing them to move. There was something in his abdomen which was forcing him to have evil thoughts and to carry out wicked acts. God was trying to protect him. He called on God to save him. He complained of difficulty with vision. There was a blackness which slanted obliquely before his eyes. At times everything about him looked small. He became excited, claiming he was Christ. He exposed his penis and shouted "Look how beautiful it is." He claimed he could destroy or save the world as he chose. He was aggressive and attacked a nurse. He trusted no one—everyone was evil and intent on harming him. In this respect he generalized his own fear of evil to others. This was but one aspect of the tendency to merge self and object. He complained that he could not sleep at night for fear of being attacked. Snakes came into his bed and passed into his body.

The intrusion into consciousness of unwanted and frightening thoughts, the automatic repetitive execution of limb movements and the awareness of auditory percepts (the hallucinations) can be explained as following from the dissolution of the ego. A similar explanation accounts for the loss of command over thinking, feeling and voluntary movement. Self-awareness was equally disturbed with the loss of the sense of identity, faulty recognition of external objects, loss of sense of time and orientation for place and person. Size constancy in visual perception was also deranged. These phenomena appeared concurrently with manifestations which must be attributed to a withdrawal of libidinal cathexes from the representations of real objects (for example, his delusion that his parents were dead) and a hypercathexis of both bodily and mental aspects of the self-representations (the grandiose delusions and the overvaluation of the body).

In similar cases of acute onset these are also transient misidentifications, the misuse of words and the creation of new words. Thinking proceeds in accordance with the sound of a word rather than with its meaning. There is a divorce between the things and their verbal representation. When these phenomena occur relations with external objects proceed on the level of need satisfaction. Bodily needs are intense and must be satisfied immediately. Oral and genital needs are outstanding in this respect. Frustration of the need usually leads to anger or violence. Alternatively there may be a complete withdrawal into the self. In some cases of chronic schizophrenia an opportunity is afforded of witnessing the same kinds of cognitive functioning in association with the demand for the immediate satisfaction of needs.

In both acute and chronic states the cognitive and drive behavior belong together. They result from the action of drive derivatives whose mode of mental representation is by way of the primary process. The instinctual drive cathexis finds an outlet in motility and through word and memory representations as well as in perceptual registrations. The libidinal cathexis is not confined to an object or to a group of related object representations but passes easily from one to another each of which may be connected by only the most meager common factor—usually of a perceptual nature. The result is a prolonged or transient misidentification of an external object due to condensation of cathected representations. In the case described in Profile No. 1 the patient reported that at the time of his admission he believed all the nurses were homosexuals and he could see them engaging in homosexual practices. He was certain that one nurse was in fact the young man whom he had known at the Agricultural College, and who was a homosexual. In some cases the libidinal cathexis leads to the hallucinatory revival of the object representations either in the visual or auditory modality.

At the onset of such a psychosis the ego, being a subsystem of the self, is immediately involved. The regression which occurs results in a qualitative alteration of those libidinal drives which ordinarily activate the ego functions. The libidinal drives now more closely approximate those of the id and hence follow the primary process. The loss of the most advanced functions of the ego—volition, attention, conceptual thinking and reflective awareness—is due to the loss of the secondary process. The libidinal (id) cathexis simultaneously finds a path to action through the motor system without the intervention of conscious decision. The status of the bodily and mental aspects of the self-representations are altered simultaneously.

Psychotic states arise when there is a severe change in the quality and distribution of the ego libido. The ego disorganization is a consequence of this development. An ego defect follows the general libidinal regression and so cannot be regarded as the primary cause of the psychotic symptomatology. This hypothesis is strengthened by the finding that in a large number of cases of diffuse cerebral degeneration (Alzheimer's Disease, Pick's Disease, Korsakow's Psychosis, Senile Dementia, etc.) the ego deterioration is not accompanied by the distortions of interpersonal relations and the disorders of self-perception which characterize the functional psychoses. In these organic mental states the capacity to attend, perceive, register external impressions and recall the immediate past is defective. Speech may be limited in quantity and disorganized by perseveration and by paraphasias. There is a loss of volition and intentionality. The patient cannot recall words at will. He forgets the names of parts of his body. In that the connections between speech and voluntary movement are disturbed the patient cannot carry out simple instructions. He may respond to an instruction with an echo reaction (echolalia). There is evidence to suggest that verbal percepts find a mental registration but these traces cannot become conscious because of the defect of voluntary recall. There are times when they appear automatically in speech but are typically inappropriate in the context in which they arise. A defect of attention cathexis can be postulated to account for this loss of function.

In cases of diffuse cerebral degeneration interpersonal relations more closely, approximate those of the mentally healthy than those suffering from functional psychoses. Delusions and hallucinations are extremely uncommon (Bleuler, 1923). Most patients are eager to join in conversation however limited their capacity and to establish a friendly contact. They show an interest in those who appear interested in them. The defect of memory provides a serious obstacle to verbal communication. However even when a name or word is inaccessible the patient will often find a verbal symbol with which the correct one is associated. These observations suggest that real objects remain cathected with libido even when their verbal representation is damaged by the disease process. A further confirmation of this is to be found in the misidentifications which are common in these states. Doctors and nurses are mistaken for fathers, brothers, mothers, wives, sisters, etc. The object cathexis remains intact. In spite of misidentifications the behavior of patients is in keeping with their situation (e.g., hospitalization). They maintain ties with others in spite of disappointments and upsets. This will continue until the disease process is very far advanced. Their object relations are therefore not dependent on need satisfaction in spite of the ego deterioration.

In a small number of cases of diffuse cerebral degeneration delusions with a persecutory content make their appearance. In these instances the delusions follow a progressive defect in the ego. The most common delusion is the patient's belief that others are stealing his possessions. This delusion is based on a short-term memory defect which the patient refuses to acknowledge. Such denial is made possible by externalization—by attributing responsibility to an external object. The vast majority of patients with a cerebral disease do not react in this way. There is, in the initial phases of the illness, a "denial" of the memory defect or an acceptance of it. As the illness proceeds the patient usually becomes indifferent to the fact that he cannot remember recent events. When persecutory delusions arise on the basis of ego damage the patient's pre-illness personality was possibly one which made free use of externalization and projection. The psychoses associated with epilepsy provide yet another instance of the fact that an ego defect does not immediately lead to the appearance of delusions and hallucinations. In epilepsy the ego defect may consist of repeated attacks of loss of consciousness or of states of altered consciousness in which speech and action proceed automatically. Between bouts of illness the relationship with others remains intact and there is no evidence of psychosis. Psychosis characterized by delusions and hallucinations makes its appearance only years after the initial epileptic attack. Two explanations are possible—the first that the ego defect increases in its extent resulting in a disintegration of repression, which is substituted for by projection, externalization and other defenses. The second possibility is that the defective ego functions so disturb object relations that danger situations are provoked which lead to a regression of the libido.

The sequence of events influencing delusional formation is quite different in the functional psychoses. Delusions and hallucinations occur contemporaneously with the appearance of phenomena due to ego regression and disorganization. Patients who accuse others of stealing their possessions also demonstrate a simultaneous change in interpersonal relations. In addition the nature of the memory defect is different. In the organic psychoses which present with persecutory delusions the short-term memory defect is obvious during clinical examination. It is also detected by psychological tests. In a functional psychosis there will be no evidence of such a memory defect either during clinical or psychological examination. The faulty memory which resulted in forgetting or misplacing a personal possession which the patient subsequently claims was stolen or hidden is a transient phenomenon. It is due to the withdrawal of cathexis from the object representation, a phenomenon which occurs on a widespread basis at the beginning of functional psychosis.

The defect of cognition which occurs in organic mental

states can be understood as resulting from damage to the physical basis of those intellectual functions brought together by Hartmann in his concept of "the conflict-free ego sphere." In the functional psychoses similar disorders of cognition appear as a result of the changed character of the ego libido. These changes disorganize "the conflict-free ego sphere." Here different pathological processes lead to similar clinical manifestations. Similarities which occur in organic mental states as well as in certain forms of functional psychosis can be illustrated by an examination of the disorders of attention which occur in both these states (Freeman, 1969a).

In both categories of illness there is often a loss of active attention. When this occurs the patient has difficulty in comprehension and he cannot pursue a train of thought to completion without its being interrupted by apparently irrelevant ideas or impressions. Attention is no longer at the patient's disposal but is automatically taken up by internal or extraneous stimuli. This imparts an incoherence to speech and leads to a breakdown in verbal communication. For example, a patient suffering from an amnesic syndrome due to cerebral arteriosclerosis was listening to a fellow patient talking about his work as a *shoemaker*. Some minutes later another patient who also suffered from a cerebral degeneration began talking about quite a different subject. The first patient spoke again and interspersed between his phrases was the word "shoemaker," giving his utterances a nonsensical quality. This patient had been affected by the earlier conversation although he had been unable to take part in it. In another case, a patient assimilated into his speech reference to two coat-hangers suspended from hooks on the wall in the following way: "As you grow older," he said, "you can find more things for yourself . . . that's all you need to worry about as long as they can be neatly hung up . . . you don't need to go and iron them if you hang them up nicely."

Identical phenomena can be observed in cases of functional psychosis. A patient suffering from chronic schizophrenia was given a box of chocolates. This patient presented a disorder in both the form and content of his speech. Without uttering a word he inspected the box of chocolates from all angles. After some time had elapsed he walked over to a table and picked up a temperature chart which he had looked at the previous day in order to determine the day and the date. He made some remarks about the name of a ship's captain and concluded by asking if the writer knew a man called Duncan. The box of chocolates which he had ignored was manufactured by Duncan, the name having been plainly marked on the box. A further example illustrates how an extraneous stimulus may even affect behavior. The writer was walking to the consulting room with a patient. The nurse commented on the fact that it was a wet day. Upon reaching the door of the room the patient excused himself and returned to where he had been standing when the writer entered the ward. When asked why he had behaved in this way he replied that his feet were wet; in fact he had not been out of the ward all day.

The capacity to attend and intend is dependent on a special state of consciousness which is to be distinguished from that of dreaming, from that which occurs in undirected thinking, in day dreaming, in acute and chronic organic mental states and in the functional psychoses. Perception of external reality requires an adequate cathexis of what Freud (1900) originally called the system Perceptual Conscious. As long as the cathexis continues its investment of the Perceptual Conscious there is consciousness and perception of the immediate environment and mental contents (Freud, 1925). If an act of direct attention is to occur, whether to the exterior or interior, something more is required. It has been demonstrated that in the mentally healthy the registration of extraneous stimuli occurs on a wider scale than could have ever been imagined on the basis of what is observed to appear in consciousness. An external stimulus which has gained mental registration as a preconscious idea, will only achieve consciousness when it becomes the focus of a cathexis. Active attention thus depends not only on a cathexis of the system Perceptual Conscious but also on what Klein (1959) has described as the deployment of attention cathexis. In the waking state the adequate dispensing of attention cathexis enables the individual to maintain a conscious train of thought apparently undisturbed by percepts, verbal ideas or images.

From a descriptive standpoint little difference exists between the expression of disorders of attention in cases of diffuse cerebral degeneration and in certain cases of functional psychosis. In both the capacity to deploy attention cathexis is deficient. Coincidentally thinking, speech or perception are disturbed by the intrusion of external impressions. It is as if the registration and perception of a stimulus merge with one another instead of occurring in sequence. The loss of active attention and the automatic intrusion of percepts into consciousness is one outcome of the disturbance in the ego. The result is that the ego functions which are concerned with making those changes in the self and the environment that will create favorable conditions for drive satisfaction are deficient. The immediate causes differ in organic mental states and in the functional psychoses. In the former there is a defect in the physical foundations of the ego while in the latter there is a malfunctioning of the ego.

In organic mental states there is a progressive withdrawal from external reality, while the drives increasingly invest memory traces of object representations. Hence the preoccupation with the past, the substitution of the past for the present and the misidentifications, denials and misinterpretations of reality. In the case of the functional psychoses the change in quality of the libido has the same consequences for the ego functions. The consequent loss of attention cathexis accounts for the disinterest and withdrawal shown by some patients. With the appearance of an ego cathexis which follows the primary process, condensation will have an effect on verbal ideas, images, memory traces and all forms of preconscious representation.

In diffuse cerebral degenerations the trend is toward the continuing deterioration of all cognitive functions while in the functional psychoses there can be a return of normal function. This may be permanent or transient. It is in cases of chronic schizophrenia that observations can be made which throw some light on the nature of the ego cathexis which, in the healthy, is required for active attention. These patients are usually withdrawn, present disorders of speech and thinking, defects of perception and memory. Periodically there is a brief return to what at first sight seems to be normal levels of cognition. The patient shows interest in those about him. Speech may be coherent and logical. There is usually an associated intense affectivity. Such improvements in cognition thus occur along with the overt expression of drive behavior. From a descriptive standpoint then interest arises at the same time as bodily needs or aggression. These manifestations can be understood as determined by the action of drive derivatives which have found expression in consciousness and in action. In finding an object the drives provide the cathexis necessary for active attending. This suggests that attention cathexis will only be available whenever there is a drive cathexis of object representations. Once the object cathexis disappears so does the attention cathexis. Such a formulation implies that the ego will only become operative whenever it is cathected with libido. For optimal activity in the mentally healthy, that is, an activity which ensures environmental adaptation along with the satisfaction of needs, the ego libido must have become desexualized and have lost its instinctual aims. In cases of chronic schizophrenia the libido which "energizes" the ego and so gives the impression of normalcy does not have the secondary-process qualities. Although the patient now attends to a real external object as a consequence of the deployment of attention cathexis the aim is immediate drive satisfaction alone. These transient improvements in cognitive functions cannot be regarded as a return to a normal level of ego functioning. At best it is a restoration of an ego state analogous to that existing in the young child.

Reality Testing and the Ego

Reality testing is usually taken to be that function which enables the individual to differentiate between subjective experience and environmental events. Ideas, images and affects are distinguished from sensations and perceptions which have their origin in the environment. Reality testing rests on a distinct separation which has occurred in early development between self and object and their mental representations. The capacity that separates self from nonself does not however prevent a movement of unconscious mental contents from one to the other and back again. This results in distortions of self-perception and enhances nonrealistic attitudes to objects. In cases of neurosis and in primitive peoples it is possible to observe how these inappropriate attitudes develop as a consequence of the action of externalization, projection and identification.

In mental illness patients experience the object world and the self as changed. These changes are of different kinds but they can be ordered according to whether or not the patient retains the capacity to see himself as a distinct entity vis-à-vis other entities. This criterion leads to the inclusion of the phenomena resulting from the merging of self- and object representations in one group but it excludes from that group patients who believe that they are being influenced, bodily or mentally by known or unknown persons or influences. Where the distinction between self and object is in abeyance the perception of real persons is altered due to condensations with the memory traces of real and fantasy objects. The result is misidentification. These persons are thus endowed with attitudes which have no basis in fact. As a consequence of the loss of the boundary between the self and nonself the patient cannot easily distinguish his own bodily and mental sensibilities from those of an external object. There is an externalization of attributes of the self and a merging of the object with the self-representations. In addition the patient's body may be experienced as changing in shape and sexual identity. Sensations of all kinds impinge on his awareness.

The other group of cases is a much wider category embracing a greater variety of phenomena. In every case the distinction between the self and the object is secure. There is no evidence of misidentifications. The first subgroup within this category comprises those patients who believe that their minds and bodies are being influenced against their will by a persecutor. In the second subgroup patients are convinced that they are continually observed and spied upon.

They do not believe themselves to be the subject of influence. The third subgroup consists of those who believe that they are hated and despised by those they care for. In part they feel this condemnation is deserved but they cannot recognize its irrational nature. The fourth subgroup comprises those who are convinced that they suffer from a bodily disease. The fifth are the patients who no longer perceive the self, environment or both as lively, interesting, colorful or having meaning. One or both have become flat, affectless without sensation and monotonous. The latter are the syndromes described as depersonalization and derealization.

When the state of the ego organization is assessed in each of the two main categories it is evident that the ego functions are seriously disorganized when the differentiation between the self and object is lost. The ego functions are better preserved in those cases where the distinction between self and object is maintained. These are the cases usually categorized as paranoid schizophrenia or paranoid psychosis. The clinical phenomena reflect the basic defect in judgment and reality testing. The fact that there is faulty reality testing which consists of a misinterpretation of events in paranoid psychoses and in certain cases of manic depression—the clinical groups falling into the second major category—indicates that this function may be disturbed even when the self and object have been differentiated.

The wide variety of psychoses which have been studied shows that a defect of reality testing may be associated with different forms of disorganization and regression of the ego. The failure of reality testing consists in something more than a complete acceptance of psychical reality. It enables the patient to continue in the belief that he is perfectly well and in full command of his faculties. The necessity for hospital or outpatient treatment is regarded by him as incomprehensible and an unwarranted intrusion into his freedom as an individual. Loss of reality testing is also related to the inability to recall significant memories. The importance of these factors will be referred to again later.

In the acute psychotic attack the failure of reality testing is associated with a sudden alteration in the relationship existing between self and object and between ego and id. The rapid redistribution of libido and its change in quality precipitates a regression which leads to the loss of the boundary between self and object. The cathexis of the ego and superego suffers similarly. There is a fusion of ego and superego while the margins of the ego and id become blurred. The hypercathexis of the self (ego-id-superego) provides the basis for the failure of reality testing. The ego is lost and consequently there is no longer the capacity for self-awareness or the ability to initiate thinking or acting voluntarily. Thought and action become automatic.

In cases of less acute onset the changes in distribution and quality of the libido are not such as to prejudice the discrete nature of the self- and object representations. Regression and disorganization are limited. There are neither misidentifications nor disorders of word form. From a descriptive standpoint the defect in reality testing revolves around a misinterpretation of the object world. The patient has a sense of self-awareness and unless interfered with by persecutors or by the superego he can selectively attend, think at will and act. In these cases the object libido follows different paths. Once withdrawn from real persons it may return to other object representations by way of projection. The outcome is one kind of paranoid psychosis with characteristic persecutory ideas. Another form of restitution takes the form of the retention of the lost object. The responsibility for repudiated instinctual needs is attributed to the object and a different form of paranoid psychosis results. Another possibility is the retention of the object through complete identification. Whether a depressive illness will result or not depends on the relationship with the superego.

The disorder leading to faulty reality testing does not wholly lie in the ego but rather in the nature of the data which is presented to perception. This data compels belief in the same manner as the hallucinatory images of the dream. The failure of reality testing in both psychosis and dream depends on the fact that cathexis is withdrawn from the representation of material reality (Freud, 1917). The argument in favor of the view that the ego is not solely at fault in paranoid psychosis and in severe depressions finds support in patients who briefly undergo a falsification of experience and then recover the ability to test reality. These are the patients who, suffering from a depressive illness, become terrified of spouses, doctors and nurses. These persons are endowed with a harsh severity which then motivates the patient to act and feel toward them on the basis of this belief. Judgment is defective and reality testing temporarily or permanently lost.

Case 12

This situation can be illustrated by reference to a woman patient of 40 years of age who suffered from a severe depression. Nausea was a prominent symptom and led to acute anxiety and agitation. She feared that the nausea would continue endlessly and that she would starve to death. To avoid this disaster she felt compelled to eat. Thin people frightened her. She believed that her husband and the writer were antagonistic to her because she would not eat. Every word or gesture they imparted was interpreted as the threat

—"Eat or you will die." In this state reality testing was suspended. Only when these acute phases passed could the patient recognize that neither husband nor writer were her persecutors and that they had no interest in forcing her to eat. The psychical reality in which this patient believed was rooted in fantasies centering on her mother and sister. The sister, two years older than the patient, had died at the age of nine. Vomiting had been a prominent feature of the sister's terminal illness. There was therefore an element of fact in the fantasy deriving from the mother's anxieties about ill health, vomiting and eating. In childhood and adolescence the patient had been frightened by her mother whenever she felt sick and could not eat. Nausea was a frequent occurrence throughout her early life and only disappeared after her marriage.

The enmity which the patient experienced as being directed against herself on account of her nausea and difficulty in eating was a result of the process whereby huband and writer had been condensed with mother (then a superego figure) representations endowed with oral-sadistic libido. This condensation product made its appearance as a function of the patient's defensive partial withdrawal of cathexis from real persons. The defense was initiated by a danger provoked by genital frustration. Initially this was a real frustration imposed by the husband's impotence. A regression of the libido to oral-sadistic fixations provoked further danger to the real object (the husband). A defensive decathexis followed. The perceptual functions of the ego were then taken up by the object representation of the oral-sadistic mother which had become the recipient of the libidinal cathexis.

Both this sequence of events and its outcome are characteristic of the various forms of paranoid psychosis (see case

13) although there the falsification of reality may continue indefinitely. The restitutional complex is comprised of the object representations which are in receipt of libidinal cathexis deprived of access to objects in the real world. In the absence of a cathexis of real objects the ego acknowledges the restitutional complex as real.

In psychoses of acute onset and in those chronic psychoses where there is extensive cognitive deterioration the ego is virtually out of commission. This is not so in the other psychotic states. There the ego functions are intact but the nature of the mental stimulus is such as to convey belief in its reality. In this respect the ego is a passive agent as it is in all those circumstances when the drive derivatives break through to libidinal or aggressive action.

Case 13

The "imprisonment" of the ego by delusional experience was to be seen in the case of a 41-year-old single woman who, over a period of a few months developed the idea that she had been recruited by British Intelligence to assist in the drive against the I.R.A. She felt herself to be in telepathic communication both with the Intelligence Agency and with certain members of the I.R.A. At the time of her admission to hospital she stated that she was magnetized and that if she came into contact with metals electrical impulses passed through her body. A week or so before admission to hospital she had been in London in her professional capacity and while there, according to her statement, had received instructions regarding her duties as a secret agent. Her admission to hospital was predicated on the fear that the I.R.A. was about to blow up her house and kill her mother and herself. While in hospital she explained that her instructions from the Intelligence Agency had not come by way of a voice but rather through a mechanism by which her thoughts appeared to be mixed up with those of another person. At these times she felt as if she were simultaneously two persons. During all these weeks she did not acknowledge that she was mentally ill.

Miss W. was an only child. Her father had suffered from chronic ill health throughout the latter part of his life which resulted in considerable financial hardship for the family. In her early adolescence Miss W. suffered from pulmonary tuberculosis which gradually remitted only to recur again at intervals until she was in her late twenties. Because of this illness she had few social contacts. Such energies as were available to her in the periods of good health were devoted to professional training. In childhood and thereafter she was frequently in conflict with her father because she felt he restricted her activities. Nevertheless she was devoted to him and shared many mutual interests with him. She never had a male friend or any sexual relation with a member of the opposite sex. She could not recollect ever having experienced intense sexual feeling.

The patient grew up in a remote part of the country estranged from companionship with the exception of her parents. She read extensively and was very imaginative. At about the age of ten she had an imaginary companion who was rich, travelled to London and abroad and led an exciting, interesting life. The companion was involved in espionage on behalf of the British government and was sent to France and other parts of the world. The material for these fantasies came from the newspaper reports on the progress of the war (1941-1944). The companion was most in evidence when Miss W. felt lonely or rejected after a disagreement or disappointment with her father.

Psychotherapeutic work with the patient led to recognition of the fact that the psychotic attack was preceded by the following experiences. A man, Mr. B., distinguished in the patient's profession, came from London to present a short course in some new technical procedures. Miss W.'s position made it incumbent upon her to entertain Mr. B. in his free time. He was about 15 years older than the patient and was married. Miss W. was quite fascinated by him as he possessed all the qualities and accomplishments which she admired. He was widely travelled—one of the patient's most dearly held ambitions. During their few days together Mr. B. made sexual advances to the patient which simultaneously pleased, excited and frightened her. After Mr. B. returned to London they corresponded regularly and occasionally telephoned. One morning Miss W. was wakened from a dream about Mr. B. by a telephone call from him, whereupon she had the thought that they must be in telepathic communication.

Some weeks later Miss W. had to make one of her periodic trips to London on professional business and arranged to meet Mr. B. Again there was some slight sexual contact. Apart from social activity she accompanied him to his laboratory where she observed several large magnets. While in the laboratory she became aware of tingling sensations passing through her body. She wondered if she had been magnetized (hypnotized). From this time on she became increasingly preoccupied with the idea of telepathic influence. This terminated in her delusion about British Intelligence and the I.R.A. Mr. B. disappeared from her mind.

In this case the ego organization did not disintegrate. The patient behaved normally during the weeks she was under the influence of the delusion and it was only when she felt threatened that the content was revealed. The psychosis was initiated by the danger of genital arousal. This was expressed in the fear of explosions which found an outlet in an anxiety dream the night before she was hospitalized. The explosives represented her feared sexual wishes. The defense which operated against the danger was that form of repression characterized by withdrawal of cathexis from the object (Mr. B.). As in her childhood, the withdrawn libidinal cathexis returned to fantasy object representations. The libidinal cathexis, failing to find an outlet, revived the fantasies associated with the imaginary companion—those of the secret agent. Again, as in childhood, following disappointment, the libido found some gratification in the excitement which the fantasy provoked.

The failure of reality testing in this case did not lie in the ego organization—neither the ego functions nor the defense deteriorated. It was the withdrawal of libidinal cathexis from real persons which resulted in a hypercathexis of the self and the fantasies of childhood. They provided the restitutional complex which then acted as a defense preventing the patient from remembering Mr. B. and her sexual wishes for him. The intensity of the cathexis which invested the fantasies led to their being acknowledged as real.

It can be said that reality testing has only partially returned when the positive symptoms of a psychosis (delusions, hallucinations, catatonic signs) disappear. The complete return of reality testing can only be presumed to have occurred when the patient acknowledges that he has been ill, is aware of the fact that he no longer enjoys capacities which were present prior to the illness and has some recollection of the experiences of the illness. When these criteria are fulfilled the patient may be considered to have passed from the psychotic phase of the illness and to have the potential for a complete remission. The inability to recognize the fact of having been ill is usually associated with a disinclination to have any further contact with the hospital or the doctor and nurses who undertook the treatment of the illness. It is quite impossible to encourage such patients to engage in psychotherapy. At best they are willing to attend the Outpatient Clinic but their disinterest and uncooperative attitudes are apparent. It follows from these considerations that although the ego organization, particularly in its cognitive aspects, has returned to its prepsychotic level of efficiency there still remains a disturbance in the sphere of interpersonal relations. This can only be explained as resulting from the incomplete resolution of the libidinal regression which occurred during the psychosis. The residual regressed libido continues to act on the ego and leads to reactions which allow a falsification of knowledge of the illness.

In this chapter reality testing has been studied from the pathological standpoint. The conclusion reached is that the defect in reality testing cannot be attributed to a deficiency in the ego alone. In psychoses the ego stands in danger of losing all those characteristics which distinguish it from the id. The trend is toward a return to a state similar to that envisaged in infancy prior to the differentiation of the ego from the id. In cases of acute onset the ego virtually disappears and is replaced by drive cathexes which seek immediate outlets. Verbal representations, perception and memory are distorted. There is an immediate reaction against this need for instinctual satisfaction with the appearance of phenomena due to the action of defenses. This sequence was to be seen in the case described at the beginning of this chapter. In cases of more gradual onset the ego retains the integrity of its cognitive functions—particularly perception. However the alterations in the quality and distribution of the libido and ensuing restitution cause the emergence of certain object representations which command the perception of the ego and a belief in their reality, no different from the situation in the dream. In psychoses the disorder of reality testing—the loss of the capacity for self-perception, volition, memory and self-object differentiation—cannot be attributed to a disorder of one psychic institution alone, namely the ego, but to a regression which affects the drives, the ego and the superego.

CHAPTER 7

Defense in Psychoses

A study of the various defense organizations which occur in psychotic states starts from the premise that the symptoms arise whenever repression fails to contain those drive derivatives whose quality has been altered as a result of regression. The regression is initiated to relieve an internal frustration but its result is a revival of conflicts and the promotion of a danger situation. In both neurosis and psychosis repression is the first means employed to dissipate a danger situation and to annul anxiety. In the initial phases of psychosis only the preliminary phase of repression is possible, namely the decathexis of drive and real object representations. The anticathexis which is established in neurosis fails to develop. The result is the emergence of other defensive maneuvers. In the section of the Profile dealing with the defense organization an account is required of the extent to which repression has acted or failed along with a description of the other defense mechanisms. This statement provides insight into the nature of the defense organization characteristic of the particular stage of the illness.

Examination of the defense organization at onset, remission, relapse and in chronicity shows that different mechanisms are operative at these stages. It is these mechanisms that determine the form and content of many symptoms but not all. Remission can be attributed to the restoration of defenses which partially or wholly limit a danger situation and relapse to the reappearance of the same danger situation. In the course of an illness, therefore, many different defenses may come to the fore. One purpose of the Profile is to give a clear description of the defenses characteristic of the particular stage of the illness under examination and their relationship to specific danger situations. This can then be compared with the defense organizations which may rise in a different stage of the same illness and with defensive organizations which appear in illnesses with similar clinical manifestations. Further an understanding of the defense organization permits of a distinction between those symptoms, superficially alike, which are due to defense activity and those which are not. A further use of the Profile is to illustrate the connection between specific conflicts on the one hand and the actual symptoms of the illness. An evaluation of the defense organization reveals that different conflicts and different dangers can lead to the employment of one defense mechanism. Therefore symptoms arising in different patients which are identical in form and content may result from entirely different conflict situations even though their representation is mediated by the same defense mechanism.

In this study representative groups of psychotic syndromes will be reviewed in order to delineate the kinds of defense organizations which arise in the initial phases of a psychosis, at relapse, remission and in chronicity.

DEFENSE IN THE INITIAL PSYCHOTIC ATTACK

The defense organization which can be delineated in the first psychotic attack is the final development in a sequence which begins with an internal frustration. This frustration resulted in a regression of the drive derivatives. The initial danger situation created by frustration is followed by a second danger caused on this occasion by the change in quality of the drives. The defense organization which appears has the aim of countering these regressed drive derivatives with the hope of removing the danger situation and the reactive anxiety. Details of the defensive operations undertaken immediately prior to the outbreak of the symptoms are rarely available and therefore the defenses which will now be described are those associated with the full development of the illness. These defenses are motivated by a danger which is sustained by the pressure of drive derivatives.

I

The first group of illnesses to be examined are those characterized by psychomotor overactivity with or without elation of mood. The onset is usually sudden or follows an attack of depression. These illnesses are placed within the diagnostic entity of manic-depression. Only rarely is there controversy about the diagnosis and this will only arise when the clinical picture also includes phenomena which are to be found in cases whose illness is regarded as schizophrenic.

In manic states the defense organization is one where repression no longer exerts a controlling influence on the drive derivatives. Oral and genital drive representations have free play as do the aggressive drive representations. The danger which they nevertheless provoke has the effect of leading to the operation of defenses the purpose of which is to both limit the intensity of the danger situation and the expression of the drives themselves. Many of the symptoms result from this defensive activity. Data will be referred to later which show that from the onset of the danger situation efforts are made to bring about a repression of all those drive and object representations associated with the danger situation. These efforts consist of a decathexis of representations and of perceptual experience.

Externalization in one or more of its forms plays a major role in defense. First externalization has the effect of allowing the patient to believe that the drive representations which are under condemnation are to be found in others. Frequently this form of externalization is accompanied by an identification with the aggressor, with the patient becoming furiously angry with these others. The drive derivatives are also countered by another variant of externalization—attribution of responsibility. When the patient expresses an idea or carries out an action which is unacceptable he blames another person or fantasy object for its occurrence. A third form of externalization which may or may not occur in states of psychomotor overactivity comprises the externalization of unacceptable features of the bodily representations. This defense is more likely to appear when a depressive mood is associated with the overactivity. The patient will then state that the unpleasant changes which are taking place in his body are also affecting the external object.

The defense in overactive states is vigorously directed against the drive derivatives which provoked the danger situation and led to the regressive movement. The affects and the memory traces with which they are associated are dealt with by decathexis the effect of which is akin to that of repression. It is, however, an unstable mechanism. This instability results in a periodic appearance in consciousness of the unwanted affect. Denial also plays a role in removing from awareness all those impressions and experiences which would activate the disturbing affect. The denial is also a form of decathexis but of percepts. Through this decathexis of both external and internal impressions the patient can maintain a denial of illness. A further means of avoiding painful affect, particularly when object loss provokes the initial danger situation, is through the merging of self and object. This merging is a further development of the process of generalization as a result of which thoughts, wishes and affects are believed to be shared by external objects. The merging has the aim of restitution and of restoring the lost object. Another process which also has a restitutive function and which serves as defense against affects associated with object loss is the appearance of visual hallucination and misidentifications. The content of these phenomena is the lost object.

In states of psychomotor overactivity the defensive operations appear to act predominately against the source of origin of the drive derivatives rather than against the aim and object as occurs with projection. It is of course possible to encounter states where projection does occur. Where projection is operative persecutory ideas follow. The defenses which have been described do not have the reliability of repression. The consequences are that neither externalization nor decathexis, whether of external or internal impressions, can consistently remove awareness of anxiety, guilt and other painful affects. It is because of this instability of the defense organization that the overactive patient becomes depressed in mood and self-reproachful. The psychomotor overactivity may disappear and be replaced by a state of withdrawal or one of psychomotor retardation.

II

There is a large group of psychotic illnesses beginning in early adult life which present a wide range of symptoms including delusions of various kinds, behavioral abnormalities, disorders of motility, disturbances of thinking and perceiving. The diagnosis which is made will depend on the psychiatrist's preferred nosological classification. The result is that these cases are either categorized as schizophrenia, schizophreniform psychosis, mixed manic-depressions or schizoaffective states. For the present purpose they can best be classified in accordance with the type of onset and the nature of the previous personality. This latter subdivision has the authority of clinical psychiatry which places greater emphasis on these characteristics than on the symptomatology when giving consideration to the eventual outcome of the illness.

In those patients who present with a gradual withdrawal from the world of reality there is always some evidence of delusional ideas. These may be more or less explicit with a characteristic persecutory content. There may also be some catatonic signs although at this stage of the illness they may not be pronounced. There are patients in whom catatonic signs become the leading clinical manifestation particularly in those cases where the psychosis follows a relapsing course. The defense organization in such cases will be described under the heading "Defense Organization at Relapse." The account of the patient's illness obtained from the relatives reveals that for some time there had been an increasing disinterest in life and a morbid self-preoccupation. Medical help was sought whenever the patient could no longer be persuaded to comply with the ordinary rules of living or when he suddenly expressed irrational ideas with or without strange erratic behavior.

Case 14

A typical example is provided by this patient, a woman of 18, whose gradual withdrawal from others eventually came to a head with outbursts of weeping during which she shouted "I hate him, I hate him." She complained that a man whom she once knew was trying to get into her room at night through the window. He was also spreading nasty stories about her. When interviewed she was found to have difficulty in expressing her thoughts which she said was due to an inability to make connections between phrases and sentences. She said she could hear her own voice arguing with her. Communication was difficult because of the withdrawal and disinterest. In this case, as in others of a similar kind, repression failed to contain the drive derivatives which had been altered in quality as a result of regression.

Clinical phenomena present ample evidence in favor of the view that a constant attempt is made to repress all those aspects of mental functioning which would increase the intensity of the danger situation. This repression is, however, limited to a decathexis of object and drive representations. Insofar as the anticathexis is lacking, only minimal stimuli are required for these representations to enter consciousness. In the case described, as in others, the administration of electroshock therapy resulted in the emergence into consciousness of the proscribed ideas. This young woman heard a voice in her head accusing her of being promiscuous, of being a prostitute, guilty of various perverse acts. She was convinced others could also hear this voice.

In such cases the blocking, the deflection of thoughts and the forgetfulness are the results of a decathexis of representations which might lead to the appearance of the danger situation. The decathexis of real object representations is the cause of the withdrawal, detachment and disinterest in external reality. Similarly decathexis of genital drive representations results in a lack of awareness of genital sensations and so resolves, for example, conflicts over masturbation. In the absence of an anticathexis the drive derivatives are influenced by reversal of aim and projection. The result is that libidinal drive derivatives comprise the content of persecutory ideas. Thus the patient may complain that others are attempting to influence his thinking in the direction of hetero- or homosexuality or trying to alter his sexual identity or merely insulting and criticizing him for sexual misdemeanors. The scant information provided by these patients during the first phase of the illness constitutes a serious obstacle in the way of providing a full account of the defense organization. This can only be achieved by the examination of a number of such cases or by close observation when the illness has passed into a chronic stage. In this way an insight is gained into the fact that the externalization, displacement and primitive forms of identification all play a part in the struggle to limit the danger situation and its expression in castration and separation anxiety.

It is in those patients whose illness is relatively acute in onset that the defense organization is most clearly observed. In contrast to the withdrawn cases these patients are more communicative, present with affective responses and at times are restless and overactive. In patients who speak freely the outstanding characteristic is the alteration which has taken place in their appraisal and judgment of external reality. This change may be accompanied by anxiety, depression or a mood of apathy. Interest is wholly concentrated on a delusional reality which as a rule involves the self as well as others. These others may be the product of fantasies or real persons. As in the previous categories of illness described the withdrawal from external reality can be attributed to attempts at repression by means of a decathexis of real object representations.

Externalization plays an important part in the defense

organization. In conjunction with identification and projection an attempt is made to fill the gap left by the faulty anticathexis. The following forms of externalization are found. The patient attributes responsibility for both aggressive and libidinal thoughts and actions to external objects—real or fantasy. He believes that others are responsible for genital or aggressive affects which occupy his mind and which occasionally are acted upon. Again there is a trend toward the externalization of unwanted aspects of the bodily aspects of the self-representations. The patient will observe changes in the bodily appearance of external objects. He will tell the psychiatrist, for example, that he has changed. This change may or may not be paralleled by changes which the patient experiences in his own body. In part, the cause for his preoccupation with homosexuality is to be found in a pronounced identification with a parent of the same sex.

Projection and reversal of aim do not necessarily play a prominent part in the defense. In some illness projection may lead to symptoms of the kind described above but often projection plays no part at all. It is in these cases that recourse is made to misidentification and hallucination to avoid the expression in reality of drive derivatives. Libidinal drive representation whose object is in the patient's immediate environment are deflected and find expression through the cathexis of an object representation from the past. This leads to a misidentification of the external object or a visual hallucination. Hallucinatory experiences do not necessarily serve a defensive function except in the circumstances of the kind described.

III

The third category of cases to be studied is comprised of those where persecutory delusions occupy the center of the clinical picture. These conditions may make their appearance at any time after the beginning of the third decade. The delusions may be accompanied by auditory and other kinds of hallucinations. The content of these psychotic phenomena is usually of a sexual nature. It is in cases of this type that projection, reversal of aim and attribution of responsibility play a leading part in the attempt to deflect the regressed libidinal drive representations from their aim and object. Identification with the aggressor is commonly encountered when the patient externalizes the unwanted libidinal impulse. Externalization is also employed to dismiss from awareness those aspects of the mental and bodily self-representations which are a potential source of anxiety and guilt. Thus the patient may complain of changes occurring in the physical and mental characteristics of external objects. The fact that the persecutor or persecuting agency appears to possess features similar to that of the patient has been described in the literature. The mechanisms of externalization serve the purpose of easing superego anxiety. It is in cases of this type that difficulty is encountered when it comes to distinguishing between persecutory delusions due to projection and those due to externalization of the superego.

Patients who are preoccupied with persecutory delusions reveal more clearly than others suffering from psychoses that it is delusional object representations which become the focus of libidinal drive cathexes. When these cases are observed during the first psychotic attack it is possible to witness the gradual loss of interest in real objects and the concentration of attention on the delusional ideas. This is due to the patient's need to withdraw cathexis from real object representations as a defense—namely as an attempt at repression. The drive derivatives, having regained their instinctual quality as a result of regression, are deflected from real object representations. They are directed to fantasy object representations by means of projection and so come to constitute the delusional reality. This delusional reality assumes a defensive role and assists in turning the patient's attention from the real object representations to whom the libidinal cathexes were directed.

In some "persecutory" psychoses evidence is frequently available of identification having taken place with the object who has come to play the role of persecutor. Such patients are a special category within the group of persecutory illnesses and, as will be discussed later, have their initial precipitation in situations of object loss. It is in cases of this type that a depressive illness may ensue following a remission of persecutory delusions. The identification which occurs and which is to be regarded as an expression of the trend toward restitution is to be distinguished from the transient identifications which occur in manic states and in schizophrenic and schizophreniform reactions. In the former those aspects of the patient which are the focus of persecutory tendencies belong to the introjected object. In the latter the primitive identifications are not subject to such persecutory influences.

IV

Severe depressive states present a more limited range of psychotic symptoms. In some patients there is intense self-reproach, a sense of guilt and a belief that they are the object of criticism. In a smaller number there is in addition delusional ideas the content of which constitutes the belief that they have damaged or injured those near to them or even others with whom they have no connection. The consequence of this delusion is a fear of being persecuted by the friends of these people or of being arrested by the police and punished. Patients vary with respect to the ease with which they can communicate these thoughts and fears.

In the least disturbed group repression has remained intact so that the drive derivatives which have been subject to regression following on the internal frustration do not lead to faulty reality testing and to delusional thinking or hallucinatory experience. Nevertheless the "pressure" exerted by the drive derivatives is such as to lead to the action of a number of defenses which give the symptomatology its characteristic features. The withdrawal and the retardation of thought and action are the consequences of the further action of repression whenever the drives on the one hand and the superego on the other provoke anxiety and guilt. The decathexis of object and drive representations allows the patient a refuge from the threat imposed by the instinctual forces. This decathexis is to be observed in the patient's loss of genital libido and in anorexia. Aggression is the drive which presents most obviously as the cause of the danger situation in these cases. It is deflected from its aim by identification. Identification results in the patient hating himself. Repression allows the patient to feel free of aggressive intent. It is necessary to add that the basic problem in these states is one of libidinal frustration the result of which is the appearance of the aggressive tendencies to which reference has just been made.

In the more disturbed group repression is less efficient in its function. The situation is akin to that found in the other psychotic states and especially similar to the group of psychoses characterized by persecutory delusions. Interest is wholly taken up with the delusional content. Decathexis of real persons occurs which accounts for the disinterest in external reality. Unlike less severe cases of depression the detached cathexes find expression in delusional ideas because of the failure of repression. Again, as in the first group, aggression is the drive which first presents itself to the onlooker. Aggressive fantasies provoked by libidinal frustration become realities as a consequence of the regression. Projection acts against the aggressive drives with the result that the superego, already externalized, becomes endowed with this aggression. The patient feels hated and despised.

Defense Organization at Remission

It is not always easy to decide whether a patient who has suffered from a psychosis has achieved a complete remission or not. This is because of the tendency toward a gradual disappearance of the positive symptoms (see Chapter 9). In a complete remission not only do these positive symptoms (delusions, hallucinations) vanish from sight but the patient regains his premorbid level of mental functioning. He is able to work, engage in social relationships and make a reasonable adjustment to his environment. Many patients are to be found who having lost the positive symptoms, are unable to participate in life, have difficulty in concentrating adequately on work and seem to be without initiative or drive. They do not complain of any particular symptoms. Again there are patients who are free of psychotic symptoms yet have developed one or more neurotic symptoms such as phobias or obsessional manifestations. It would appear therefore that the quality of the remission varies from patient to patient. In one case the remission is complete and in another it is only partial. Patients who continue in a state of partial remission for a long period of time are difficult to distinguish from those in whom the illness has assumed a chronic state.

A remission in a psychosis has its onset whenever symptoms lose their intensity and there is the beginning of affect and drive control. This is due to the restoration, in varying degrees, of the anticathexis which ensures the stability of repression. The means by which remission occurs can best be understood through an examination of those cases where the remission is only partial in extent. Positive symptoms completely disappear but their place is taken by neurotic manifestations. These may be hysterical, phobic, compulsive or hypochondriacal in character. As in a neurosis these symptoms indicate that drive derivatives are actively seeking an outlet but this is prevented by the presence of the anticathexis. Again as in a neurosis these drive derivatives had become active following regression. Fantasies are cathected and drawn into the conflict from which the symptoms are ultimately derived by way of condensation and displacement. In these cases where partial remission occurs the anticathexis may have been restored but the drive derivatives are still affected by regression and continue to sustain a danger situation.

Under current conditions of psychiatric practice the vast majority of partial remissions occur following the use of tranquilizing drugs.

Case 15

In the following example it was possible to trace the connections between the symptoms of the psychotic phase and the hysterical symptoms which were present during the remission. The patient, a single woman of 24, was admitted to hospital on account of loss of interest, depression of mood alternating with excitement and impulsive behavior. She had made sexual advances to her father. Although this acute state was resolved, soon after she had to be readmitted to hospital on account of depressive symptoms. This time she became sexually interested in the psychiatrist as she had previously been with her father. When this doctor left the hospital the patient accused him of impregnating her and giving her a venereal infection. Within weeks she transferred these ideas to the person of the Medical Superintendent who she said looked like her father. She maintained that he was turning her into a prostitute, forcing her to have unnatural sexual feelings (homosexual) and making her submit to sexual indecencies. The patient further claimed that he was having intercourse with the matron of the hospital and that this affected her brain. The result was a progressive blindness and the loss of the capacity to think clearly. Later she developed the delusion that she was the daughter of George the Sixth. She refused to acknowledge her true identity and her parentage, maintaining that she had been abducted at birth and left with the people who claimed to be her parents.

Treatment with the phenothiazine drugs led to the loss of the delusional ideas. She was able to mix freely, converse with others and enjoy a reasonable existence. However she insisted that she was no longer fit to work because of poor physical and mental health. She complained of bodily weakness, dimness of vision, headache and deafness. Claiming that her memory was defective, she wondered if this had been caused by the pills she received or whether she had cancer of the brain.

This patient fell ill after discovering that her father was having an affair with his housekeeper. She had accidentally discovered them in the act of lovemaking. The inner reaction to this discovery was the promoting of a danger situation compounded from the various components of the oedipal conflict. There was a regression of libidinal drive derivatives with oedipal fantasies being recathected. The concomitant failure of the anticathexis resulted in sexual advances to the father. In hospital the oedipal conflict was repeated again but this time pregnancy fantasies appeared as delusions. Other "retributive" fantasies associated with the oedipal conflict appeared in the dread of being blinded and in the belief that she had been infected. At this stage projection and attribution of responsibility were employed as substitutes for the disorganized anticathexis of repression.

The remission of symptoms resulted from the reimposition of the anticathexis. However, the drive derivatives and fantasies continued to find expression in hysterical-like symptoms. She no longer believed that her brain was being injured or that she was being blinded. Instead she complained of headaches and dimness of vision. There was an amnesia for the precipitating events of the illness and the psychotic experiences themselves. The effects of the repression was to give the impression of a progressively failing memory. Condensed within the symptoms and the hypochondriacal preoccupation were the fantasies which had found an outlet in the delusions.

Attempts to engage this patient in psychotherapy were of no avail. She objected to meetings except on those occasions when she was pleased to speak about her symptoms. Characteristic of her resistant attitude was the remark—"I don't want to talk to you for hours and hours." A dream she reported might have been an allusion to her dislike of interviews—"I had a dream of being shown photos of myself, it's no good."

The return of premorbid interest, attitudes and a freedom from symptoms which occurs in a complete remission presupposes the disappearance of the defense mechanisms which were activated to deal with the danger situation caused by the regressed drive derivatives. This hypothesis is supported by the data elicited from those patients who recover from severe depressive states and from manic or somewhat similar forms of psychotic illness. In severe depressions the genital organization is recathected with libido as are real object representations. In manic reactions repression is restored whenever the genital and oral libido is no longer necessary for restitutional purposes. In manic and depressed patients who fall ill after real disappointments the forward movement of the libidinal cathexes from the fixations to which they had regressed becomes possible once there is a relinquishment of the cathexes attached to the lost object. In cases where the danger situation consisted of castration fear the diminution of this anxiety permits a similar movement of the libidinal cathexes to the most advanced stage of the sexual organization reached prior to the illness. The restoration of genital primacy, however unstable, removes the need for an anticathexis which was directed at the regressed form of the libidinal drive derivatives.

Lastly reference should be made to those patients whose remission is associated with the development of a new real object relationship. It is when such patients relapse once more into illness that some insight can be obtained into the role of the object relation as it affects remission.

Defense Organization at Relapse

At least two conditions are conducive to the recurrence of psychotic symptoms. There are those patients whose remission is apparently dependent on continuing drug therapy. Failure to persist with this treatment leads to relapse. Then there are patients who remain well after drug therapy is terminated. These patients may relapse when confronted with events which lead to an internal frustration. In the first category the conditions for the emergence of the symptoms remain but the effect of the drug therapy is to reduce anxiety and psychomotor overactivity with the result that those defenses which substituted for the anticathexis of repression are no longer necessary. The upshot is the disappearance of those symptoms whose expression was dependent on projection, externalization, etc., as long as treatment continues. In the second category the internal frustration leads to regression and to a failure of repression as occurred in the first psychotic attack.

The abandonment of drug therapy and the occurrence of a significant stress have the same result—namely, the loss of the capacity to contain the impact of the regressed drive derivatives. In the case of drug remissions the quality of the derivatives has not altered from its regressed condition while in those cases where remission is independent of drugs the regression has been resolved. An insight into the events which probably occur when relapse takes place after the cessation of drug therapy can be obtained when a reduction of medications is made in cases where the effect of the treatment has been to bring about a removal of positive symptoms. The attempt to find the minimal yet effective dosage frequently leads to the reappearance of symptoms.

Case 16

An illustrative case is provided by a woman of 28 years of age who, when well, was by temperament quiet and retiring. She was admitted to hospital following the onset of her third attack of mania. The first bout of illness began at 18 following a disappointment in love; the second at the age of 26 when she was already married with two children. The third attack occurred some months after a separation from her husband. Data is only available about the two latter attacks. Both were characterized by a heightened eroticism. In each she believed that a man whom she had only met once would meet her need for love and genital gratification. In the second bout of illness she criticized her husband for neglecting her and failing to satisfy her sexually. In the third she complained of loneliness and lack of sexual satisfaction. Disappointment was the feature common to all the psychotic attacks. This patient was overactive but neither elated in mood nor overtalkative. Her speech was often difficult to understand and frequently there were signs of depression of mood. Following administration of a phenothiazine drug the overactivity subsided with speech and thinking returning to normal levels. No reference was made to the man she longed for in the attack. The medications were quickly reduced as in the earlier attack, the effect of which was to induce a relatively severe depression. Some days following the reduction of medications the patient returned home for a second weekend to visit her children who were living with her mother at the time. On return from the weekend the manic symptoms recurred.

It may be assumed that the visit to her children provoked a reaction which the lessened quantities of drug could not contain. The first weekend visit had passed off quite successfully. In this case the increase in the genital libido and the associated fantasy had the aim of removing from awareness the danger situation which object loss and separation provoked. The effect of the drug treatment was similar to that of repression which had been disorganized at the onset of the attack. As in the case of repression drug therapy removed all evidences of the heightened genital libido. The absence of this drive derivative left the patient vulnerable to depression. Withdrawal of the drug or failure of repression permitted the reappearance of the eroticism which acted as a defense against the danger situation. Nothing had changed in the patient's inner life apart from the effect of the drug on the expression of libidinal drive derivatives. This is equally true of all patients whose relapse follows a remission which is wholly maintained by drug treatment.

In those cases where relapse takes place long after drug treatment has been stopped the situation both externally and internally is no different from that which led to the first attack of illness. Often the attack is provoked by an obvious libidinal frustration as may occur in a patient who, when confronted with a danger of heterosexual experience, cannot tolerate the cathexis of homosexual fantasies. Failure of repression leads to the homosexual drive derivatives finding expression in consciousness and in the content of delusion and hallucinations. A further defense against the emergence of the homosexual trends is the appearance of catatonic symptoms. The hypertonia and the rigidity of the musculature prevents any kind of voluntary movement.

Relapse may also occur if the patient is exposed to a situation which creates an internal danger. There are patients who cannot tolerate the stress of living alone, living with parents or with the parent of the opposite sex. There are others who fall ill when marriage is impending. Individuals who by virtue of their work are mainly confined to the society of their own sex may also relapse into a psychosis. In each instance the danger situation leads to the same sequence of events as took place during the first attack, that is, to regression and failure of repression. This may be illustrated by reference to a woman patient aged 58 (case 17) whose illness became manifest after approximately 12 years of reasonable mental health. The patient lived alone with her mother who was aged 83.

Case 17

Miss X was an art teacher by profession who had first been admitted to a mental hospital in 1953. It is likely that the illness had been present at an earlier period but a remission had occurred spontaneously. The precipitant was a disappointment in love. In 1953 she was overactive, excited and believed that she possessed supernatural powers. This illness was regarded as due to schizophrenia and was treated by insulin coma therapy. The symptoms disappeared and she remained well until 1956 when she fell ill once again. The clinical notes at that time revealed the presence of excitement, overactivity and persecutory as well as grandiose delusions. On this occasion treatment consisted of electroconvulsive therapy. Although discharged from hospital the illness did not remit and she had to be readmitted for the third time in 1957. On this occasion she complained that her possessions had been stolen from her and that her family and others were meddling in her affairs. She alleged that when in the hospital on the first occasion she had been sexually assaulted following an insulin-coma treatment. She also accused her brother of having exposed her to the sexual advances of a young man while they were having lunch in a restaurant. While engaged in conversation with this young man he showed her a photograph of his mother. The patient realized this was a photograph of herself, that in fact the young man was her son.

The patient left hospital early in 1958 having lost all her symptoms. She had to abandon her teaching career but obtained different posts which she held for varying lengths of time. At the end of 1969 she lost her position due to redundancy. As a consequence she and her mother sustained considerable financial hardship. Periodically she would obtain remuneration for some artistic work but after payment would fear that officials from the insurance agencies would prosecute her for having received payment. She began to believe that a man was watching her outside her house. This was followed by the belief that her room was being searched while she was out of the house. She noticed that she was losing many of her possessions and took steps to protect her room from intruders. At night she would barricade the door. She confided to her mother that her belongings were being stolen. Soon thereafter she had the idea that her mother may have stolen them or given them away and proceeded to accuse her of this. The extent of the patient's anger alarmed her mother. When her brother came to visit the house at his mother's request the patient told him that she was married and had a son. She visited the family solicitor inquiring about a box which she claimed her father had left with him for safe keeping. The box was supposed to contain a child's suit and other items appertaining to her marriage. This marriage, according to the patient, had taken place when she was about 18 years old. The supposed husband was a doctor. She blamed her parents for being against the marriage and for its eventual disruption. At no time was she aware that all these ideas were purely the product of fantasy. She was particularly angry with her mother and brother whom she believed wanted to get rid of her by incarcerating her in a mental hospital.

The shortage of money had, in this case, the significance of a danger situation. The loss of resources was equivalent to object loss. It will be recalled that the patient's illness had become manifest following a disappointment in love. The threat of loss evoked libidinal frustration. In the absence of possibilities of libidinal gratification a regressive movement affected the drive derivatives. The effect of this regression was to be observed in the loss of personal possessions. This was the result of a weakening of the cathexis of real object representations. A further consequence of the regression was the cathexis of wishful fantasies which had until this time been dormant. Their conversion to delusions followed from the failure of repression. These delusional ideas in their turn acted as a defense against awareness of the realities of her situation. Not only was she supposedly married but she was rich and in a position to call on resources from her father's estate as well. The defensive reversal was accompanied by externalization of aggression particularly to her brother and mother who were regarded as standing in the way of her being reunited with her "husband."

Reference was made above to patients whose illness remits when they succeed in establishing a new object relationship. If this relationship disintegrates then relapse occurs. The observation of such cases shows that the remission becomes possible because the real object comes to serve a purpose not unlike that of repression. Unacceptable wishes and affects are externalized. Jacobson (1967) has shown how the behavior of the new object can be so manipulated as to provide a vicarious satisfaction of needs that otherwise would find expression in psychotic symptoms. Once the relationship comes to an end the patient is utterly exposed to the danger created by the regressed drive derivatives and psychotic symptoms result.

Defense in Chronic Psychotic States

The patient whose illness has passed into a chronic state is incapable of making even a modest adjustment to life. He can neither work efficiently nor maintain an independent existence. These patients are either hospitalized or live at home entirely dependent on their families. In the schizophrenic group the usual clinical picture is one in which the patient is apathetic, without interest or initiative. His speech is limited and he is disinclined to communicate. In some cases the speech is incomprehensible. In others the catatonic signs are the leading clinical manifestations. Periodically these schizophrenic patients burst out of their withdrawal becoming elated and expressing grandiose ideas. Sometimes there is only anger at imagined persecutors. The result is attacks on nurses, patients or relatives. There are patients in whom the phases of activity approximate normalcy. Speech becomes rational and there is a return of affect and interest. These episodes are, however, short-lived. The next major group of chronic patients comprises those who are continuously dominated by delusional ideas of one kind or another which may or may not be of a persecutory nature. As a rule these patients are reasonably well preserved and at least show some interest in their personal appearance. Last are the chronic depressive illnesses where the patient alternates between a state of psychomotor retardation and one of agitation. Delusions of guilt and hypochondriacal preoccupations are frequent.

In chronic schizophrenic states the defense is instituted against the constant pressure exerted by the drive derivatives. These derivatives, regressed in their quality, are easily activated by external stimuli which arise from any kind of interpersonal contact. External reality comes to offer as great a danger as that caused by internal reality. Hence the negativism and hostility to all attempts to establish communication. In the absence of an anticathexis which would ensure a stable repression of the drive derivatives a decathexis is undertaken of both object and drive representation. It is this decathexis which enables the patient to maintain his disinterest and withdrawal from external objects. Decathexis is the principal defense operating during the quiescent phases of the illness. It is a vulnerable defense and sensitive to the slightest stress. This is reflected in the patient's inordinate fear of doctors, psychotherapeutic endeavors and any mention of mental illness.

The decathexis becomes ineffectual whenever the intensity of the drive derivatives reaches a certain height or when, as in some instances, the antipsychotic medications are discontinued or reduced below a critical level. The result is a partial breakthrough of the drive derivatives. Latent fantasies become delusions. There is psychomotor overactivity and a free expression of libidinal drives. Concurrently defenses are called into play to offset this irruption of instinctual drives—namely, attribution of responsibility, denial, etc.

Case 18

A case in point is provided by a female patient who had suffered from a schizophrenic illness for about 15 years without remission. She was usually negativistic in manner, disinterested in her appearance, in her environment and completely apathetic. She resented any attempt to engage her in speech. Periodically she would become overactive, elated in mood, grandiose and present a heightened eroticism. If a man came near her she would rush at him and attempt to grasp his genitals. She would exhibit her breasts in a seductive fashion. Masturbation was openly undertaken. She voiced numerous erotic wishes and ideas. She claimed she was a Princess of India. Her manner was arrogant and overbearing. The patient lived at home with her parents and on this account it was very difficult to obtain any information about circumstances which may have led to the periodic exacerbation of symptoms.

In other cases where a similar upsurge of positive symptoms occurs it is often quite obvious that there is an increase in the quantities of the libidinal drive cathexes as a result of an external stimulus.

Case 19

A woman of 41 who had been ill for nine years with a schizophrenic illness passed from a state of withdrawal to one of overactivity and delusions after some months of psychotherapy with a member of the hospital nursing staff. For a time the patient was friendly, communicative and helpful. She explained that her husband had left her for another woman and thought this was because the woman had been better educated than herself. Subsequently she became depressed. Within a few days she became aggressive, complaining that she was being made to experience genital sensations. She said, "They make me lie down and put a pillow under my hips." And "They are throwing my husband and children at me." She was unable to accept the guilt feelings attendant on the breakthrough of the libidinal tendencies. She smashed a print hanging on the wall—a picture of a handsome man. She shouted, "You are dirty, getting inside me." At an earlier time she had commented on how much she liked this picture and how handsome she thought the man—"I like that man in the picture; I like his appearance."

In chronic delusional states projection, attribution of responsibility and simple externalization are the defenses which influence the drive derivatives. Where projection acts as a substitute for repression the patient constantly feels persecuted. Attribution of responsibility is found associated with projection in these cases. These patients do not make use of the defense of the decathexis of object and drive representation and can therefore continue in some sort of contact with external reality.

There is a further group of chronic delusional states where externalization appears to be the principal defense. These patients attribute to external objects all aspects of the self-representations which are considered unacceptable. They are not the subject of victimization or persecution but believe that they are surrounded by evil. Both libidinal and destructive drive derivatives are thus disowned as well as aspects of self-awareness which are liable to provoke anxiety. The externalization appears to substitute for the anticathexis of repression. This is borne out by the fact that prior to the development of the externalization the patient was consciously aware of, for example, alterations in his body scheme or persecutory ideas of various kinds. These externalizations can be observed when such patients are seen regularly over a period of time.

Case 20

The patient who provided an illustration of this defense was a man of 53 who had been mentally ill for about 20 years. For many years he had entertained grandiose and persecutory delusions. He believed that his body was being changed in shape and rendered lighter. He was convinced that his thoughts, feelings and actions were those of another person, identical to himself. This person spoke and acted through him even though all these expressions were against his will and inclination. Inanimate objects also changed in size and shape altering perception which he attributed to persecutors. After some years the persecutory elements disappeared. Instead he constructed an elaborate delusional system in which he played the part of onlooker. He believed that "very brainy criminals—the very greatest of doctors and surgeons"—enticed unsuspecting persons to their lair and after "doping" them cut up their bodies and, according to the patient, "cannibalized and suck the rest and guts it." They then constructed a double of the individual—a "slip" as he called it. In his own words, "slipism is the whole key . . . without slipism they can't do it . . . they suck the blood . . . take the whole flesh and body over and make it up to look like for example F (the writer) and put it on strings and work it . . . the slip is a mere reflection of a man." These "slips" once inserted into an individual allowed the criminals to control his thought, action and appearance. The patient himself was untouched by all this—"I am immune to it" he said . . . "they never gave me host hospitality . . . I was always skeptical . . . I agree with Shakespeare all men are liars and rotters I am not." Every crime perpetrated in the land was committed, according to the patient, by criminals using unsuspecting victims into whom they had inserted "slips."

He was forever commenting on the writer's appearance or mental activity—"Someone was speaking through you . . . someone was interfering with your speech"—or he was in contact with the writer's double. He would move his lips without speech. When asked what he was doing he replied, "Speaking to a man behind you . . . he is another man of you . . . very like you . . . he's a double of you in appearance and disguise . . . he is a familiar of you . . . the more familiars a man has the more successful he will be . . . they strive all the time to keep you from slipism automation . . . that's why you are as free as you are."

The externalization of drive and self-representations which occurs in chronic delusional states is similar to that found in patients whose remission from psychosis is dependent on the cathexis of a real person. In the former the externalization alters the content of the psychotic reality while in the latter it enables the patient to disown representations which would disrupt adaptation to external reality.

In chronic depressive states the defense organization is similar to that found in recent cases. Self-representations are cathected with aggressive and libidinal drive cathexes. Real object representations are decathected with the result that the patient is withdrawn and refractory to influence. Oral-sadistic drive derivatives which have resulted from regression lead to conflict. The outcome is anorexia, nausea and sometimes vomiting. The anticathexis is maintained against aggression so that this drive only finds expression through turning in on the self and being introjected into the superego.

Psychotic Symptoms and Defense

By examining the defense organization characteristic of different stages of psychotic illness it became apparent that the symptoms may either be the result of a failure of repression or the outcome of the action of specific defense mechanisms. In both acute onset and relapse many of the symptoms and behavioral abnormalities follow the disruption of repression. The defense mechanisms which act to counter the failing repression determine the form and content of much of the symptomatology. Projection, by altering the aim and object of the drives, leads to persecutory delusions. Attribution of responsibility has a somewhat similar result in that the patient can avoid acknowledging the origin of drive and affect. He does not, however, experience the drive derivatives passively as occurs in projection. Externalization of different aspects of the self-representations enables the patient to disown thoughts, feelings and bodily sensations which would provoke anxiety. Displacement is used to deflect the drive derivatives from objects as occurs in neuroses. Additionally it participates with condensation in those hallucinatory phenomena which also have the purpose of redirecting drive derivatives from the appropriate external object. Identifications enable the patient to avoid reactions from object loss and may also act as a defense against dangers provoked by incestuous wishes. Denial and decathexis lead to a withdrawal of cathexis from external reality as well as from drive and object representations and so diminish the possibilities of a danger situation arising.

All psychotic symptoms cannot be attributed to either a failure of repression or to the activity of specific, defense mechanisms. Many symptoms are the result of regression (see Chapter 8). The nature of these symptoms will depend on the extent of the regression and on the fixation points which are recathected by the regressing libido. There are again other symptoms which cannot be easily related either to defense or to regression. The frequency of symptoms due to one or another form of externalization has already been commented upon. Patients easily attribute their own feelings, fantasies, wishes and bodily attributes to an external object. These kinds of phenomena consist of the patient believing that the object possesses omnipotence, strength, happiness, extraordinary powers just as he does himself. The object is felt as sharing thoughts and even bodily sensations. Similarly the patient who makes passing identifications with a loved or admired object does so because he wishes to be the same as the object. *None of these manifestations can be regarded as defensive in their origin.* Both categories of phenomena are the result of regression which has affected object relations. A primitive mode of relating has been reconstituted where self and object are not readily differentiated. Externalization and merging characterize this form of relating and when present can easily be employed for defensive purposes as has already been described.

There are many varieties of delusion whose form and content are not due to projection. These delusions result from the cathexis of childhood and adolescent fantasies which comprise aspects of the ego-ideal. These delusions are a product of libidinal regression. Wishes become facts. The patient believes himself to be a poet, doctor, famous scientist, etc. The delusions are not created in order to serve the purpose of defense. On occasion, however, they may be so employed. They can be used to protect against a sense of hopelessness and a crushing sense of inferiority. Delusions, merging phenomena and manifestations resulting from externalization of aspects of the bodily and mental self provide some clues as to the site where fixations and arrests may have taken place during the course of libidinal development. A form of narcissistic fixation is presupposed in the case of delusions which are relatively stable and coherent. The delusions are based on a pathological narcissism which is most likely to have occurred in those who were able to create a constancy of object cathexis. In merging phenomena and those due to externalization the libidinal cathexes are of a nature akin to that existing at the need-satisfying level of development suggesting fixations at that stage.

Hallucinatory experiences and misidentifications result from the cathexis of memory traces of objects, of past acts of instinctual gratification and of fantasies of libidinal satisfaction. Hallucinatory phenomena allow some outlet for libidinal cathexes which are unable to find a way to real objects. These wishfulfilling phenomena are in themselves a danger. They lead to anxiety and to defense. The result is attribution of responsibility. Someone else is blamed for the genital or oral-genital fantasies which provide the content of the hallucination. Hallucinatory wishes do not necessarily provoke anxiety or guilt, a phenomenon which is particularly true in manic states. On occasions, as has already been mentioned, the hallucinatory experience is evoked as a defense. The drive cathexis is deflected from the real object representation. In psychotherapy the patient hallucinates so that he can avoid awareness of a libidinal wish directed toward the therapist. Similarly hallucination of the image or voice of the lost object will act as a defense against the painful affect of loss. It is essential to add that auditory hallucinations and ideas of reference can be due to the externalization of the superego and bear no relation whatever to the defense organization.

The survey of defenses undertaken at different stages of a psychotic illness not only revealed that certain defenses are responsible for certain clinical symptoms but also that the defense organization may change radically during the course of the psychosis. First there are those patients where the defense changes from one bout of illness to the next. Characteristic of this group are patients who in the first episode present a depressive syndrome but in the second exhibit a persecutory symptom complex. This sequence may be reversed with the persecutory symptom complex occurring first and the depression second. In both episodes there is a withdrawal of cathexis from real object representations. In the persecutory illness projection leads to the development of the delusional reality on the basis of real or fantasied representations while in the depression the libidinal cathexes are taken up in complete identification with the object.

Second, there are those patients in whom the defense organization alters during the one bout of illness. This is usually to be observed during chronicity. Examples have already been cited of patients who have presented symptoms arising principally from a decathexis of drive and object representations. Sometime later phenomena due to an abolition of this decathexis occurs. Externalization and attribution of responsibility are employed to deal with the irruption of instinctual drive derivatives. The resultant persecutory delusions will gradually die away and the patient will return to his former withdrawn state. In several of these chronic patients the libidinal cathexes are taken up in identifications which have a considerable stability. These identifications are usually with object representations which at one time were the object of drives. When such patients have, even if only for a brief period, a free expression of drive derivatives the identification is partially resolved with the patient constantly referring and expressing wishes regarding the object representation. The reaction to this is a projection of the forces opposed to the object choice. The patient then blames parent, doctors, etc., for preventing his union with the love object. In addition to these chronically ill patients there is the further category where projection is gradually replaced by externalization as the principal defense. An instance of this kind was described.

SYMPTOMS, CONFLICT AND DEFENSE

Behind both symptoms and defense lie the danger situations from which they have their origins. These danger situations are the result of regression and arise from the cathexis of unacceptable drive representations. The process of symptom formation is set in motion by economic factors. The danger situations bear a relationship to the defense mechanisms which is different from that existing between the symptomatology on the one hand and the defense on the other. A particular symptom, irrespective of the symptom complex of which it is a part, can always be attributed to the action of one defense mechanism (for example projection and persecutory delusions). This would be the case in a given patient and from patient to patient. When patients are compared, one to the other, it becomes apparent that the different danger situations may make use of the same defense mechanism while different defenses may be activated by the same danger situation. For example superego anxiety and castration fear may give rise to identification as the principal defense in two different cases while projection and externalization may be the consequence of separation anxiety and object loss. Understandably each patient will make use of those defense mechanisms which have habitually been employed to counter internal dangers throughout the course of his development.

The differences which exist between patients manifesting similar symptom complexes (paranoid, catatonic, depressive, psychomotor overactivity) must be sought not in this sphere of the defense organization but in the kinds of danger situation conflicts which have sprung up in the individual case. Patients cannot be adequately differentiated either by symptom or by defense organization but only by the particular danger situation which is unique for each patient.

Psychoses in which persecutory delusions are the leading clinical feature may be taken as an example. These states may fall into the clinical category of schizophrenia or paranoid psychosis. The persecutory phenomena can be traced in one group of cases to the danger provoked by castration fear. Illustrative is the case of a young man of 21 who fell ill following an unsuccessful attempt to initiate a heterosexual relationship. Regression led to the cathexis of passive feminine and oral-sadistic fantasies. The failure of repression caused the former to find conscious expressions in the idea that he was turning into a woman. The ensuing conflict resulted in the delusion that he was being poisoned and preyed upon by a hermaphroditic creature. The influence of externalization of bodily aspects of the self-representations on the content of the delusional objects is clear enough. In female patients the equivalent situation to the danger incurred by castration is obtained when masturbation fantasies are hypercathected with resultant phallic-masculine tendencies (see case 22, page 252). The libidinal regression which follows eventually leads to conflicts which are dealt with by projection and externalization.

In a second group of paranoid illnesses the danger situation is caused by superego anxiety. For example, a young man of 20 fell ill following his father's death. He believed that his mother had killed his father. Guilt led to externalization of aggression and jealousy and also to regression from the oedipal conflict. The revived fantasies brought about a projection with the resultant belief that he was being poisoned. The third group of patients suffering from persecutory delusions sustain their illness following separation or object loss. The loss of the object exposes the patient to the stress of libidinal frustration. Regression follows. A case in point is that of a woman who developed persecutory delusions after being abandoned by her lover.

Cases belonging to the one syndrome can also be differentiated on the basis of whether or not the defenses and the subsequent symptoms have contained the danger situation and achieved a form of restitution. In both recent and chronic cases of psychoses patients are to be found where the danger which was provoked by object loss or castration fear and which led to the regressive cathexis of fantasies, and so to conflict, is overcome by projection or externalization. These defenses allow for cathexis of fantasy or object representations. This psychotic reality can be supportive and reassuring as well as persecutory. In other illnesses the cathexis which was detached from real object representations is not taken up by representations of objects or fantasy objects. There is no restitution in these cases. The patient does not relate to delusional objects except insofar as he is persecuted by them. The part played by aggression in converting the attitude of the delusional objects from love to hate cannot be entered into here. Chronic catatonic states can also be distinguished, one from the other, on the basis of how far the danger situation has been allayed by the defenses characteristic of this particular symptom complex.

The investigation of the defense organization at different stages of the psychotic illness leads on the one hand to an examination of symptomatology and on the other hand to the study of conflicts and danger situations. Psychoses appear to find their expression through a limited number of syndromes or symptom complexes which at times are not too sharply distinguished from one another. Each of these symptom complexes can be regarded as a final common path through which different forms of conflict can find representation. This representation is mediated through the defense mechanisms. This formulation emphasizes the fact that the symptoms of a psychosis like those of a neurosis are the end products of the process of illness and are essentially surface manifestations.

CHAPTER 8

The Problem of Regression in Psychoses

In previous chapters considerable emphasis was placed on regression as a major factor contributing to symptom formation in the psychoses. The clinical phenomena were attributed first, to an alteration in the quality of the libido, second to the loss of the differentiation between self and object, third to the disappearance of distinguishing features between ego and id and fourth to the dedifferentiation and externalization of the superego. All these changes are the result of regression. The negative symptoms (the loss of volition, reflective awareness, etc.) were regarded as a direct effect of the regression while the positive symptoms (delusions, hallucinations and catatonic signs) were the final result of the same backward movement of mental function.

Deep and Extensive Regression

The effect of regression is to reveal modes of mental activity appropriate to early phases of development. In those cases of psychosis which can be designated "simple mania," the effect of regression is to bring about a state where there is a merging in varying degrees of self and object, where the ego is barely distinguishable from the id and where the superego merges with the "ego-id." In such a state there is no evidence of mental conflict. It is a state where need satisfaction predominates, the libido being characterized by instinctual aims. There is an easy externalization of thoughts, wishes and affects which are generalized to external objects. Aspects of the bodily self are also attributed to others. Cognition will be subject to the primary process in those cases where the regression has been sudden as well as extensive. Speech will then be fragmented and lose its function of communication. Memory and perception will be similarly affected with a fusion of memories and misidentifications.

Mania does not present such a simple picture when complicated by phenomena other than those which reveal the uninhibited, conflict-free expression of drive derivatives and concomitant object relations. There may be guilt feelings, phases of depression of mood, periodic states of withdrawal and psychomotor retardation and an accompanying tendency to attribute blame to others. These symptoms cannot be understood as resulting from regression alone. Their presence suggests conflict and the activity of defense mechanisms. Such a conflict must have arisen because of the partial activity of both ego and superego. Attribution of responsibility absolves the patient from guilt and a withdrawal of drive cathexis from objects as well as a decathexis of the drive representations themselves annuls a potential danger. In such a case the regression has been arrested at a stage prior to that which would have completely inactivated the ego and superego or the regression has been partially resolved with some return of ego and superego function. However it must be concluded that the regressive process had uncovered a conflict already existing in the patient.

Case 21

In the following case of mania such a conflict could be discerned behind the clinical phenomena. The patient was an unmarried man of 22 years of age. He had become deeply depressed following his mother's death. In the months prior to her death he had been unemployed, which had apparently led to a mild depressive reaction that had been a source of anxiety to his mother. It was only after her death that he was referred for psychiatric treatment. He blamed himself for his mother's death, suffered from insomnia and was without appetite. At this time he refused to attend the psychiatric clinic for further treatment. Four months later he became elated in mood, overactive in speech and action and expressed numerous grandiose ideas.

In the initial phase of the illness speech was rapid, one theme quickly replacing another. There was an overvaluation of mental and physical powers. He could read minds; he was able to provide for everyone; he could light a match without striking it or fill a glass with water without taking it from a tap; he was as strong as the sun—"I have enough electricity in my body to keep London alight." He identified himself with Christ. He expressed himself as follows—"It's pure agony I'm in, nails through your hands and feet. . . ." His attitude to external objects was based for the most part on need satisfaction. His needs were urgent and imperative—"Get my girlfriend immediately or I will smash up the place." He was impatient and irritable if kept waiting. He generalized his conscious mental contents to external objects —when he felt happy the object was happy. The object partook of his own physical characteristics—"As soon as you shake my hand you get 10 years younger." Even his occupation was transferred to the writer—"You are a mechanic (his trade) . . . you used to be a doctor." At other times he appeared concerned about the welfare of those about him. He said he would resolve the problems of everyone and relieve their depression and suffering.

He denied the fact of his mother's death insisting that he had seen her in the hospital. He fantasied a girlfriend who assumed a delusional reality. This was a girl he had admired from afar who had died some months before his mother. He was forever searching for her in the female wards of the hospital. Other women were frequently misidentified as his mother or the fantasy girlfriend. There was a free expression of libidinal drives. Genitality was heightened—"I go to bed with a girl every night." He was forever making sexual advances to female nurses and women patients. He attributed an equal genital urge to God—"He's a sexy man." God was in him and told him what to do.

The mood of elation, the psychomotor overactivity and the other phenomena described above were not consistent in their expression. Interspersed was depression with self-criticism—"I'm all depressed, downhearted, I'm not well, it's pure agony I'm in . . . it's like falling into a furnace." Another comment descriptive of his "black mood" was, "I'm down the well, there's no light and I can't get up." He claimed that he deserved to be in hell. It was a just punishment for having brought about his mother's death. She had known there was a devil in him, having seen it in his eyes. She had been unable to stop him from corrupting the morals of those about him. At other times the overactivity gave way to withdrawal and inactivity. He would remain silent and if he did speak it was only to utter one or two phrases or sentences. His behavior reflected the presence of some degree of psychomotor retardation.

During the periods of overactivity he said there were

evil, destructive forces at work in the world which had to be contained. God had set him this task. He had to test people to see if they had integrity or were already corrupted. When he had an outburst of sexual excitement or aggression he put the responsibility on the deity—"God told me to wreck the place." The conflict between the drives on the one hand and the remaining ego organization and superego on the other was even evident when he was elated. The conflict was partly resolved by externalization and if more drastic measures were required, by a withdrawal of cathexis from drive and object representations. This led to the inactivity and to the retardation.

Prior to the illness the patient was a quiet, conscientious young man who had sustained a disappointment in being unable to reach the intellectual standard required for the profession of his choice. He had to accept a less satisfying occupation. Prior to his mother's death he was unemployed. Although usually cheerful in manner and sociable he was sensitive and had pronounced inferiority feeling particularly with respect to young women. He had revealed during the illness that his mother had acted as an "auxiliary ego" assisting in the maintenance of defense against the eruption of the drive derivatives—in his own words "she knew he was evil." Her death left him defenseless. Once the depression due to her loss had subsided a rapid and extensive regression ensued as a means of dealing with the danger created by the libido. This regression was rapid and extensive. It brought to light the conflict which heretofore had remained unconscious.

It may be assumed that this conflict was part of a fixation now activated by the regressive movement of the libidinal cathexes. The preoccupation with genitality pointed to a fixation at the phallic phase, while the numerous wish fulfillment fantasies suggested a fixation at a narcissistic stage where self and object are still competing for libidinal cathexis. There was evidence to favor the view that this narcissistic fixation had arisen as a substitute for and a defense against a libidinal cathexis of the mother. On the basis of this formulation the regression drew cathexis away from real object representations and resolved an immediate danger. At the same time it provoked a new danger by returning to fixations of which conflict was an integral part.

A further regression ensued leading for brief periods to the clinical picture of a simple mania. The natural tendency toward progression ("evolution" in Hughlings Jackson's terminology) revived the conflict and the danger. Defenses set in, leading to the appearance of depression and withdrawal. The sequence regression-progression-regression was repeated on numerable occasions over a period of many months.

In the case just described the manifestations of a simple mania were complicated by the effects of conflict. The question is whether such an explanation—the revival of conflicts arising from fixations—holds for cases of psychosis where there are delusions and hallucinations. In these states are the fixations specific for each case or are they identical in every case? Clinical observation supports the view that persecutory delusions and hallucinations follow from regression to fixations unique for the individual case. Before presenting clinical data which supports this hypothesis it should perhaps be pointed out that the fixations which give the symptoms their peculiar stamp need not have been created in the earliest phases of infancy (Niederland, 1959).

In order to study how the fixation of the libido contributes to the form and content of psychotic symptoms—particularly delusions and hallucinations with a critical and persecutory content—it is necessary to examine in detail cases where the clinical phenomena were more extensive than those of the patient just described.

Case 22

The case which will now be presented is that of a single, 21-year-old woman, an only child. The illness commenced three months after her mother's death. Symptoms appeared in 1963 when she was working in London at a temporary post until the University term began. The illness had an acute onset. She stopped eating and remained in bed. Her withdrawal, which reached a state of stupor, led to her being admitted to a mental hospital where the symptoms were relieved by electroconvulsive therapy. The illness was diagnosed as depression. She returned home and started at University. Although failing examinations at the end of the first year she passed on the second attempt. At the beginning of the second year she complained of nervousness which rapidly became intense.

At the time of this admission to hospital (now in her home town) in 1964 she presented with considerable anxiety and agitation. She revealed that she was very frightened of her father with whom she was living alone. She was obsessed with thoughts about homosexuality, a preoccupation which she attributed to books on psychology which she had to read for her degree course. She was convinced that her father had become a homosexual since her mother had died. At the same time she could not rid herself of the idea that she was also a homosexual. She said that for some days prior to coming to hospital she had a fear that her father might sexually assault her. Additionally she believed that her father was involved in some kind of criminal activity and that he would be put in jail.

After two months in hospital these ideas disappeared and she was discharged. Unfortunately she did not remain well. She was depressed in mood and worried about her health. She believed she had cancer (her mother had died of cancer). This state, which continued for some weeks, was replaced by elation of mood and psychomotor overactivity. It was this which led to her readmission to hospital. She was distractable, would not answer questions directly and would mutter to herself. When asked if she was depressed she pulled a face, let her head fall on her chest and suddenly burst into laughter. This elation passed and was replaced by disinterest and apathy. She neglected her appearance, was inattentive and self-preoccupied. Again the psychomotor overactivity and elation returned to be replaced once again by withdrawal. This sequence of symptoms was similar to that reported in the case described above. Gradually she recovered and was discharged after a period of eight months. During that time she did not express any of the ideas about homosexuality or about her father as on the previous admission.

Three months after discharge (1966) she fell ill once again. This attack occurred on the third anniversary of her mother's death. She had obtained work in a shop shortly after her return home from the hospital at the end of 1965. While at work she began to complain about the customers, accusing them of speaking about her in an unpleasant manner. The irrational nature of these accusations led to her dismissal. She told the doctor at the hospital that women who came into the shop were saying that she was a homosexual. She thought this must be true as she did feel attracted to some women. In the street she had the idea that a neighbor knew that she masturbated. At this time she was inactive and there was no elation or overactivity. However these phenomena appeared soon thereafter to be followed by the same cycle of mood and behavior changes as had previously occurred.

During the periods of psychomotor overactivity her thinking was omnipotent with resultant grandiose delusions. She generalized her affects and thoughts to external objects in just the same way as did the previous patient. During psychotherapeutic sessions with the writer there was a free expression of genital wishes. The frustration either led to anger or to withdrawal. The following material is illustrative—"Is it a good thing for an unmarried man and woman to live in the same house?" She was sure she embarrassed her father. At that moment she heard a voice say "dirty old man."

She freely admitted having genital feelings for her father. This frightened her. At this time curiosity about her father's sexual life and her wishes concerning him provided a vehicle for transference fantasies. She wondered if her father masturbated, did he think about women, etc. The first indication of her sexualization of her relationship with the writer was a joke about the door of the consulting room—"I didn't use to trust you . . . you know," she said. Soon she was declaring her genital needs—"I am attracted to you . . . are you a lecturer . . . perhaps a lecherer . . . I can see it in your eyes." While talking in this humorous vein she heard a voice saying "he's married." She continued, "I'm sexually frustrated . . . that E.C.T. made me lecherous." This latter remark indicates that her notion as to the writer's sexual arousal was a generalization of her own heightened drive state.

The increased tension due to genital arousal found expression in a constant need to micturate. She repeatedly had to excuse herself and leave the consulting room. She smoked incessantly. The smoking apparently relieved her feelings.

She accused the writer of causing her to have a headache—"You don't love me, you hate me . . . you are hurting me . . . frustrating me . . . you are hurting my head." She could not accept the idea that the writer was not excited by her and attracted to her. "You're attracted to me now," she said. When asked how she knew this she replied, "Do you hear the vacuum-cleaner [it had been switched on in the hall outside the consulting room]—it's the cleaning woman's movements causing it . . . she's a lover."

The patient was subject to auditory hallucinations which had a sexual content. Young men were talking about masturbation or a woman's voice said "she's a virgin." Usually the hallucinations made her laugh. She complained that television announcers interfered with her thinking. Again the interference was concerned with sexual topics—both heterosexual and homosexual.

In the overactive state sexuality found its principal outlet through masturbation. She exhibited herself in addition to masturbating. The frequency of micturition was a masturbatory equivalent. Innumerable fantasies accompanied masturbation. At home she had become excited at the thought that the young couple who lived below were having sexual intercourse. On one occasion she "heard" the man make a sound like a cow mooing. This was done by him, she explained, to convey the idea that she was a cow for eavesdropping. The masturbation carried considerable guilt and anxiety—"It has always made me feel I was odd . . . I wish I had no feelings." When anxieties were uppermost the psychomotor overactivity disappeared and she spoke quietly and at a normal speed. The fear of the inability to control her masturbatory urges found expression in the wish that she had someone to help her control herself. This applied to smoking: "I smoke too much—is morality behind it? . . .

I have indigestion from smoking . . . I smoke more than 20 a day . . . it's because of the stress, that's why I smoke so much in here." "What stress?" she was asked. "Sexual feelings . . . I feel about any man."

The illness arose when the patient's mother died. This event left her vulnerable to the threat of libidinal drive derivatives (fantasies and affects) as expressed through masturbation. Guilt from death wishes against the mother played a part in the depressive coloring of the initial phases of the illness. The danger provided by the libido was increased by the fact of her living alone with her father. For some time the danger was contained. The patient was depressed in mood and preoccupied with thoughts about homosexuality. Eventually a sudden and extensive regression occurred with the appearance of the psychosis proper.

The regression affected the quality of the libido, the ego-id, self-object differentiation and the superego. Fixations were at the phallic-oedipal phase and were recathected. The conflicts inherent in this fixation resulted in further regression to a preconflict stage. Recathexis of the conflict was reflected by the recurrence of misinterpretations and auditory hallucinations with a critical content. These manifestations emanated from a superego which had become externalized as a result of regression. In this case the merging of ego with id resulted in the loss of repression and the free outlet of libidinal wishes. Similarly the loss of the boundary between self and object precluded the employment of projection as a substitute for repression. In such a regressed state only generalization was possible as a defense against the superego.

In cases where there is extensive regression the loss of the ego results in hallucinatory phenomena which have as content memories of past acts of libidinal arousal and gratification. These hallucinations may occur in the auditory, tactile or visual modality. In the last case the patient experienced the sensations caused by an erect penis pressing against her lower abdomen. In another case which will now be described a male patient, when in bed at night, felt hands on his genitalia. The hands were usually those of a man but they frequently changed to those of a woman. This patient's illness was initiated when he hallucinated his penis being touched by a woman's hand. According to this patient an "electrode" had been placed in one or both ears while he was listening to his wireless by means of an earpiece. It was when he removed the earpiece that he felt the woman's hand on his penis. He believed that this "electrode" allowed certain persons to control him as they would a magnetized piece of metal. He claimed that he was being controlled by the church and the Archbishop in particular. He heard voices which suggested that he was Christ or that it was his task to populate the world. He felt that his entire body was controlled—both the voluntary and involuntary musculature. At times he was forced to walk like a woman and feared he might be turning into a woman. He believed that the influence could be removed if a probe was put into his ear and the "electrode" removed.

Here the regression in the sexual organization and in object relations was halted at fixations which had been created at the phallic and anal levels of the libido. A strong attachment to a grandmother and later to his mother had encouraged the development of passive sexual aims and so predisposed him toward an inverted Oedipus complex. Thus the fixation was in part composed of pronounced identification with the preoedipal mother. These object ties had obstructed the development of heterosexual relations of a permanent nature. The illness first occurred following his father's death. On recovery from this his feminine identifications found an outlet in looking after his mother and the house.

With the ego merging into the id and the failure of repression there was a revival of the wish to be a woman and the desire for passive sexual aims. This was reflected in his wish for a probe to be inserted into his ear and the "electrode" removed. A conflict developed once these passive-feminine drive derivatives were recathected. The outcome was the externalization of the drives. While externalization could not abolish the conscious impact of the drive derivatives as repression or projection would have done it brought about a dissociation of the affects and ideas from intent. The patient was now free of any wish to act like a woman or have passive genital wishes. The cause of whatever was experienced in the physical or mental spheres could now be safely attributed to outside sources.

In the psychoses it is the fixations which largely determine the content of delusional phenomena. Fantasies which were created in childhood on the basis of fixations of the libidinal drives and object relations will find a means of representation in the delusions. The patient may therefore disclose delusions with an oral-sadistic, anal-sadistic or phallic content. In the same way fantasies based on fixations affecting the object relations (family romance, rescue fantasies) can lead to delusions with an oedipal, preoedipal or narcissistic content. The way in which the content will finally be represented will depend on the extent to which the recathexis of these fantasies gives rise to conflict.

LIMITED REGRESSION

The study of psychotic states which result from an extensive regression shows that the changes which affect the self, the ego and superego may vary considerably from case to case. In some the disturbance of self-object discrimination is confined to an unimpeded movement of almost every aspect of mental and physical experience from the self to the object and vice versa. The patient does not appear to have lost the sense of self as such and he retains the ability to distinguish the self from the object. In other cases there is a loss of the capacity to view the self as quite distinct from the object. The elucidation and clarification of these phenomena is frequently obstructed by the patient's difficulty in clearly describing his subjective experiences. This makes it hard to know whether or not the generalization of mental and physical attributes is or is not accompanied by an actual physical merging with the object.

Changes within the ego vary with respect to the extent to which the ego abandons its secondary process characteristics and functions as part of the id. The degree to which this occurs will be governed by the limit to which the ego libido has regained its instinctual quality. The depth of the ego regression can be gauged by the occurrence of those hallucinations the content of which constitutes the memory of previous acts of libidinal arousal or gratification. Such phenomena reflect the action of drives governed by the primary process. They were observed in the second and third patients described above. In the female patient there was no sign of an ego defense. In the male patient the special kind of externalization which led to the formation of the persecutory delusions arose from an ego which was not sufficiently integrated or differentiated from the id to promote the action of repression or projection.

The regression which affects the superego may lead to different consequences. In some psychoses there is a complete decathexis of the superego. This may be transient or continue for a long period of time. Alternatively the superego may be externalized and sometimes decomposed into its constituent objects. The result will be misinterpretations of overheard speech, ideas of reference and auditory hallucinations. The effect of the regression is to abolish the sense of guilt. Its only expression is in the feeling of being criticized, spied upon, followed and talked about or the experiencing of auditory hallucinations. As will be seen later it is possible for a regression to take place in the superego while the ego functions remain virtually intact.

There are a variety of psychotic states where the regression is not as extensive or as deep as the cases which have been described. In these states the regression is confined to the libidinal cathexes with only a secondary effect on the ego and superego. As these psychoses have a relatively gradual onset it is possible to observe the connections which exist between the changes in quality of the libido on the one hand and the alterations in its distribution between self and object on the other hand. In those cases where there are sudden and extensive regressions it is easy to regard the changes in the ego and the superego as the decisive factor leading to symptom formation. In fact the ego disorganization is secondary to the changes affecting the quality and quantities of the libido. In the following case the relationship between the withdrawal of libidinal cathexes from real object representations (the change in libido distribution) and the libidinal regression (the change in quality) can be followed from the onset of the illness to the development of the delusional reality.

Case 23

The patient, Miss D., fell ill when she was 27 years of age. She was working as a bank clerk. About a year previously, at the age of 26, she was extremely upset when a man with whom she had been keeping company for about a year and a half and from whom she had expectations of marriage gave her up. She became depressed in mood, lost interest in work and in social activities. There was a slight improvement but about eight or nine months after the disappointment she announced to her family that her former lover had begun visiting her at the bank and at home. This mystified her parents as they had not seen him since he had abandoned the friendship. They were all the more concerned because the patient had taken to blaming herself for the termination of the affair and she would weep endlessly. She was taken on holiday but while at the hotel continued with her fantasy about Mr. K. (the friend). Convinced he was at the holiday resort, she was forever wanting to go out and look for him.

As these ideas did not disappear the patient was seen by her doctor who recommended that she be seen by a psychiatrist. The increasing preoccupation with the fantasy had led to an inability to concentrate at work and it was suggested she be admitted to hospital for treatment. This proved unsuccessful, the patient demanding that she be permitted to return home. As she was now quite unrealistic in her attitudes and refractory to rational argument a nurse companion was employed to look after her. After some months this nurse was substituted by a cousin (Miss B.) who later came to play an important part in the patient's delusional reality. The illness increased in severity with the appearance of negativism, inattention and complete self-preoccupation. Management at home became impossible and she was again admitted to hospital.

At this stage of the illness a complete withdrawal of libido from the representations of external objects had taken place. The libidinal cathexes were wholly invested in the representation of the lost love object (Mr. K.). There was no libido available to promote interest in people, things or activities. From a descriptive standpoint the ego was decathected. The withdrawal and the negativism were also motivated by intense hatred directed against the parents and relatives who were regarded as being the cause of her separation from the love object. The reproaches which were later made against the relatives in the delusional reality consisted of the memories of the criticisms which she made of them at this early phase of the illness. Periodic outbursts of anger and the demand for an immediate union with her lover pointed to the fact that some degree of change had already affected the quality of the libido. On such occasions of rage it was clear from the state of the cognitive process (speech, etc.) that the ego functions had not succumbed to regression.

Miss D. remained in hospital for a period of about a year and three months. The admission note recorded that "she is depressed and negativistic . . . she speaks in a low voice in a hesitating manner, quite coherently and without any formal disorder of talk other than retardation (thought blocking) which is marked. She states that she is very unhappy and she looks depressed . . . her only spontaneous remark was that she did not want to be here, that she wanted to go home." When asked how long she had been ill she did not reply but after a minute or more said quite inappropriately—"I thought I heard him last night" (the night following admission).

During her stay in hospital she continued feeling resentful about her commitment and remained uncooperative. On several occasions she insisted that someone was downstairs waiting to see her. She angrily accused medical and nursing staff of preventing her from seeing a "certain person" whom she would not name—presumably Mr. K. Her mental condition deteriorated with increasing withdrawal and refusal to eat. She admitted to hearing her relatives' voices and she would get angry. A gradual improvement took place and she was discharged from hospital. She remained at home for about two years. During that time she kept house for her father and brother. The mother to whom she was deeply attached had died when Miss D. was 20 years old. A relapse was announced by her accusing her maternal uncle, Mr. A., of interfering in her affairs. She became abusive and impossible to manage. This led to her readmission to hospital.

The content of Miss D.'s utterance prior to her readmission to hospital and a letter which she had written to one of the doctors indicated that the preceding period in hospital had provided new material for the delusional reality which now found expression. A new love object had been cathected. This was Dr. P. who had been concerned with Miss D.'s treatment. This object cathexis was confined entirely to fantasy and never had a reality basis. The letter which was found read as follows: "Dear Dr. P., Do come for me, I would be glad if you would take me to 'C.' I would be an assistant maid in the doctors quarters. I have my print frock to take with me. Yours sincerely." Further details of the delusional reality will be described below. For several years Miss D. remained in hospital where she continued to be uncooperative, negativistic and aggressive in manner. She hallucinated and would sometimes refer to the "voices" as her enemies. Later she lived at her sister's home until her disturbed condition required that she be hospitalized once again.

Miss D. had little interest in real persons except insofar as they may have been able to bring about the realization of her fantasy wishes. It was this possibility that encouraged her to tell the writer the details of her psychotic reality. Miss

D. had converted Mr. K.—the former lover—into the role of persecutor. He was in league with her uncle Mr. A. and her cousin Miss B. They conspired to prevent her from being reunited with Dr. P. Miss D. was not put out by the fact that Mr. K. and her uncle were now dead. She said they were evil spirits and continued their victimization of her. They talked to her and this made her angry. She explained that K. hated her because she had preferred Dr. P. K. cursed her and said evil things. She had never liked him but he had always pushed himself upon her. Now K. never leaves her in peace. Her cousin, Miss B., was jealous of Dr. P. B. had chased the patient into hospital so that she could get Dr. P. for herself. Miss D. was particularly annoyed by the fact that K., her uncle and cousin constantly criticized Dr. P. to her—"You wouldn't like it," she said to the writer "if you were going with someone and others talked about you all the time. They say Dr. P. takes drink."

In contrast to the criticism and aggression from K., A. and B. all the communications from Dr. P. were pleasant and agreeable—"He says nice things to me." She would not reveal details beyond saying that she had him in her mind's eye. He was handsome. She was not disturbed by the fact that she had not seen him for a great many years. The content of the auditory hallucination attributed to Dr. P. usually reflected her own wishes—"He says he is coming to take me away." After Dr. P. had spoken to her, either K., B. or A. would speak. What they would say always upset Miss D. Usually it was to contradict everything Dr. P. had said. Miss D. said they pretended to be friendly, particularly K., but he hated her because she had rejected him in favor of Dr. P. She easily transferred feelings from the persecutors to doctors and nurses. A doctor and a ward sister were hated because they interfered with her affairs. She accused one doctor of not telling her when Dr. P. had come to the hospital to take her away—"I hate Dr. L. and Sister Q.; they are deceitful and enemies."

When Miss D.'s illness had reached its full development the libidinal cathexes wholly invested the delusional object representations. There was little cathexis available for external objects except when they became involved in the psychotic reality. The withdrawal of cathexis from real persons had occurred concurrently with a change in the quality of the ego libido due to regression. This regression brought about a partial loss of the ego. Repression failed and there was a concomitant disinterest in external reality and in the means of communicating with that reality (i.e., the cognitive functions). At no time was there a loss of the capacity to differentiate between self and objects. It was perhaps because of this that projection was the principal means whereby contact with the object representations was regained and the defense against unwanted drive derivatives instituted.

In this case the initial defense against object loss was withdrawal of object cathexis. The aggression engendered by the disappointment was turned in on the self. Later projection had the effect of removing the memory of the loss and its effect from consciousness. At the same time it allowed for externalization of the aggression thereby changing love to hate. The underlying libidinal cathexis remained although altered by the impact of projection and as a result of having found a substitute object in the representation of Dr. P.

The content of the delusional reality suggested that narcissistic fixations had occurred in childhood to act as a defense against traumata associated with the Oedipus complex (the patient, Mr. K. and Miss B.). The regression which occurred led to the cathexis of these fixations and determined the content of the delusions. Such information as was available pointed to the likelihood that Miss D. had reverted in the psychosis to preoedipal fixations which comprised a deep, dependent attachment to the mother. The choice of Mr. K. was based on narcissism and the mother attachment. As in all cases of psychosis it was the fixations which determined the content of the delusions and hallucinations whereas the psychotic reality was the outcome of the libidinal drive toward the restitution of object relations.

Regression, Defense and Symptom Formation

Psychoses begin immediately after unsuccessful attempts to bring about repression. This failure occurs because the regression which has affected the libidinal cathexis of the ego eliminates wholly or partly the distinction between ego and id. The ego functions (cognition) are no longer cathected by libido in the service of the secondary process. The result is a virtual decathexis of the ego functions with a resultant loss of active attention, conceptual thinking, differentiated perception and control over motility. These ego functions are then cathected by instinctual libido with the appearance of disorders of word form, misidentifications, etc.

The failure of repression permits the entry into consciousness of regressed drive, self- and object representations. Whether or not conflict will be provoked depends on the depth as well as the extent of the regression. There will be no conflict or defensive activity if the regression proceeds to a stage where self and object merge and where the libidinal drives have purely instinctual aims—a state akin to the infantile phase of need satisfaction. Once ego and object become partially redifferentiated conflict will occur and defense ensue.

The form to be assumed by the defense will depend on

whether or not the regression has or has not caused a far-reaching fusion of self and object. In those cases where the merging is considerable that form of externalization will act as a defense which permits the attribution of responsibility to real or fantasy objects. This defense does not prevent the affects or the ideational derivatives of the drives from reaching consciousness. In other psychoses where regression is limited and self-object discrimination remains (see case 23) projection substitutes for faulty repression. Where projection is operative there is no awareness in consciousness of the drive derivatives. In this respect projection acts like repression (Glover, 1949).

The close relationship which exists between regression and defense may be observed in the aims of the defense mechanisms. In the healthy, and in patients suffering from neuroses, attribution of responsibility (externalization) and projection act purely in a defensive role. When these mechanisms function in psychoses they also act defensively and in so doing determine the content of delusions and the misinterpretations of overhead speech and environmental events. The prior withdrawal of object cathexis, its change in quality and the concurrent regression of the ego libido provide the preconditions for such developments. Such movements and changes in the libidinal cathexis of object and ego do not occur in the neuroses. Under the regressed conditions existing in psychoses the libido cannot find its way to the real object because of the conflicts and dangers associated with it. Projection and externalization then become the means of restoring the libidinal cathexis to the object. The primary process nature of the cathexis leads to the belief in the reality of the object relationship. The mental mechanisms which act as defenses in the neurotic or in the healthy individual also carry out the task of restitution in psychoses.

Psychotic symptoms can be classified with respect to their relationship to the predominant defense organization, to danger situations and to conflicts. They can also be categorized in accordance with their relationship to regressions and fixations. Regression creates two different groups of symptoms. The negative symptoms result from the effect of the regression on the ego functions and the drive derivatives which are necessary for harmonious interpersonal relations. Some positive symptoms are similar in their form to the mental functions of early childhood. Merging of self and object, need-satisfying behavior and the results of the primary process are illustrative. The regression also leads to the cathexis of fixations which arose in the course of the development of the sexual organization and object relations. The positive symptoms to which these fixations ultimately give rise—delusions, hallucinations and catatonic signs—do not spring from regression alone but are the consequence of the defensive actions which follow conflict. The speed and the extent of the regressions provide another dimension along which symptoms can be classified.

The cathexis of fixation points by the regressing libido probably occurs no differently in psychosis than it does in neurosis. The decisive difference is that in the psychoses the libidinal regression may include object and self-representations, drives, the ego and the superego. Once the fixations are cathected they lead to conflict. The fixations are specific for each case and to some extent determine the depth of their regression. It is unlikely that the content of all psychoses can be traced back to fixation points common to all at the earliest periods of infantile life. Such a view is not supported by the heterogenous nature of the clinical phenomena or by the analytic study of individual cases.

In Chapter one an alternative explanation was presented

to account for the appearance of undifferentiated and primitive forms of drive and ego activity in psychoses. Reference was made to the theory that these manifestations did not result from one or another kind of regression but rather from a dissolution or destruction of the advanced levels of mental life which subserve psychosocial and psychosexual activity. Such an explanation, however, does not negate the proposition that these clinical manifestations are nothing other than the reappearance of modes of cognition and object relating which predominated at some point in the childhood of the individual patient—that in fact the effect of the dissolution is to expose fixations of the drives and the ego.

The use of such concepts as regression and dissolution implies that in the individual case a more advanced state of mental development is present in the preillness period than existed during the psychosis. Anna Freud (personal communication) has pointed out that psychoses may appear first, as a consequence of an arrest in the advance of the drives and the ego in early or late childhood; second, after considerable development has occurred as in adolescence and early adult life and third, after the development of the personality seems complete as in adult life. Only in the last two instances would regression be involved as an explanatory concept. Here as has been demonstrated patients frequently exhibit phenomena which have the characteristics of the oedipal period and the genital organization of the libido. The significance of these findings has been a constant source of controversy. Do they indicate that the patient had, prior to the illness, reached such an advanced developmental level or do they have some other significance?

In some cases, as illustrative clinical data have shown, the libido has advanced to an oedipal-phallic level but it has failed to find expression in the initiation and maintenance of a real object relationship. Neurotic symptoms and inhibitions of various kinds typically characterize such patients prior to the psychosis. In these cases the clinical phenomena, i.e., the oedipal content of delusions can be understood as resulting from the loss of repression. In other cases this explanation is unsatisfactory. Here the oedipal fantasies are accompanied by drive activity which is more appropriate to early phases of the sexual organization. Ideas and behavior are driven by libidinal cathexes whose sole aim is immediate satisfaction; there is an intolerance of frustration and a relative indifference for the object. The genital zone acts merely as a means for the expression of these pregenital libidinal drives. The differences between patients can be attributed to the effects of regression on the one hand and to the kind of libidinal and ego development (including the fixations) which obtained prior to the illness on the other.

CHAPTER 9

The Profile, Symptomatology, Treatment and Research

The majority of the cases of psychosis described in earlier chapters were studied by means of the completion of profiles. The profiles amplified and connected the clinical phenomena which ordinarily would be obtained by routine case taking. Many of the cases presented with psychomotor overactivity or with a paranoid symptom complex. In those patients where psychomotor overactivity was the leading clinical feature the completed profiles provided details of the phenomena which constituted the content of the abnormal motility. Impatience for the immediate satisfaction of needs, the aggressive reactions to disappointment and frustration, the heightened sexuality, both genital and pregenital, were correlated with the existing cognitive state and with conflict, if and when it was present. These manifestations were more readily identifiable as were their interrelationships whenever they were recognized as reflecting special modes of action of the object libidinal cathexes, of the ego and superego, and were recorded in the appropriate sections of the profile schema.

Symptomatology

When dramatic changes occurred in the symptomatology, profile studies revealed the continuity between one phase of the illness and that which followed. If overactivity was replaced by withdrawal, retardation, negativism and catalepsy or elation was followed by depression of mood, completed profiles demonstrated that the new phenomena were the consequence of attempts to provide a defense organization by means of which the regressed drive representations could be contained. The cause of this defensive activity in individual cases could not always be attributed to the superego. In some patients the depression of mood which occurred during or following a period of psychomotor overactivity was not necessarily accompanied by self-reproach.

In the case of patients presenting with persecutory symptom complexes the profile facilitated a comprehensive description of the clinical state. Beyond this, however, profiles showed that persecutory syndromes have a much more complicated development than the syndrome of psychomotor overactivity with its wishful delusions and elation of mood. Except at acute onset or relapse regression was not the only significant influence in (persecutory) symptom formation. Conflict, the influence of the superego or its regressed equivalent and defenses could be discerned and the distribution of libido between self and object correspondingly affected. In some cases further regression occurred as a means of relieving conflict. When this happened there was a change in the clinical picture. Psychomotor overactivity in varying degrees, instinctual expression, affect and grandiose delusions appeared. Here again the profile revealed the essential continuity of the process of illness. Additionally the profile helped in the differentiation of paranoid cases with respect to the extent to which the superego played the major role as the instigator of conflict.

From the profile studies it was possible to identify different forms of interpersonal relationship as they existed during the psychosis and correlate them with the remaining clinical phenomena. Symptom complexes were not characterized by one specific form of relating to others. Relating at the need-satisfying level, for example, occurred equally often in a paranoid syndrome as it did in one in which there was an abnormal psychomotility. The same circumstance applied in the case of patients whose relating was less with real persons than with delusional figures or where there was a residue of reality-oriented drive behavior, thinking and affect. The form assumed by the pathological modes of relating and any changes which occurred were shown by the profiles to be the result of changes in the cathexis of self and object, to regressions and to defenses.

The case of Mrs. A. described in Profile No. 2 provided an illustration of how the changes in libidinal distribution altered the manner of relating and the clinical manifestations. After the period of hospitalization during which the profile was constructed Mrs. A. returned home. She was free of the symptoms described in the profile. Gradually she became withdrawn, showed signs of psychomotor retardation and complained that the neighbors were against her and her children. She felt alone and a stranger in the housing estate where she lived. She agreed to return to hospital although she was reluctant to leave her children. While in hospital she did not show the heightened eroticism or the misidentifications which were detailed in the profile. She complained of a loss of interest, depression of mood and wanted to return home to her family. Here there was neither the radical redistribution of libidinal cathexes between self and object nor the change in their quality as had occurred during the previous admission. The representations of her children and husband retained their cathexis. On this occasion Mrs. A. talked about her dissatisfaction with her husband and home, her loneliness, her attachment to her mother and the bitterness she felt against her father for squandering the family resources. The conflicts which had led to the earlier attack were apparent. In the psychotic state described in the profile the reaction to the dangers created by libidinal frustration and fear of object loss was a cathectic upheaval involving the redistribution and change in quality of the libido. This did not occur in the relapse. Object cathexis was retained.

Profiles are not primarily concerned with problems of nosology. They do however offer a means of examining psychoses which on descriptive grounds are allocated to the categories of schizophrenia, paranoid psychosis and manic-depression. The cases described in earlier chapters confirm the widely held view that each of these nosological entities is in fact a heterogenous collection of abnormal mental states. Only the presence of a particular symptom complex and a characteristic course of illness allows widely differing conditions to be brought together under one of the three diagnostic categories.

Although many more profiles will need to be completed before firm conclusions can be reached there are indications that the psychopathological process which results in the break with reality is identical in every case. The course of the illness, the nature of the symptomatology, its manner of expression, form and content, however, depends on many other factors which are unique for the individual patient. Profiles make allowance for the isolation of these factors in directing special attention to the dynamics and economics of the drives, to the ego and the superego characteristic of the prepsychotic personality. This requires information about childhood fantasies, experiences and conflicts. Many of these fantasies and experiences find their way into the psychotic reality. It is knowledge of the prepsychotic conflicts which shows that the psychosis is the outcome of an alternative method of dealing with a danger situation which previous measures have been unable to contain. Whether a remission will occur, whether there will be a change in the symptomatology or ensuing chronicity, will depend on the extent to which the threat caused by the libidinal and aggressive drives can be relieved.

TREATMENT

Provision of a systematic psychoanalytic evaluation of the individual case profiles should be able to supply material assistance in the selection of cases for treatment and contribute to all forms of therapeutic endeavor. In particular the profile helps to differentiate those cases where there has been an actual arrest of libidinal development or where the ego functions have failed to complete their maturation. Patients presenting phenomena due to such ego deficiencies may be easily confused with cases of functional psychosis where the regression of the drives, ego and superego, and the reactions which are engendered, leads to the clinical manifestations. In cases of arrested libidinal development treatment presents special problems. Where there is an actual defect in the ego due to faulty maturation therapy has only a limited value.

Patients suffering from psychoses can be differentiated descriptively according to whether or not the illness is in an acute phase or in what Eissler (1951) described as a "state of relative clinical muteness." The acute phase corresponds, as Eissler points out, to that phase of a psychosis where the libidinal drives have abandoned real persons, changed their quality, and cathected aspects of the self- and object representations which come to comprise the delusional reality. This acute phase may be transient or persist for many years.

When the patient is in the "acute phase" possibilities of a systematic psychotherapy or psychoanalysis are virtually nonexistent. The regression which has affected the drives and the consequent restitutional tendencies bring about a complete break with previous mental experience. It is as if the patient has become a completely different person and one who is divorced not only from reality but from his immediate and distant past. He is totally preoccupied with the delusional ideas and is convinced of their reality. He is refractory to all attempts to bring him into contact with his immediate environment as he knew it prior to the attack. It is at this time that the patient will generalize, attribute aspects of the self or project unwanted drives to the physician. The degree of response to nonspecific psychotherapeutic measures will in part depend upon the extent to which there still exists libidinal cathexes which follow the secondary process (the nonpsychotic elements).

In the majority of psychotic illnesses the symptoms of the "acute" phase diminish in intensity or vanish altogether. This may occur spontaneously or with treatment usually of a physical kind. This change is due, as was described in the chapter on defense, either to a diminution in the intensity of the drives or to the reinstatement of adequate defensive measures. When these defenses provide only minimal safeguards against potential inner dangers the patient passes into the state of "relative clinical muteness." This condition is easily mistaken for a remission. It is the patient's sensitivity to others, his disinclination to reflect on his subjective experiences, his lack of interest, volitional inadequacy and continued belief in the reality of the earlier delusional ideas which betray the fact that the illness is still active.

The stage of "relative clinical muteness" is not an invariable sequel to the acute psychotic phase. In a large number of psychotic states the quality of the remission is such as to allow the patient insight into the fact of having been ill and also of recognizing the irrational nature of the preceding thinking and behavior.

Case 24

The following case is illustrative. The patient was a married woman, aged 37, who had recently obtained a divorce from her husband. They had been married for 15 years. There were two children of the marriage, a boy aged seven and a girl of five who was mentally retarded. Prior to the attack, which will now be described, the patient spent three brief periods in a psychiatric hospital throughout the previous year. She was hospitalized because she believed that her husband was gradually becoming effeminate, turning into a homosexual and that he was going to attack and kill her. There was considerable anxiety and periodic depression of mood. The present attack to be described was characterized by psychomotor overactivity. Her mood alternated between cheerfulness and sadness. The content of her speech was limited to her husband, children and omnipotent ideas. The following was illustrative of her speech at this time—"Do you know what the 11 November means? It is the day I died . . . I divorced my husband . . . I won my husband back . . . his secretary is only 24 and he is 38. She told me she liked my children. . . . I have a mentally retarded daughter . . . I am going to commit suicide . . . my brother wanted me to believe in God but I could not . . . I want to appear on television hand in hand with my husband and say we believe in God. Neither of us could understand the other. I am God . . . I am the son of God. . . . I have no religion but I can prove that I am God."

The overactivity subsided within a few days, the patient becoming tearful and anxious. She thought the nurses were going to poison her because she talked too much. She was self-reproachful. This state was followed by a phase during which she rarely spoke, refused to eat or take any form of medication. She continued to gesture and exhibited cataleptic phenomena. During this period the following words were expressed—"My mother has put a tape on my mouth and has forbidden me to say anything. I loved my husband and tried to be a perfect wife . . . I am speaking the truth . . . mother please forgive me . . . if I die the whole world crashes." Speech was rare while she remained in this state. Within a week, however, the psychomotor overactivity returned.

While the overactivity remained real persons were cathected by libidinal drives which sought immediate satisfactions. The primary process nature of the drives had the effect of causing a condensation of real persons and the representations of son and husband. The patient misidentified the attending psychiatrist. She addressed him as her seven-year-old son. She overcame the discrepancy in the ages of psychiatrist and son by saying that he had now grown up and had become a doctor. She freely expressed her need for genital satisfaction—"I can't stay here with you . . . I want your father . . . I don't want to do it alone, I want to do it with your father . . . I want to be with your father not with you." Later this preference for her husband disappeared and she continually made sexual advances to the psychiatrist while still identifying him as her son. Pregenital needs, mostly of an oral type, with active aims appeared. The wish for sexual satisfaction was accompanied by pregnancy fantasies which had a delusional intensity—"He is giving me a baby," she said. References to pregnancy and the need to have an abortion were frequently made.

She misidentified the writer with an older man she had met when previously in a mental hospital. In the postpsychotic period this object representation served as a means for the expression of transference thoughts. While misidentifying the psychiatrist as her son she would frequently become tearful and unhappy—"P. . . . my son . . . do I have to tell anything more . . . you are my son, my son . . . I want you." Concurrent with these misidentifications the grandiose delusions appeared as a result of the cathexis of ego-ideal representations. She was God, Christ and President Nixon. This cathexis of masculine representations accorded with the predominant sexual organization and with fixations which characterized the prepsychotic personality.

The externalization of various aspects of the bodily and mental self onto real persons did not have a defensive aim. External conflict was frequent usually because of the genital frustration from which she suffered. She became angry when these needs were not met—"I'm fed up . . . why are you scared of me . . . will you marry me . . . I know I am pregnant . . . I haven't had a man for six months. . . . I am the Lord Jesus Christ. . . . I love you . . . my husband married that bitch. . . . I am the Lord Jesus Christ." In these utterances was reflected the process whereby libidinal (phallic) drive cathexes, failing to find an outlet through a real person, returned to the self and caused a grandiose delusion. This change in the distribution of cathexes between self and object acted as a defense against the danger caused by frustration. Similarly the decathexis of the real person and the cathexis of the representations of son and husband alleviated the effects of object loss. The self-cathexis also had the aim of alleviating the danger of object loss.

In the prepsychotic period the object cathexis was narcissistic in nature. Both husband and son represented the masculine, active, phallic aspects of the self. The birth of a defective daughter had impaired this narcissism, predisposing the patient for subsequent attacks of depression. These depressions were initially due to fear of object loss (the husband's frequent absence from home) and to its ultimate occurrence (his taking up with another woman). The psychosis began shortly after her divorce proceedings were finalized. The immediate precipitant of the manic attack was the following incident. While she was working as a waitress she served a woman who was accompanied by a little girl who appeared to be mentally defective. The woman told the patient she had cancer and feared for the child's future. It was immediately following this that the patient fell ill.

This patient's psychotic symptoms gradually disappeared. In the subsequent period she appreciated that she had been mentally ill and recognized that her thinking and behavior had been the product of illness. She complained of feeling tense, ill at ease, anxious and occasionally depressed in mood. She felt the need for further help.

In contrast to this kind of case there are others, as previous examples have illustrated, where the reaction to object loss or some other danger situation consists of the sudden appearance of grandiose and persecutory delusions with auditory hallucinations. There may be psychomotor overactivity or withdrawal and negativism. The completion of profiles in such cases throws light on the state of the libidinal distribution which followed the libidinal regression. Significant is whether or not the drive derivatives cathect real persons (identified correctly or not) or whether they cathect the representations of real or fantasy objects. The former situation will be reflected either in need-satisfying behavior or anxiety in relation to real persons who may or may not be condensed with other representations while the latter leads to a preoccupation with delusional objects and auditory hallucinations. This state of the libido distribution can be compared with that which obtained in the prepsychotic period as can the sexual organization and the ego.

Profiles will show whether or not fixations have been recathected with the consequent action of defenses. As has been described in previous reports these are the cases where the conflict which led to the danger situation was not relieved by the regression. The conflict finds a new representation following the regression with an ultimate expression in delusions and hallucinations. When these acute symptoms subside the situation most adequately fits the concept of "the phase of relative clinical muteness."

In the chapters on "Object Cathexis" and on "Defense" reference has already been made to the reactions which patients in an acute state present when they are offered the opportunity of systematic psychotherapy and the likely reasons for their occurrence. A case in point is provided by a young woman patient whose acute symptoms consisted of passivity experiences, grandiose delusions with acute excitement alternating with profound withdrawal and catatonic signs.

Case 25

The patient, a single woman of 21, was admitted to hospital following an outburst of excitement. She had previously been unwell but the dramatic symptoms had subsided after a period of treatment. In hospital she strutted about the wards in an exhibitionistic manner claiming all kinds of exceptional powers. Mostly, however, she refused to get out of bed where she would lie stiffly, occasionally adopting unusual postures. She was often incontinent of urine and was observed to masturbate almost continuously.

As the severe manifestations abated it was possible to obtain some details of the psychotic reality. At times she gave the impression of having some insight into the fact of being ill while at other times she was quite unaware of the irrational content of her speech. She said that her actions, thoughts and feelings were being controlled by mysterious forces which she did not understand. She misidentified the other patients as agents of these powers and this led to her attacking patients and nurses. In a clearer phase she said that she had thought the hospital was a concentration camp and that the writer wanted to gain power over her mind. She had the delusion that a Goddess—Athene—was protecting her. Even she, however, controlled the patient's actions. When she twisted her fingers together she said—"Athene is moving my fingers . . . it's not me." After a silence she said, "I am struck with lightning again . . . I can't talk I was lightninged before I came to the hospital."

During this acute phase the cathexis of reality was totally abandoned. Cathexes invested the self- and fantasy objects only. The regression which occurred revived fixations characterized by oedipal-like (family romance) fantasies. In its regressed state the libido found an ideational expression through these fantasies and a physical outlet through the act of masturbation. The regression, instead of resolving conflict as had occurred in other cases, led to new dangers. The sexual stimulation was attributed to outside forces as was any other unwanted action, thought or affect. In the prepsychotic period the patient had cathected real persons as a possible means of need satisfaction but they remained purely in the realm of fantasy. As in previous cases the cathexis of wishful fantasies formed in childhood and adolescence acted as a defense against disappointment and object loss.

The acute phase was followed by a state in which the patient was without interests, inclined to neglect her appearance and remain apart from others. She showed no intiative of any kind. When approached she was quite friendly but never showed signs of animation facially or in speech. Over a period of two years repeated attempts were made to encourage her to participate in psychotherapy. These attempts which lasted for weeks or months all ended in failure. The coherent and intelligible speech which was in evidence during casual contact was rarely sustained in the "treatment" sessions. Soon she would begin to speak so quietly that it would be difficult to hear what she said. One sentence would merge into the next or there would be no continuity between phrases. After some days normal speech would return but then it would be limited in quantity only appearing in reply to questions. For the most part she sat in silence. This reluctance to participate increased until she refused to attend further.

Another attempt was made some months later when the patient gave the impression of having improved mentally. She had become friendly with some other patients, was holding conversations with them and seemed to be taking an interest in her appearance. When approached by the writer she was cheerful and agreed to resume meetings with him. She said that she realized that she had not been well. She felt the cause for her illness was her overimagination but stated that she now had "a more sensible head." During the ensuing weeks she continued to be communicative but the content of what she said consisted of a repetition of a few themes—about her parents' new house and looking forward to going home. Gradually she became silent but in addition it was noticed that she was becoming restless and agitated. The nursing staff reported that she was irritable with them and had taken to marching up and down the ward in the exhibitionistic fashion which had occurred after her admission. She threatened to strike other patients and on one occasion impulsively attacked a television engineer who had come to repair a television set. One day the writer found her some distance from the ward in a disturbed condition. He suggested that she return to the ward and come to the consulting room for a talk. She did not respond to this suggestion. For want of something to say he asked her if her mother was visiting on that day. This made her very angry. She shouted—"Why should I want to see her?—I don't like her, she's too bossy." This hostility, displaced on the writer at that moment, became more apparent in the succeeding days. It eventually led to her refusing to see him any more.

Some time later when she had settled down another attempt was made to resume the meetings. On this occasion the reason for the eventual break was clear in contrast to the two previous times. After some weeks she accused the writer of making her masturbate by causing her to have sexual feelings. Neurotic patients undergoing psychoanalytic treatment may also express this fantasy but they do not believe it to be true. This accusation was followed by the reappearance of passivity experiences and by the delusion that she was pregnant. At this time she gave the impression that she was rapidly passing into an acute stage of the illness. This was avoided by the use of drugs which led to a reversion to the previous state of apathy and disinterest. Several further attempts were made to promote a treatment relationship but all failed because usually she would neither speak nor attend.

With the first patient described above, the opportunity

to engage in a systematic psychotherapy was readily taken up. Her attitude and approach was little different from that of a patient suffering from a neurosis. Awareness of the fact of having been ill and the persistence of anxiety acted as an incentive to participate in treatment. Unlike some patients whose remission is not materially different in nature she was not unduly anxious about the therapy itself. She did not repeatedly ask for reassurance as is often the case or advice as to how she should conduct her life. During the first session she quickly entered into an account of her relations with her husband and children. In this she showed that the continuity of mental experience had not been damaged by the illness. However, she still believed that her husband had altered insofar as he seemed to be more effeminate and in her mind femininity was equated with homosexuality. This change toward effeminacy was not accompanied by any loss of potency on her husband's part and she could not account for it. She was, however, willing to examine this supposed change. Subsequently it became clear that the change occurred when her husband was spending a lot of time away from home with the woman he was eventually to marry. The change in the husband which the patient experienced was no doubt brought about by an externalization of the masculine (phallic) aspects of the patient's self-representations. This can be regarded as the first sign of the regressive (defensive) trend which came to affect the libido and the ego organization. At the same time the delusional idea acted as a defense against the fear of object loss. If the husband was a homosexual then he could not be interested in another woman. This interpretation based on dynamic considerations was acceptable to the patient and led to insight.

The behavior of the second patient stands in contrast to what has just been described. She feared contact with real persons. The third attempt to initiate psychotherapy showed that one reason for this dread sprang from libidinal arousal. Here the libidinal drives were almost entirely instinctual in their quality. Only a fraction of these drives followed the secondary process and allowed some degree of ego functioning. The defense against the arousal, as was noted in similar cases, consisted of a detachment of cathexes from both drive and object representations. The decathexis of the drives resulted in apathy and volitional defect while the decathexis of real persons led to the inattention and the disinterest in external objects. The alteration in the quality of the ego libido, when there was arousal, led to that disorganization which disrupts the communicative function of speech.

The hypothesis that it was libidinal (heterosexual) arousal which led to the reemergence of acute symptoms and disruption of the treatment received support from the observation of the patient's reaction to psychotherapy when offered by a female psychiatrist. The initial behavior was quite different from that encountered by the writer. The patient was relaxed, talked freely and only occasionally was the flow of speech disturbed by thought blocking or inappropriate associations. Over several weeks she revealed more of herself and her life experiences than she had during numerous periods of hospitalization. This information confirmed earlier speculations regarding the significance of "oedipal-like" conflicts in promoting the symptoms of the illness. Unfortunately the treatment could not be continued as the dramatic improvement resulted in the patient's being taken home by her parents.

When patients suffering from schizophrenic illnesses of this kind are compared with cases of hysteria (hysterical depressions, etc.) the outstanding difference consists in the absence, in the former, of clinical manifestations which can be attributed to a resistance to the emergence of transference fantasies with a sexual content. Prior to the appearance of these fantasies in cases of neurosis there is a period of intense resistance which may take the form of aggressive attitudes, silences, critical remarks and accusations against the analyst. At times the treatment is in jeopardy. It is this resistance which points to the presence of an effective anti-cathexis. Following the resolution of the resistance the repressed ideation and affect emerges initially in connection with the analyst. In severe psychotic states such a stable anticathexis is lacking. The upsurge of libidinal drives has to be countered. The result of the measures directed to this end are withdrawal, negativism and persecutory delusions.

The fact that there are patients suffering from psychoses who can join in a systematic psychotherapy indicates that the passing of the acute phase is accompanied by the reconstitution of the anticathexis (repression) which holds the drives in check and guarantees the integrity of the ego. However when repressed libidinal drives are subsequently activated in the therapy, with the psychiatrist as their object, the resulting manifestations are quite different from those found in the treatment of a neurosis. Phenomena similar to those characterizing the more severe psychoses occur and they may be passing in nature. It is as if there is a momentary return to the acute phase. When the treatment survives the danger situations which led to the acute phase, symptomatology can be alleviated. The means by which this takes place is still a matter for speculation. For some it is the outcome of the working through of infantile conflict in the transference while for others it is the result of identifications with the therapist which help to strengthen the anticathexis.

RESEARCH

Metapsychological studies of psychotic states provide an alternative to the descriptive approach on which reliance is usually placed in research in this field. Much current research suffers because the subjects of study are erroneously held to be suffering from the same abnormality, for example, schizophrenia. Profile studies show, and an illustration will be provided below, that identical symptomatology does not by any means indicate a similarity in the underlying psychopathology. Symptom complexes (catatonic, depressive, manic, paranoid) are all too easily equated with disease entities.

In order to achieve a formulation which embraces the symptoms as well as the patient, patients should be examined according to the following criteria. Each case must be studied in terms of the degree to which the drives, ego and superego have attained, in the preillness period, that level of development which provides an optimal measure of psychosocial and psychosexual adaptation. A distinction can then be made between cases where the symptoms result from an arrest in drive or ego development (sometimes based on faulty endocrine or neurological development) and those where the clinical phenomena are due to regressions affecting drive and ego functions.

The second criterion encompasses the effect of regression, its speed and extent. The speed can be gauged by the manner of onset of the illness, while the extent of the regression depends upon whether or not ego-id differentiation, self-object discrimination and the superego are all affected or not. The depth of the regression will be reflected by the presence or absence of internalized conflicts and the kinds of fixations which have been revived by the libido. It can also be assessed by noting the state of the libidinal distribution between self and objects. The cases can then be distinguished according to whether or not there is a continuing cathexis of real object representations, whether the objects cathected are of a fantasy nature or whether the libidinal cathexis is confined to one or more aspects of the self-representations.

The kind of danger situation which resulted in attempts at repression and so to regression comprise the third criterion. Cases can be distinguished on the basis of whether or not the danger arose from heightened libidinal cathexis or from the fear of or actual object loss. With regard to the former danger the specific libidinal drive involved and the nature of its objects and aims may spring from any one of the forms of the sexual organization. With respect to the latter danger the loss may be real or fantasy. Awareness of the specific danger (heightened drive, object loss, superego) allows a connection to be made with the predominant distribution of libido between self and object.

The fourth criterion is the state of the defense organization. This is dependent on the extent and depth of the regression—for example, projection will only be found when self-object discrimination remains intact. In its absence the defense is limited to different kinds of externalization, further regression, turning in on the self and reversal of drive aim. Danger situations and defenses cannot be considered apart from conflicts. The recognition of conflicts can often be achieved by examination of the ego and object cathexis as it exists in the psychotic state. In some cases the conflict arises from active or passive libidinal aims, in others from the aggression provoked by object loss, by frustration or from the pressure of the superego. It is the isolation of the internalized conflicts which opens communication between the psychoses and the prepsychotic personality.

The fifth criterion consists of the assessment of the object libido which unaffected by regression continues to follow the secondary process. This cathexis fluctuates in its quantity as does that which has regained its instinctual form. The relationship existing between the two forms of drive cathexis will depend upon such factors as the intensity of the danger situation, regression and defense. The result is that during the acute phase of the illness there is a constant fluctuation in the extent to which the patient presents evidence of a functioning reality ego with insight into the fact of being ill.

By employing the metapsychological criteria just described it is possible to distinguish descriptively similar clinical states from one another. Paranoid psychoses can be taken as illustrative. There is a group of paranoid illnesses occurring in women the content of which consists of the complaints of being persecuted by a former lover. Four cases will be referred to in this discussion, three of which have already been described (Profile No. 2 and cases 5 and 23).

From a descriptive standpoint these patients present an identical clinical picture. The illnesses usually begin after the age of 25 and occur in married as well as single women. The patients state that a man with whom they were emotionally involved at some time in the past has returned to press his claim for their love. Three patients actually had an affair with the man in question. The fourth patient (case 5) wished for such a relationship but it never materialized. According to all the patients the man, unwilling to accept their lack of interest, now engaged in their persecution as an act of revenge. He might stand outside the house at night and shout insults or follow the patients in the street encouraging others to stare at them or make disparaging remarks. The result was a state of mental distress such that all the patients feared at one time or other that they were being driven mad. The following differences and similarities were noted between the four patients when they were studied in terms of the criteria detailed above.

(1) *Developmental*

Two patients were married thus revealing their capacity to make a heterosexual object choice in reality. In one case (Profile No. 2) the sexual organization had phallic-genital qualities. Her sexuality had active masculine characteristics. She was nevertheless able to achieve orgasm under favorable circumstances. The second married patient had a potential for full genital functioning as was indicated in her ability to achieve orgasm with her lover, although never with her husband. In the remaining two patients (cases 5 and 23), both of whom were unmarried, one had established a heterosexual relationship but this did not lead to coitus and was not sustained (see case 23). The other patient (case 5) never proceeded beyond a fantasy love object. In neither case did the patient acknowledge to having experienced genital affects prior to the psychotic attack.

The narcissistic nature of the objects (real and fantasy) in the case of these two single women was pronounced. The objects chosen by the unmarried women (cases 5 and 23) possessed physical and mental attributes which were admired, valued and wished for. In both cases this narcissistic form of object choice could be traced to the tendency, arising out of adverse early life experiences, to take the self as the love object. In contrast the two married patients had made object choices based partly on fixations at the preoedipal phase. In the case described in Profile No. 2 the patient had the same expectations from the husband as she once had from her mother. In both cases a close relationship with the mother had existed in childhood although development had been marred by parental discord and instability in the home.

The unmarried patients had failed to reach an optimal level in object relations and drive adjustment but whether this was due to regressions or to an actual arrest in ego and drive development could not be ascertained. In the case of the married patients there was sufficient proof of regressions having affected the drives with their cathecting fixation points at the phallic level of the sexual organization. It was the subsequent conflicts arising from such regressions which provoked the danger situations and led to symptom formation. Prior to the onset of the illness in all cases there was a lack of libidinal satisfactions which resulted in defensive maneuvers (regression) to avoid the dangers of frustration and object loss.

(2) *Regressions*

Psychotic symptoms appeared when regression affected the libido and the ego organization. In none of the patients was the speed of the regression so great as to result in a complete disorganization of the drives, of the ego and superego. The self-object and ego-id differentiation remained thus indicating the limited extent of the regression. This did not prevent the externalization of the conflict provoked by the arousal of the libidinal drives. In all four cases there was no awareness of a conflict over sexual needs, projection having brought about its externalization with the patient remaining guilt-free.

The effects of the drive regression were to be seen in the state of the libido distribution between self and objects. Real persons lost their cathexis in object relations and assumed an entirely new status. Redistribution and regression of the libido led to the cathexis of the longed-for fantasy object. This became a reality as a result of the hypercathexis of the self and the creation of a pathological narcissism. In the unmarried patients projection not only acted as a defense but by altering the direction of the drives it facilitated the cathexis of the delusional object now carrying the unwelcome instinctual demands. The object was thus regarded as a persecutor. In the single patients real persons were almost devoid of cathexis. In the married patients there remained some cathexis of real persons. The two sets of patients could be distinguished by the intensity of the preoccupation and attachment to the delusional objects.

(3) *Danger Situations and Conflicts*

In the married patients the principal danger was caused by sexual frustration. This eventually resulted in regression as has been mentioned above. When the frustration was eventually overcome as occurred in the case reported in Profile No. 2 there was a pronounced improvement in mental health. Aggression played a much greater role as a source of danger in the single patients. In these cases object loss (factual in one, fantasy in the other) resulted in an aggressive reaction. This aggression directed at the love object, combined with the projected libidinal wishes, tends to increase the intensity of the persecution. Where libidinal frustration acted as the main source of danger, as with the two married patients, the aggression was consciously aimed at the real object of the frustration (the husband) or turned in on the self leading to depression of mood and periodically to self-reproach. These patients did not react against the persecutor with hatred as did the unmarried patients.

(4) *The State of the Defense Organization*

Projection was the main defense employed in all the four cases. It enabled the patients to remain unaware of their sexual longing for the delusional object. As a consequence of the projection the "torturing" demands of the libido could be located outside of themselves.

(5) *The Nonpsychotic Part*

The incapacity of the unmarried patients to take an interest in anything other than their delusional ideas indicated that the libidinal drives, in almost their entirety, cathected the fantasy objects. This state remained constant over many years. These patients forever attended to hallucinatory voices and consistently misinterpreted environmental events. Material reality only assumed a significance when it offered some connection with the psychotic reality. On such occasions the ego functions were cathected with libido following the secondary process consequently enabling the patients to take some interest in the environment.

In the married patients preoccupation with the delusional reality was phasic in its expression and did not last beyond a few months. Even during the delusional period contact was, as has been mentioned, maintained with real persons. In this respect therefore it can be asserted that only part of a libidinal drive cathexis had been subject to regression, the remainder cathecting material reality. In accord with this situation these two patients periodically recognized that their thinking and experiencing was delusional and was due to mental illness. Thus, the course of the illness followed significantly different paths in the two sets of patients. In the single women there was no remission of symptoms while in the married patients the delusional ideas disappeared. This occurred most strikingly whenever their sexual needs were met as in the case described in Profile No. 2.

The schema can also be used as a research instrument in

cases where there is a dramatic change in the symptomatology either during the one attack or in succeeding attacks of illness. The change from psychomotor overactivity to withdrawal, psychomotor inhibition and catalepsy is illustrative of the former while the emergence of a persecutory symptom complex in an attack which follows an earlier one in which depressive phenomena predominated is illustrative of the latter. When Profiles are completed in these cases there is much to be said for the view that the appearance of the new symptomatology has resulted from changes in the extent of regressions and defenses.

A further use of the schema is to compare and contrast psychotic states in adults and children. The study and treatment of children suffering from "borderline" states and psychoses have revealed phenomena which are almost identical to those found in adult patients (Rosenfeld and Sprince, 1963; Thomas, 1966). This is particularly so with respect to interpersonal relations and cognition. Like some adult patients the children use the real object (therapist, etc.) as a source of need satisfaction or as a means of drive control. Again like adult patients they show the same tendency to merge self- and object representations. Cognitive defects (speech disorders and perceptual upsets) are also similar.

When these pathological childhood phenomena are examined from the metapsychological standpoint (Rosenfeld and Sprince, 1963; Thomas, 1966) they can be understood in exactly the same manner as obtains for those appearing in the adult cases. The children are either unable to sustain object cathexis or have difficulty in doing so. The self is cathected at the expense of real objects whenever there is the slightest endopsychic stress with a resultant movement toward the kind of primitive identification (merging of self- and object representations) as is found in the adult patient.

A further similarity consists in the quality of the libidinal drives in the two categories of patient. In both the drives function in the service of the primary process, seeking immediate outlets, their derivatives (ideation and affect) being subject to displacements and condensation. It is this which leads to the cognitive disturbances and the inappropriate affective expression.

These studies point to the fact that the adult patient who has achieved a fairly satisfactory psychosocial and psychosexual adjustment has regressed to a state almost identical to that found in the child whose libidinal development has either been arrested or has itself been affected by regression (e.g., as in the pubertal or adolescent patient). It may be that comparisons of child and adult patients in conjunction with a follow-up of treated and untreated psychotic and "borderline" children may throw light on the most difficult area of the metapsychology of adult psychoses—namely, the form and content of the fixations which had affected the patient's libido and ego in the course of his childhood development.

The reliability of the schema will depend on the experience, knowledge and integrity of the clinician. Profiles completed early in an illness will be incomplete. They will at best ". . . alert the diagnostician's mind to the many possibilities which exist and to ask him to make a choice between them" (A. Freud, 1967). When the patient is better known it is possible to confirm or refute these provisional hypotheses. Detailed Profile studies reveal the complexity of psychotic illnesses. They counteract the tendency to regard the symptomatology of psychosis as the direct expression of cerebral dysfunction.

CHAPTER 10

Some Comparisons Between Childhood and Adult Psychosis

The psychoanalytic study and treatment of children suffering from psychoses and borderline states (Rosenfeld and Sprince, 1963, 1965; Thomas, 1966) has revealed data which are almost identical to those found in psychoses occurring in early or middle adult life. The children who were treated (Thomas, 1966) presented nearly all the categories of symptomatology and abnormal behavior which are regarded by Creak et al. (1961) as characteristic of the schizophrenic syndrome in childhood. The adult patients who present phenomena similar to those encountered in children are those in whom the psychosis has an acute onset (mania, schizophreniform psychosis, reactive psychosis) with a relatively short course as well as those where the psychosis is in a state of chronicity (chronic schizophrenia) but is capable of sudden eruptions of affect and delusion.

Descriptive Aspects

Interpersonal Relationships

(a) Treatment of the children over a long period of time allowed the therapists to recognize the different ways in which the young patients acted in an interpersonal situation.

In every case the therapist came to be regarded as a vehicle for the satisfaction of needs. These needs were of an oral, anal or phallic nature. The demands were imperative and continuous. There was thus little ability to tolerate the frustration of wishes or the capacity to be satisfied. At the outset of treatment the therapists were impressed by the fact that they were without significance for the children—"little more than a piece of furniture" (Rosenfeld and Sprince, 1963).

Even when the treatment had continued for some time the therapist was not regarded as an individual in her own right who was valued by the patient. The therapist was only of importance insofar as she provided a service. Rosenfeld and Sprince (1965) describe a child whose reactions in the clinic and outside conveyed the impression that the therapist had come to assume a special significance for him. Later, however, it became apparent that it was the therapy that was valued, not the therapist. When told about a forthcoming holiday break the child asked "Who will be my therapist then?" The authors comment that at no time did this boy show interest in or curiosity about the therapist. In other cases (Thomas, 1966) the therapist was confused with other persons.

In contrast to the tendency to regard the therapist in terms of her function alone and as a means of need satisfaction there was also the wish to utilize her as an instrument for the control of affect and motility. In such instances the presence of the therapist was essential because of the child's inability to prevent unwelcome wishes and affects passing over into action. Thomas (1966) describes the case of a boy who saw the therapist not as a person but as a function which prevented him from breaking into pieces. He expressed some of his feelings as follows—"I feel like electricity inside. What I need is a fuse box to give warning before I get too excited and wild. Getting excited is like breaking in two" (Thomas, 1966). The need which these children had for help in controlling sexual and aggressive affects was emphasized by the occasions on which these affects found free expression in action.

A further series of reactions was the tendency to confuse the self with others and others with the self. This confusion included the belief that others experienced the same thoughts and feelings, had the same bodily sensations, as changes in identity and an inability to discriminate bodily boundaries. In the case of the inability to retain identity Rosenfeld and Sprince (1965) quote the instance of a boy whose identity changed whenever he was in the presence of someone who held a significance for him. He was, for example, a participant in a television play, a neighbor who frequented a pub nearby, etc. In other cases there was evidence of body merging as with the boy who said, "When I am with mummy I feel we are one" (Rosenfeld and Sprince, 1963).

The inability to acknowledge that the therapist could have different feelings was sometimes accompanied by resentment that the child and therapist were separate individuals. The therapist of one child wrote—"Ever since I have known Stanley he has envisaged a unity of feeling and experience between us. He would ask if I had washed my hair when he had washed his; if I had been to the barber when he went; if I was upset because his housemother left . . . he resented all proofs of my separate existence" (Thomas, 1966). It was also observed that the children assimilated and reproduced the speech content of the therapist without appearing to understand what he said—for example, "in the context of her own sadness Lucile always repeated explanations her therapist had given her. Their meaning was less important than the fact that they were the words that the therapist would use in this context" (Thomas, 1966).

An additional manifestation had to do with the compulsive collection of inanimate objects of all kinds, and in one case, even of words. The therapists were forever being asked for gifts of one form or another. The objects which were collected were often valueless and their possession rarely afforded lasting pleasure. Sometimes the child identified the objects with real persons. Play was always repetitive in nature even when it was quite intricate and complex. When attitudes to the inanimate and to the animate (real persons) were compared the children's preference was for the former rather than the latter—". . . our children have an over-riding preference for the inanimate and impersonal" (Thomas, 1966).

(b) All the phenomena described above can be seen in adult psychoses. Patients suffering from chronic schizophrenia show similar behavior to that observed in the children at the beginning of treatment and at periods of relapse. Although some description of the behavior of chronic schizophrenic patients has been given in earlier chapters ("Object Cathexis" and "Cathexis of the Self") it can be supplemented by a further account.

Chronic schizophrenic patients have little interest in other persons except insofar as they might satisfy a need. Even then the other person makes little or no impact except as an individual who appears at certain times and then goes away. A clear image of the other person is not retained with resulting poor recognition. A patient, a single woman of 26, who had been seen regularly by the writer for some months said, as he left one day, "You will be going to your work . . . in the town . . . are you in business? . . . have you a job in the town? . . . do you work in a shop?" At another time she said, "I'll see you tomorrow . . . will it be the same man . . . I thought maybe there were two of you."

Unless interest in the other person is stimulated by the possible satisfaction of a need he will be ignored in favor of some more likely source of satisfaction—usually of an auto-erotic nature. For a long time the patient just described would give priority to a cup of tea or a cigarette, refusing to see the writer or abruptly leaving an interview—for example, "I have nothing to say to you . . . I am waiting for a cigarette." Only when she knew she would get cigarettes from the writer and that he might be able to procure her discharge from hospital did she willingly come to daily meetings.

The free expression of sexuality and aggression which is so frequently observed in psychotic children is also to be found in adult psychoses—both in chronic schizophrenia and in acute states (for example, mania). Genital and pregenital phenomena are to be observed in both categories—child and adult. As has been reported in earlier chapters these expressions of sexuality may appear, in patients whose clinical condition was previously characterized by withdrawal, disinterest and negativism. The sexuality may be entirely auto-erotic in character or it may be directed to heterosexual or homosexual objects.

When aggression appears, whether in an acute or chronic illness, it is usually, but not invariably, a reaction to frustration or disappointment. Failure to obtain the satisfaction of a need will result in aggression and at such times lack of awareness of the other person as anything other than a potential source of satisfaction becomes apparent. The aggression is expressed without regard for the effect of the action or the consequences.

In many cases of acute and chronic psychoses the adult

patient, like the child, shows that he fears the loss of impulse control and looks to others for help. Two examples were quoted in chapter three ("Object Cathexis"). A further illustration is appropriate here. The patient was a single man of 23 who had been unwell for a period of four years. At the beginning of treatment he was unresponsive. Sometimes he would begin to answer a question and then break off in the middle of a sentence. He sat uncomfortably examining his right forearm and hand. Postures were held for varying lengths of time. He was extremely sensitive to the presence of the writer. This he explained later was due to a terror of loss of control. He dreaded that the relationship might assume a homosexual character. He was afraid of perverting the writer if by chance he touched him. Similarly he feared loss of control over aggression—"I'm frightened I might punch someone . . . no I wouldn't punch anyone." A habit of asking to go to bed resulted from this fear. In bed he was safe and free from the temptation to strike out or make a homosexual contact. Thus the writer became an auxiliary control and was only valued as such. This did not necessarily prevent the emergence of anxiety even in the presence of the writer, thereby revealing the conflict between the sexual and aggressive impulses on the one hand and the dread of the consequences of their expression on the other.

The tendency of the adult psychotic patient to merge self with object images has already been illustrated (see chapter four). These phenomena are almost identical to those observed in psychotic children. Manic patients and withdrawn chronic schizophrenic patients attribute their own thoughts, feelings and sensations to the psychiatrist or nurse. Simultaneously they may assume the physical and mental characteristics of those with whom they are frequently in contact. As in the case of the child described above, a chronic schizophrenic patient assumed the identity of real persons with whom he came in contact—"Did I tell you how I became Dr. F.? . . ." or "I was Mr. P. [a male nurse] the week you were away." Similarly he "identified" with television actors and other patients.

In the days prior to the introduction of occupational and social therapies in mental hospitals it was commonplace to find patients who ceaselessly collected useless and valueless articles. Today this is less frequent. Nevertheless there are patients who are obsessively preoccupied with inanimate objects. Sometimes the article is factual and at other times a product of fantasy. Preoccupation with such articles is more common in withdrawn patients whether or not the illness is in an early or late stage.

Perception of the Self and Sense of Identity

(a) All the children showed defects in the way in which the self was perceived and in the sense of identity. There was a loss of the integrity and the autonomy of the self. This embraced both the mental and physical representations of the self. The inability to use pronouns correctly reflected the failure to perceive the self as distinct from other entities. Lack of the capacity to clearly distinguish boundaries of the bodily self led to the belief, on the part of one child, that his clothes were an integral part of his body. In one example of the merging of body boundaries a girl would open her own mouth when she fed the therapist from a spoon. It was observed that the children had great difficulty in differentiating between emotions and peripheral sensations. Illustrative is the child who when afraid of being angry asked for a swimming cap to protect her hair. Thomas (1966) believes that the replacement of the child's perception of emotions by the perception of peripheral (including visceral) sensations is the result of a partial arrest at a primtive form of pre-emotional experience.

Instability of the boundaries of the self was a constant finding. Apart from easily assuming the identities of others as has been described (see Interpersonal Relationships), some children feared the loss of personal (physical and mental) characteristics as a consequence of merging with others—

> . . . under the impact of a small shock Derek's fear of becoming his therapist broke through. When she had to restrain him from attacking her, she held his wrist firmly and inadvertently scratched him slightly. Derek broke into panicky sobs and he feared that he would become, like the therapist, a dark haired woman with a long nose [Rosenfeld and Sprince, 1963, p. 630].

The impermanence of bodily boundaries was also reflected in fears concerning loss of bodily contents.

In some of the children omnipotent fantasies were observed. One boy said, "I felt like opening that door, stepping right out and turning myself into a giant and pushing all the traffic out of the way" (Thomas, 1966). In another case, that of a girl, the omnipotence was reflected in the idea that she was the cause of any mishaps which occurred in the hospital where she was a patient. The boy just referred to described himself as the most popular boy in the hospital.

(b) In recent cases of psychosis and in chronic schizophrenia the self is perceived in ways little different from that described by Rosenfeld, Sprince and Thomas for psychotic children. In recent adult cases and in manic states in particular the patient appears to be incapable of regarding himself as a separate and independent entity. His thoughts and feelings are shared by others as are his bodily sensations.

Features of his body seem to belong to those about him. He assumes the identity of others as has been described in earlier chapters, while simultaneously interpreting their behavior, and discerns their emotional experience and vocational activities in terms of his own past and present.

In cases of chronic schizophrenia there is also a loss of the ability to use pronouns correctly in a manner no different from that observed in the children. The patient will typically refer to himself in the third person. This loss of the sense of "I" is accompanied by phenomena which reflect the absence of a differentiation between self and others. A patient of 26 showed, like one of the children, that he experienced his clothes as part of his body—"A nurse was brushing my clothes with a big brush and it made an awful mess of my face . . . clothes are really a part of you" (Freeman, 1969a).

This last illustration shows that the patient could not discriminate the different parts of his body. Face was confused with limbs and trunk. This confusion may in part be due to words having lost their function as referents. Similarly, bodily sensations alter in quality so that the patient feels his body to be changed or distorted—the face changes in shape, the mouth is twisted, etc. Even in early cases of psychosis such alterations in the body image occur. One patient, a young man of 19, believed that his bones had altered in their consistency and that he had shrunk in size. A sense of bodily disintegration is experienced similar in nature to that observed in psychotic children.

Other phenomena appear in chronic states which follow from the loss of the self-nonself boundary. One adult patient said, "I am the first serious patient to have this composition . . . I am made up . . . the first patient to have a complex tissue . . . I am composed of different people . . . I have the same mouth as a black nurse and another black woman . . ." (Freeman, 1969a). Even in terms of their behavior patients will reveal the same difficulty in separating themselves from another person. A patient suffering from chronic schizophrenia took a crust of bread from his pocket. He pushed the crust toward the psychiatrist's mouth as though giving it to him to eat. Simultaneously he opened his own mouth (Cameron, Freeman and McGhie, 1955). In this he acted in exactly the same manner as the girl patient who was feeding the therapist from a spoon.

Adult patients suffering from psychoses also have difficulty in distinguishing emotions from peripheral sensations. Depressive or anxiety affects can be experienced as changes affecting the body—changes of the type described above. The patient who said that he felt his mouth to be twisted was expressing the depressive, self-critical idea that he was twisted in his dealing with others.

Many of the changes in self-perception which adult patients experience lead to bewilderment, to a sense of unease and to acute anxiety (Freeman, Cameron and McGhie, 1958). Here it is reasonable to assume that these patients, like the psychotic children described, fear the loss of personal characteristics—both mental and physical—as a result of merging with other individuals. It is, however, necessary to add that all patients do not experience these changes as distressing. This lack of distress is most common where there is no indication of conflict as evidenced by the absence of delusions or hallucinations with a persecutory content.

Cognitive Functions

(a) Speech abnormalities were present in all the children, particularly at the beginning of treatment. These abnormalities were present in both the form and content of speech. Speech was slow and retarded or completely absent. Grammatical structure was deficient leading in some cases to jargon speech. Words and phrases were compulsively repeated (perseveration). The thought content was characterized by magical, egocentric and concrete thinking. Words were sometimes regarded as things which could either be a source of reassurance and pleasure or a source of great anxiety. Certain words might have special meanings which could only be known through extensive knowledge of the child. Thomas (1966) quotes examples of this. Rosenfeld and Sprince (1963) have drawn attention to the ease with which borderline children translate their wishes and fantasies into action. The authors regard this as due to an arrest in thought development.

In the sphere of perception it was noted that psychotic children appear to have lost the capacity to select those percepts which are relevant for a mental and physical activity currently at hand. Rosenfeld and Sprince (1963) report as follows—

> . . . our children find it difficult to inhibit stimuli. They seem to get swamped by them and are unselective in their choice of what is relevant and what is irrelevant . . . they [the children] appear to be overwhelmed by stimuli from outside or inside and seem incapable of sorting them out, which hinders these children from following any one theme. It may be that this incapacity to select and inhibit interferes with the differentiation between self and object representation [p. 623].

Associated with this defect is an inability to differentiate between internal and external stimuli. Rosenfeld and Sprince quote the case of a girl who when attempting to avoid thinking about anxiety-provoking ideas plugged her ears with cotton wool. Anxiety, deriving from fantasy, commonly led to children turning away from a visual or auditory percept. Finally attention should be drawn to phenomena which indicate that a close relationship exists between perceptual experiences and motility disorders (Stroh and Buick, 1964).

(b) The disorders of speech and thinking which occur in adult psychoses are almost identical to those found in psychotic children. In chronic schizophrenia, for example, there are similar disorders of speech form and content. Magical, egocentric and concrete thinking can be observed at any time. Words lose their communicative role and are used instead as concrete objects. As with the children, comprehensible speech is more likely to appear following the arousal of a need—for example, jargon will be replaced by rational speech. In chronic schizophrenia auditory and visual percepts are easily assimilated into the stream of talk, giving it an illogical character. This tendency is part of a disturbance in the capacity to selectively attend to thoughts and percepts.

In both acute and chronic psychoses perceptual disorders have been described which are closely connected with catatonic manifestations (see Chapter six). In some cases there is an inability to discriminate between perceptual modalities—"a movement in front of my eyes is like hearing a sound in my ears" (Chapman, Freeman and McGhie, 1959). It would appear that in such cases there is a failure to organize perceptual experience arising from internal or external sources. Patients have been described who have reported (Chapman, 1966) that they cannot look and listen at the same time and that they are unable to simultaneously perceive visually while attending to their thoughts. Attempts to do so have led to disorders of muscle tone and voluntary movement with the production of catatonic phenomena.

Like the psychotic child the adult patient reveals that

visual percepts easily lose their formal characteristics with resultant loss of size and shape constancies. Similarly percepts evoke great anxiety. Again the loss of the boundary separating the self from the nonself leads to internal stimuli being confused with external stimuli. As with child patients adult patients will stuff their ears with cotton wool in an attempt to dull distressing affect and sensation.

Motility

(a) The disorders of motility which occur in psychotic children can be classified into three groups. First there are the repetitive movements of the head, trunk and limbs. A long period of contact with the child may be necessary before his attention can be drawn from the movements. These simple repetitive movements bear the hallmarks of the two different kinds of perseveration which have been described by Luria (1965). Repetitive movements and the need for sameness in play are characteristics of psychotic children which have been repeatedly observed and commented upon (Stroh and Buick, 1964). The reluctance for change must be related to an "inertia" of mental processes which precludes the "switching" of attention and interest from one series of thoughts or external events to another.

The second group of motility disorders, usually occurring in association with the repetitive tendency, consists of changes in the tone of the voluntary musculature and the appearance of strange and unusual postures which may be maintained for varying lengths of time. Elkan (1969) quotes a typical example—

> . . . at home she cried and screamed a great deal (this, in the acute phase) and stereotyped repetitive behavior which had been noticed previously greatly intensified. She seemed com-

> pelled to repeatedly walk forwards and backwards through a door; to continually stand up and sit down on the chair; to hold herself in stiff postures with hands stretched out in front of her. At times she stood rigidly still for long periods without talking. At other times she begged members of the family to open a door for her but would be unable to walk through [p. 7].

In other cases the hypertonia alternates with hypotonia with the result that the child collapses to the floor.

The third disorder of motility consists of increased motor activity. This is usually accompanied by excitement and the free expression of all kinds of sexual demands. Rosenfeld and Sprince (1963) report the following case—

> . . . at the beginning of treatment Kenneth discharged attention predominately through the motor apparatus. When an activity was not immediately provided for him or when he was not immediately successful, his motor activity became chaotic, his whole body would become entangled in itself, he would hang upside down from chairs and tables, legs and arms muddled, his head popping up in some unexpected place. He would maintain such tangled postures for unusually long periods without apparent effort. He appeared to have little regard for pain or the possibilities of danger. Wild phantasies of being chased and trapped expressed in a high pitched voice and slurred speech, accompanied these activities [p. 610].

(b) Repetitive movement of head and limbs have been observed in both acute and chronic psychotic states in adults. Repetitive phenomena have also been demonstrated in writing and drawing (Freeman, 1969a). In chronic states the repetitive activity wholly absorbs the patient's attention and, as with the child, it is extremely difficult to bring it to an end. Compulsive repetition takes precedence over failure to pass from one task to another in chronic schizophrenia (Freeman and Gathercole, 1966).

As in the case of psychotic children repetitive movements in adult patients are usually associated with hypertonia of the voluntary musculature and with the appearance and persistence of unusual postures. These abnormalities can appear as easily in the recent as in the chronic case. For example, at the onset of illness in the case of a young man of 19 there was great difficulty in the initiation and completion of voluntary movements. When eating he would bring food to his mouth and then take it away. This sequence of movements would be repeated for a long time. He took a spark plug from his pocket, went to put it on a table but only got part of the way, then took it back and started again. This was repeated many times. He would stand motionless for long periods in a fixed position.

Psychomotor overactivity with excitement similar to that found in psychotic children may arise in patients who have been previously in a withdrawn, negativistic state. A man of 20 had been inaccessible for some days after admission to hospital. He suddenly became overactive, jumping and dashing about the ward. He would spin about his own axis, or spin around a pillar while grasping it with one hand. He would collapse limp to the floor. Sexual excitement found expression in masturbation, inviting nurses into his bed and in such statements as "those sexy bitches (nurses and occupational therapists) keep wiggling their bottoms, tantalizing me." He tickled other male patients and struggled with them playfully. He rushed about the ward making a noise like a machine gun and the exploding of bombs. In this fantasy he played the roles of attacker and the attacked. His behavior was exactly like that of an overexcited child.

Affects

(a) Anxiety is the affect most in evidence in psychotic children. Rosenfeld and Sprince (1963) refer to the special quality of this anxiety, that it is ". . . intense, diffuse, panic-like and seemed to involve an experience of disintegration and annihilation." The authors differentiate this kind of anxiety from that in the neurotic child and point to the fact that the psychotic or "borderline" child is without means of lessening the impact of the anxiety to which he is subject. The thought content associated with the anxiety was found to consist of fears of bodily disintegration, fear of loss of personal characteristics and fear of loss of control over sexual and aggressive impulses.

As was mentioned earlier psychotic children do not experience emotion as it is understood in the healthy child. Instead they are conscious of inner states composed of peripheral (visceral, proprioceptive, tactile, etc.) sensations. These inner states ("pre-emotional experience") can lead to acute and intense anxiety which in turn results in serious acts of aggression—"some children feel threatened with bodily disintegration, some are driven to wandering, some to killing animals, some to violent attacks on themselves or others; the person attacked may be an uninvolved person" (Thomas, 1966).

(b) Anxiety is by no means the only affect to be observed in adult psychoses. It is, however, most common in cases of acute onset. When the anxiety springs from fantasies of bodily injury outbursts of violence occur. Anxiety is less apparent in cases of chronic schizophrenia but its presence is betrayed when attempts are made to initiate a relationship with a patient. There will be an aggressive response or the withdrawal will become even more pronounced. As in the case of psychotic children, adult patients also suffer from the fact that the anxiety appears to be self-perpetuating and is not brought to an end by the appearance of new symptoms as occurs in hysterical or phobic states. Hallucinations and delusions do not succeed in removing anxiety. Only profound withdrawal with negativism seems to provide the necessary protection against this intense anxiety.

In those cases of psychosis where some degree of involvement with reality remains other affects appear as well as anxiety. Jealousy, sadness, grief and envy are representative. These affects do not, however, have the disastrous impact on the patient as does the anxiety. In common with the children, adult patients dread the effect of their sexuality and aggression on others. They fear bodily disintegration and a loss of personal, physical and sexual identity.

Observations on the Descriptive Data

The phenomena which have been described show that childhood psychoses resemble most closely those adult states where an extensive dissolution has affected mental life. Thus the most striking similarities have been found in psychoses of acute onset and in cases of chronic schizophrenia characterized by withdrawal, disinterest, lack of affect, negativism and catatonic signs. There are fewer resemblances when the childhood states are compared with cases of paranoid psychosis where cognition still operates at an advanced level and where there are complex delusions. Delusions are rudimentary or nonexistent in the chronic patient and in the psychotic child. In both they are confined to omnipotent fantasies and to isolated persecutory ideas which may be attached to anyone in the immediate environment.

The absence of organized delusional (persecutory) ideas

in childhood psychoses can be attributed to poor or undeveloped intelligence, to limited powers of conceptualization and to a poor vocabulary. Nevertheless psychotic children show that they regard the animate and inanimate environment as hostile, disappointing and frustrating. Thomas (1966) quotes a series of observations of which the following is a good example—"Stanley's therapist wrote to him, when he was ill, saying what a nuisance he had diarrhea." Stanley's reaction was "Why you say it? It is a silly word. If you write it it makes me say it. Why you say I am a nuisance. Don't write me" (p. 542).

The patient suffering from chronic schizophrenia also regards others as antagonistic and antipathetic to him. Mishaps, disappointments and failures are interpreted as purposive on the part of those about him. The aggression which may be evoked as a consequence is illustrated in the following instance where the writer took pains to show the patient his concern. The patient wanted to smoke. The writer took him to the hospital shop and bought a packet of cigarettes. On their return to the main building the patient insisted on going back to the shop because in his opinion the transaction had not been properly conducted. This conviction was connected with his delusional ideas. On arriving at the shop for the second time it was found to be closed for lunch. The patient demanded that it be opened immediately and expected the writer to have this done. When the writer explained that this was not within his power the patient cursed him, screaming and shouting that he (the writer) was inconsiderate, deceitful, coarse and crude.

It is the experience of the world as unhelpful, disappointing and hostile which acts as an obstacle to psychotherapeutic endeavors with both psychotic children and adult schizophrenic patients. These attitudes remain even when some form of attachment to a therapist appears to have developed. This was so in a case reported by Rosenfeld and Sprince (1965) —

> She attacked the people to whom she became attached and demonstrated that she could not conceive of the possibility of any relationship not leading her into a dangerous situation similar to the real one with her mother in which both were at the mercy of aggressive drives. She defended against making a new relationship partly because she dreaded the therapist's aggression and partly because of the terror of her own, which might destroy the therapist [p. 511].

The same kind of situation developed during the attempted psychotherapy of a young, unmarried schizophrenic girl whose illness had passed into a state of chronicity. Here as with the child patient the wish for an emotional tie with the writer was countered by the fear of her own hostility and the hostility which she felt was directed against her. The following excerpts from treatment sessions show the extent of this conflict—"You don't need to come unless you want to . . . to tell the truth it would be better if you didn't come. . . . I don't like men doctors. . . ." When asked in what way she would feel better if left alone she replied—"I thought you didn't like me. . . . I thought you couldn't be bothered with me. . . . I am very quiet like you. . . . I was very worried maybe you wouldn't come . . . don't you like to see me? . . . do you like to see me?" The other obstacles which stand in the way of the development of a psychotherapeutic process in psychotic children and in adults have already been described in the accounts of the way patients relate, perceive reality and communicate with it. Only when the disorders which affect these mental functions lessen in extent and intensity, as so often occurs in adult psychoses of acute onset, can progress be made toward a remission of the illness.

Metapsychological Aspects

Developmental and Economic Considerations

The metapsychological approach to the clinical phenomena requires that attention first be turned to the condition of the drives and the ego organization in the different psychotic states. In children it is apparent that the libido has retained its instinctual state and in adults it is clear that the libido has returned to this state. Once the treatment is under way the child, no longer fearing an adverse reaction from the therapist in response to the expression of his sexuality, comes to regard the latter solely as a source of instinctual satisfaction. In some cases there is a rapid development of anxiety lest the reaction to such continual demands will be one of object loss. This has the effect of the child coming to look to the therapist as a means of drive control.

The fear of object loss has the significance of a potential psychic trauma in that the opportunity to reduce heightened libidinal cathexis will no longer exist. Thomas (1966) in referring to the effects of treatment in a child says—

> as treatment progressed there was an increasingly, spontaneous and continuous recognition of the value of the human object and its specific emotional states generated by loss. However an unusually great or unexpected threat of loss could always revive the diffuse manic type of excitement [p. 511].

In chronic schizophrenia a similar state of the libido is to be found. An object relationship is wished for yet feared in view of the potential traumatic situation which may be engendered by increasing "quantities" of libido which cannot find an outlet. The tendency for the self to be cathected with libido at the expense of objects in both adult and child patients can be explained on the basis of the economic hypothesis already referred to in Chapter three ("Cathexis of Objects"). The self will always be a more reliable vehicle for the libidinal drive gratification than real objects, the experience with which has proved painful and frustrating. The extent of autoerotic activities in adult and child psychoses supports this point of view. In a footnote to her paper Thomas (1966, p. 550) states "all the children masturbate, some anally; none makes use of finger sucking. We are reminded that autoplastic modes of discharge are influential in maintaining whatever psychic unity the child may have achieved (A. Freud, 1954)."

Remission of symptoms depends on whether or not that change occurs in the distribution of libido which enables objects to surpass the self in the competition for the available cathexis. This occurs spontaneously in many cases of adult psychosis but fails to take place in those patients who eventually fall into the category of chronic schizophrenia. Clinical observation indicates that while the self is the principal recipient of libidinal cathexis, merging occurs with objects as has been described. This merging is, as has already been mentioned, a primitive kind of identification analogous to the primary identification postulated as an early developmental phase in object relations. Anna Freud believes (see Rosenfeld and Sprince, 1963) that borderline children ". . . are constantly on the border between object cathexis and identification and (she) describes how they revert to identification with the object and that this may lead to a merging with the object."

Psychotic children and adults have, in varying degrees, abandoned object cathexis. The resultant hypercathexis of the self and the tendency to merge with the object may account for the fear of loss of physical and mental characteristics. It is this anxiety which might be responsible for the negativism which is so commonly encountered in psychoses (A. Freud, 1952). Merging with the object also occurs as an expression of an instinctual (oral-incorporative) wish, the wish to possess the object, particularly in those phases of a psychosis where there is an extensive dissolution of all mental functions (see Chapter four).

When the genital and pregenital phenomena which occur so plentifully in childhood and adult psychosis are assessed in terms of libidinal phase development the striking feature is their need-satisfying character. Oral, anal and phallic manifestations must be immediately gratified. Frustration and postponement of satisfaction are badly tolerated and the state of the object is of no concern. It is this, in addition to other phenomena, for example phallic manifestations without phallic dominance (Thomas, 1966) which point to the likelihood that even when the sexuality is expressed via the genitals this does not imply that the genital organization of the libido has been reached. The extent to which sexual drives will find direct outlets varies from case to case and depends upon the phase of the illness and the condition of the therapy.

In child and adult psychoses the sexual drives become divorced from their appropriate aims and objects. For example there is always evidence of phallic activity in the form of masturbation but this is not necessarily associated with object relationships belonging to the positive or negative Oedipus complex. In adult cases active sexual drives may appear directed to real persons but their expression is chaotic, poorly sustained and rarely has coitus as an aim. Again it is commonplace to observe behavior and delusions which are based on oedipal fantasies but these fantasies are not cathected by phallic libido which has active aims.

The libido and ego of the children treated by Thomas (1966) had sustained developmental arrests. Changes in the libido, ego and superego in the adult cases were principally the result of regression. In these patients the preillness personality differed according to the extent to which a genital organization of the libido had been established with object relations appropriate to the oedipal phase.

The preillness personality of chronic schizophrenic patients often indicates that a fairly advanced level of libido and ego development had been reached. When these cases are compared with the adolescent "borderline" states described by Rosenfeld and Sprince (1963) it would seem that, prior to the attack, such heterosexual object relationships as were present were based on narcissism (see Chapters three and four). The instability of the phallic organization renders it vulnerable to regression under the impact of anxiety. However this does not preclude, in the psychosis, the employment of the phallic channel as a means of "discharging" pregenital libido.

Dynamic and Structural Considerations

The special quality of the anxiety which appears in psychotic children shows that a danger situation is almost constantly present. The danger is entirely due to heightened drive cathexis—libidinal or aggressive. This danger is somewhat lessened whenever an object relationship can be established—however fragile—through which both drive satisfaction and drive control can be obtained. In turn this leads to the danger of object loss as has been described. A further danger is created by the fear of the consequences of merging with the object. Such conflicts as occur are of necessity with external objects.

The arrest in ego development has the effect of blurring the margins between ego and id (see Chapter eight). In the presence of a danger situation the child cannot employ either repression or projection, both mechanisms being dependent on an ego organization which is clearly differentiated from the id on the one hand and which allows the self to be discriminated from objects on the other hand. The psychotic child's perception of external reality as hostile is not the result of projection but of externalization of destructive tendencies.

Externalization, displacement and the withdrawal of object cathexis when present are the principal methods of defense against the drives. The operation of these defenses is illustrated in the following example taken from Thomas's paper (1966)—

> Norma developed new ways of displacing aggression onto toys and of substituting less dangerous forms of attack for example squirting water instead of scratching. She would also withdraw from situations which aroused anxiety; and when she had failed to control herself she externalised her destructiveness onto creatures she invented. Having torn her dress she explained—"a birdie pecked it." Later she invented a jumper-caughter—a creature who caught and tore her dress—laughing mischievously she elaborated about "glove caughters" and "sock caughters" [p. 538].

Identical danger situations and defenses are found in chronic schizophrenia. Many examples have already been presented in earlier chapters of the way in which drive derivatives are countered by externalization and displacement. External conflicts are reduced by the withdrawal of object cathexis. The negativism and catatonic manifestations which are so common must also be regarded as defensive. The inability to easily initiate voluntary movements as a result of the muscular hypertonia acts to prevent the passage of instinctual wishes from thought to action.

The ego state in chronic schizophrenia is, as has been described, similar to that existing in the psychotic child but it comes into being predominantly as a result of regression. Repression and projection play no part in the defense or in symptom formation for the same reasons as pertain in the psychotic child. An equally extensive regression of drives, ego and superego occurs at the onset and during a manic attack as well as in other, possibly schizophrenic, psychoses at different phases of the illness. In those states where the ego merges with the id there is neither anxiety nor guilt indicating that for brief periods the drives are not regarded as dangerous. Once past this phase the continuing presence of the drives requires the operation of externalization and displacement. In these acute states the regression of drives, ego and superego is resolved with the return of repression and other defenses. In this respect these patients differ from psychotic children and chronic schizophrenic patients.

DISCUSSION

Only two points will be taken up in this discussion. The first relates to the relevance of the childhood findings for later adult illness. On several occasions attention has been drawn to the pronounced similarities which exist between childhood psychoses of the type described by Thomas (1966) and chronic schizophrenic patients. The question which springs to mind is whether the adult schizophrenic, in his childhood, sustained a mental disturbance similar in form, if not in intensity, to childhood psychosis. The assumption would have to be made that instead of a permanent or semipermanent developmental arrest having taken place, the libido and ego continued their maturation with later achievements in interpersonal relationships and cognition concealing the earlier pathological state.

Hence the appearance of the schizophrenic illness in early adult life would be a function of regression of libido and ego with a return to libidinal fixations and "ego states" which were established during the phase of childhood disturbance. Such a hypothesis becomes more acceptable if the disturbance is envisaged as occurring in early childhood when cognitive development is only in its beginnings and pathological relating easily overlooked. The abnormal period may only be of short duration. Under such circumstances, and these would include those instances where parental pathology enhanced the denial of abnormality in the child or resulted in indifference, it would not be surprising if there was no recollection on the patient's part or that of relatives of an early childhood period of mental abnormality.

This formulation is in accord with the psychoanalytic theory of mental illness which postulates that the kind of psychosis which appears in adult life and the course which it will follow will depend on the influences which affected the developing libido and ego. The evidence obtained from childhood psychoses indicates that the nature of the fixations is as important a contributory factor to predisposition as is the timing of their occurrence. The data from childhood psychosis suggests that the fixations, partly created by adverse environmental circumstances, must include a fundamental weakness in the capacity for object cathexis with the consequences this has for self-object differentiation and ego development as a whole. This incapacity for object cathexis must follow from large "quantities" of libido having been permanently obstructed from further participation in the developmental process. The later interpersonal behavior of individuals who develop chronic schizophrenia points to a weak capacity for object cathexis.

The situation is different in those acute psychotic states where remission of symptoms is the rule even though there may be recurrent attacks. In those psychoses the regression also occurs to fixation points whose placing in developmental terms must be in the early childhood period. It is the nature of the fixations which is different. Here less object libidinal cathexis was subject to arrest. The potential for object cathexis, even under the conditions of regression, remains much greater than in the cases of chronic schizophrenia. The result is that real objects can be cathected. Coincidentally the ego regains some degree of integration with the reestablishment of stable defense mechanisms. This does not happen in chronic schizophrenia.

The hypotheses outlined have a practical relevance in that they point to the necessity for studying adult psychoses from the standpoint of predisposition, excluding for the moment hereditary influences. This study can be undertaken not only by examining delusions and hallucinations which so often contain childhood memories and fantasies but also by scrutinizing whatever data is available from the patient's early childhood. Such an investigation must inevitably be incomplete in that it throws little light on the psychic reality of that period. It is also important to recall that in some cases of a childhood psychosis an organic cerebral factor must be included with other relevant etiological agents. Similar considerations must also be taken into account in certain cases of chronic schizophrenia.

The second point for discussion has already been taken up in an earlier chapter (see Chapter six) and concerns the question of how far it is justified to regard the symptomatology of the psychoses as basically due to a defect in the ego organization. In that chapter this hypothesis was rejected in favor of the view that the fundamental disturbance in psychoses is a disorder affecting the development of the libido with this secondarily involving the ego. It is of some interest that this is the view proposed by Rosenfeld and Sprince (1963) with respect to "borderline" children. It may be appropriate to conclude this chapter with a relevant quotation from their paper—

> . . . together with others writing about these children, we have found that the quality of ego disturbance and its variation are of greatest significance for each individual case but these factors do not in our opinion adequately explain the aetiology of the disturbances. Influenced by Anna Freud's unpublished papers on borderline states (1956, 1957) we began to direct our attention to a specific aspect, namely, the capacity for object relations, and especially the precarious maintenance of object cathexis [p. 604].

REFERENCES

BAK, R. C. (1971), Object relationships in schizophrenia and perversion. *Internat. J. Psycho-Anal.,* 52:235-242.

BLEULER, E. (1923), *Textbook of Psychiatry.* New York: Macmillan.

BOYER, L. B. (1967), Office treatment of schizophrenic patients. In: *Psychoanalytic Treatment of Characterological and Schizophrenic Disorders,* ed. L. B. Boyer and P. L. Giovacchini. New York: Science House.

CAMERON, J. L., FREEMAN, T., & MCGHIE, A. (1956), Clinical observations on chronic schizophrenia. *Psychiat.,* 19:271-281.

CHAPMAN, J. (1966), The early symptoms of schizophrenia. *Brit. J. Psychiat.,* 112:225-251.

——, FREEMAN, T. & MCGHIE, A. (1959), Clinical research in schizophrenia. *Brit. J. Med. Psychol.,* 32:75-85.

CREAK, M. et al. (1961), Schizophrenia syndrome in childhood. Progress report of a working party. *Brit. Med. J.,* 2:889-890.

EISSLER, K. R. (1951), Remarks on the psychoanalysis of schizophrenia. *Internat. J. Psycho-Anal.,* 32:139-156.

ELKAN, I. (1969), A clinical approach to borderline phenomena in children. *Report, Hampstead Clinic,* London.

FEDERN, P. (1927), Narcissism in the structure of the ego. In: *Ego Psychology and the Psychoses.* London: Imago, 1953.

—— (1943), Psychoanalysis of the psychoses. In: *Ego Psychology and the Psychoses.* London: Imago, 1953.

FENICHEL, O. (1926), Identification. In: *Collected Papers,* First Series. New York: W. W. Norton, 1953, pp. 97-112.

Flarsheim, A. (1967), The separation of management from the therapeutic setting in a paranoid patient. *Internat. J. Psycho-Anal.,* 48:559-572.

Freeman, T. (1969a), *Psychopathology of the Psychoses.* New York: International Universities Press.

—— (1969b), Psychoanalytic aspects of diffuse cerebral degenerations. *Dynamische Psychiatrie,* 2:83-93.

—— Cameron, J. L., & McGhie, A. (1958), *Chronic Schizophrenia.* New York: International Universities Press.

—— —— —— (1965), *Studies on Psychosis.* New York: International Universities Press.

—— & Gathercole, C. E. (1966), Perseveration—the clinical symptoms—in chronic schizophrenia and organic dementia. *Brit. J. Psychiat.,* 112:27-32.

Freud, A. (1936), *The Ego and the Mechanisms of Defense.* New York: International Universities Press, 1966.

—— (1952), Notes on a connection between the states of negativism and of emotional surrender. In: *Indications for Child Analysis and Other Papers.* [*The Writings of Anna Freud,* Vol. IV.] New York: International Universities Press, 1968.

—— (1954), Problems of infantile neurosis: a discussion. In: *The Psychoanalytic Study of the Child,* 9:16-71. New York: International Universities Press.

—— (1956), Unpublished papers on borderline states.

—— (1957), Unpublished papers on borderline states.

—— (1963), The concept of developmental lines. *The Psychoanalytic Study of the Child,* 18:245-265. New York: International Universities Press.

—— (1967), Personal communication.

—— (1968), Panel discussion. *Internat. J. Psycho-Anal.,* 49:506-512.

—— Nagera, H., & Freud, W. E. (1965), Metapsychological assessment of the adult personality: the adult profile. *The Psychoanalytic Study of the Child,* 20:9-41. New York: International Universities Press.

Freud, S. (1900), The interpretation of dreams. *Standard Edition,* 4 & 5. London: Hogarth Press, 1953.

—— (1911), Psychoanalytic notes on an autobiographical account of a case of paranoia (dementia paranoides). *Standard Edition,* 12:1-82. London: Hogarth Press, 1958.

—— (1914), On narcissism. An introduction. *Standard Edition,* 14:67-102. London: Hogarth Press, 1957.

—— (1915), Repression. *Standard Edition,* 14:141-158. London: Hogarth Press, 1957.

—— (1916-1917), Introductory lectures on psychoanalysis. *Standard Edition,* 15 & 16. London: Hogarth Press, 1963.

—— (1922), Some neurotic mechanisms in jealousy, paranoia and homosexuality. *Standard Edition,* 6:221-232. London: Hogarth Press, 1971.

—— (1924), Neurosis and psychosis. *Standard Edition,* 19:147-153. London: Hogarth Press, 1961.

—— (1925), A note upon the 'mystic writing-pad.' *Standard Edition,* 19:225-232. London: Hogarth Press, 1961.

—— (1926), Inhibitions, symptoms and anxiety. *Standard Edition,* 20:75-175. London: Hogarth Press, 1959.

FROSCH, J. (1967), Delusional fixity, sense of conviction and the psychotic conflict. *Internat. J. Psycho-Anal.,* 48:475-495.

GLOVER, E. (1949), *Psychoanalysis.* London: Staples Press.

HARTMANN, H. (1958), *Ego Psychology and the Problem of Adaptation.* New York: International Universities Press.

JACOBSON, E. (1967), *Psychotic Conflict and Reality.* New York: International Universities Press.

KATAN, M. (1954), The importance of the non-psychotic part of the personality in schizophrenia. *Internat. J. Psycho-Anal.,* 35:119-128.

—— (1960), Dream and psychosis. Their relationship to hallucinatory processes. *Internat. J. Psycho-Anal.,* 41:341-351.

KLEIN, G. S. (1959), Consciousness in psychoanalytic theory—some implications for current research in perception. *J. Amer. Psychoanal. Assn.,* 7:5-34.

LEWIN, B. (1950), *The Psychoanalysis of Elation.* New York: Norton.

LURIA, A. R. (1965), Two kinds of motor perseveration in massive injury of the frontal lobes. *Brain,* 88:1-10.

NAGERA, H. (1969), The imaginary companion. *The Psychoanalytic Study of the Child,* 24:165-196. New York: International Universities Press.

NIEDERLAND, W. G. (1959), The miracled-up world of Schreber's childhood. *The Psychoanalytic Study of the Child,* 14:383-413. New York: International Universities Press.

NOVICK, J. & KELLY, K. (1970), Projection and externalization. *The Psychoanalytic Study of the Child,* 25:69-98. New York: International Universities Press.

NUNBERG, H. (1955), *Principles of Psychoanalysis.* New York: International Universities Press.

ROSENFELD, S. K. & SPRINCE, M. P. (1963), An attempt to formulate the meaning of the concept "borderline." *The Psychoanalytic Study of the Child,* 18:603-635. New York: International Universities Press.

——— ——— (1965), Some thoughts on the handling of borderline children. *The Psychoanalytic Study of the Child,* 20:495-517. New York: International Universities Press.

SCHILDER, P. (1928), *Introduction to a Psychoanalytic Psychiatry.* New York: International Universities Press, 1951.

STROH, G. & BUICK, D. (1964), Perceptual development and childhood psychosis. *Brit. J. Med. Psychol.,* 37:291-299.

THOMAS, R. (1966), Comments on some aspects of self and object representation in a group of psychotic children: an application of Anna Freud's Diagnostic Profile. *The Psychoanalytic Study of the Child,* 21:527-582. New York: International Universities Press.

INDEX